leaving Pōōgah, t...  ...d corresponding des... it road to this place. ...te little Rōōpshoo Ghoont, that not only considerably preferred trotting to cantering, but whose paces were of the very roughest.

I saw a very pretty hare, fawn-coloured, with light blue hind-quarters. As I was crossing the high, grassy hill, where I saw some wild-horses last year, I observed a large troop at some distance. Shortly afterwards, near the small lake, (which is passed before the Chōōmorēēree,) a wild-horse galloped before me, not thirty yards distant. I saw it quite plainly. It was of the size of a pony, with longish ears. The colour was chesnut, and a dingy white in large patches over the quarters and stomach. There was not another horse in sight at the time, so I suppose the one I saw was the sentinel of some distant troop.

Before I ever saw these animals, imagination used to picture the realization of Byron's beautiful description of the wild-horses in Mazeppa:—

> "A trampling troop, I see them come!
> In one vast squadron they advance!
> The steeds rush on in plunging pride,
> But where are they the reins to guide?
> A thousand horse, and none to ride!

With flowing tail, and flying mane,
Wide nostrils, never stretch'd by pain,
Mouths bloodless to the bit or rein;
And feet that iron never shod,
And flanks unscarr'd by spur or rod,
A thousand horse, the wild, the free,
Like waves that follow o'er the sea,
Come thickly thundering on!"

Ah! romance and reality are not always the same thing! I would recommend any sportsman who may be anxious to shoot these animals, to visit the mountains near the route between Pōōgah and the Chōōmorēēree. There are a myriad hoof-marks in every direction, and many other traces of the wild-horse are scattered all over this line of country. One range of high mountains, about seventeen thousand feet in elevation, is called by the Thibetans the Kiâng-La, or Pass of Wild-Horses, from the troops which frequent this peculiar mountain.

TH' HUTTAH. (OOJAR.) DISTRICT ROOPSHOO.

Distance, about two miles.

Same day.—I am writing by the bank of the blue Chōōmorēēree. It is piercingly cold, a bleak wind searching every crevice of the tent.

Mrs. Hervey

THE
ADVENTURES OF A LADY
IN
TARTARY, THIBET, CHINA, & KASHMIR,

THROUGH

PORTIONS OF TERRITORY NEVER BEFORE VISITED BY EUROPEAN

WITH AN ACCOUNT OF THE JOURNEY FROM

THE PUNJAB TO BOMBAY OVERLAND,

VIA THE FAMOUS CAVES OF AJUNTA AND ELLORA

ALSO AN ACCOUNT OF THE MAHABLESHWUR AND NEILGHERRY MOUNTAINS,
THE SANATARIA OF THE BOMBAY AND MADRAS PRESIDENCIES

Volume 3

Elibron Classics
www.elibron.com

Elibron Classics series.

© 2005 Adamant Media Corporation.

ISBN 1-4021-9449-8 (paperback)
ISBN 1-4021-1037-5 (hardcover)

This Elibron Classics Replica Edition is an unabridged facsimile of the edition published in 1853 by Hope and Co.,
London.

Elibron and Elibron Classics are trademarks of
Adamant Media Corporation. All rights reserved.

This book is an accurate reproduction of the original. Any marks, names, colophons, imprints, logos or other symbols or identifiers that appear on or in this book, except for those of Adamant Media Corporation and BookSurge, LLC, are used only for historical reference and accuracy and are not meant to designate origin or imply any sponsorship by or license from any third party.

Fort of Iskardo, or Ashardo, Capital of Little Thibet.

THE
ADVENTURES OF A LADY

IN

TARTARY, THIBET, CHINA, & KASHMIR;

THROUGH

PORTIONS OF TERRITORY NEVER BEFORE VISITED BY EUROPEAN.

WITH AN ACCOUNT OF THE JOURNEY FROM

THE PUNJAB TO BOMBAY OVERLAND,

VIA THE FAMOUS CAVES OF AJUNTA AND ELLORA.

ALSO AN ACCOUNT OF THE MAHABLESHWUR AND NEILGHERRY MOUNTAINS, THE SANATARIA OF THE BOMBAY AND MADRAS PRESIDENCIES.

BY

MRS. HERVEY.

IN THREE VOLUMES.
VOL. III.

LONDON:
HOPE AND CO., 16, GREAT MARLBOROUGH STREET.
1853.

ERRATA OF VOL. III.

Page 191, line twenty, for "Rane" read "Râm."
Page 291, line fifteen, for "Simoon" read "Simoom."

ADVENTURES OF A LADY;

IN

TARTARY, THIBET, CHINA, &c.

POOGAH. (DISTRICT ROOPSHOO.)

Distance, seventeen miles.

16*th August*, 1851. *Saturday.*—This has been a long march, and the path has been very stony, though tolerably level. We passed Neupoonsum, the Oōjâr encamping ground, where we halted last year, on our way to the Chōōmorēēree Lake. There are plenty of wild sheep in this neighbourhood. At the top of a stony hill, some four or five hundred feet above Neupoonsum, I recognised the *Mânie*, which our sacrilegious hands despoiled of its flags and horns last year. Close by, the path divides; the right leading to Nâgpogoonding, and the left and lower one, branching off to the valley of Pōōgah, where the productive mines of sulphur and borax are found, of which I gave a short account last year. I have carefully avoided Nâgpogoonding, or the Black Mountain, remembering how intensely I suffered there formerly. Moorcroft calls it a "Pass," and gives its height at seventeen thousand feet above the level of the sea. Fancy people of sane mind, giving such an elevation as a halting-place, when the rarity of the air at night must be so very distressing to most people. It would be just as sensible to halt all night on the Bara Lâcha Pass!

I have just returned from a visit to the upper part of Pōōgah valley, where the sulphur and borax is found. I have not my former Journal by me, but I *think* I gave an exaggerated estimate of the length of the Sohâgur (borax) deposits along this valley. The breadth may be fifty or sixty yards, and the length from half to three quarters of a mile, though the entire length of the valley is nearly three miles. If I gave the borax a greater range, in my previous Journal, why, I apologize! It is never too late to acknowledge an error.

Having described the place last year, I am not going to enter into much detail at present, for no wonderful change has in any respect occurred, and if I failed to be instructive before, I should probably be equally unfortunate now.

There are two excavations in the sulphur mines, and I descended one of them. The smell was very powerful and disagreeable. I observed that a fragile red and also white stone or clay was largely mixed with the sulphur in the mines. There are several hot springs in the neighbourhood, and it is curious to see how the sulphur is gradually forming near these springs. I carried off four of the purified and manufactured cakes of sulphur, which are cast in a crescent-shaped mould. All these sulphur mines belong exclusively to Goolâb Singh, and he has them merely sufficiently worked for the consumption of his army, in the manufacture of gunpowder. The borax belongs to the people of Rōōpshoo, and even these illiterate and stupid people find the means to make it profitable. I could have taken away as much as I liked, of both sulphur and borax, for no one seemed to guard the valuable products of the land. There were no young geese here either, though they were so abundant last year, and I saw but one Brahminee duck sailing on a pool of water.

How very remarkably evinced is the wise beneficence of the Almighty, in these small spots of grass, water, and bushes for firewood, occurring at *convenient marching distances*, in the midst of these vast, inhospitable deserts, where the intervening spaces, whether hill or dale, are destitute of all that is requisite to support human or animal life. Even in the merciful disposition of these immense deserts, who does not recognise the hand of the all-wise Creator of the world? There are many, very many things, very striking in these wild and remote regions, and yet some people would pass them unheeded by.

TCHAKSHANG. (OOJAR.) DISTRICT ROOPSHOO.

Distance, nine miles.

17*th August*, 1851. *Sunday.*—I found breakfast here, but my camp is pitched a couple of miles distant, by the banks of the Chōōmorēēree lake. This encamping ground, though in sight of the blue lake, is fully two miles on this side of it. A considerable rivulet flows close by, and falls into the lake on the northern extremity. This stream rises in the snowy mountains above Nâgpogōōnding. A great deal of luxuriant grass, and many pretty wild-flowers, grow thickly along both banks of this little river.

This march is a very fatiguing one. After

This encamping ground is at the further end of the northern extremity of the lake, about three miles from last year's encamping ground, near Kōōrzuk, where the black tents of the wandering tribes are found during the summer months. The little lake which is passed on the left hand, before reaching the Chōōmorēēree is called Tchârrh, and Khurr, by the Thibetans, but Târa Chund, the Laḥoūl T'hâkoor, (who accompanied us as interpreter last year,) called it the Chânghur.

I observed a white deposit resembling that which is found along the banks of the Tchōō-Soowūrrh, extending thickly over twenty or thirty yards along one shore of the little lake, but the sun was too hot, and I was too tired to go out of my way to examine the substance, or to see if the water was also bitter and salt. My guide, a mounted Tartar, briefly told me that the water of this tiny lake was not fit to drink, but I did not understand the rest of his information.

I have sent my advance camp on to Chângdoom, an Oōjar encampment at the other extremity of this lake, and I purpose riding *round* to morrow, meeting my rear-camp in the evening at Kōōrzuk, having breakfasted previously at Chângdoom. I have seen the space between this and Kōōrzuk, a distance of some four miles, and my object is to make an entire circuit of the lake, rigidly keeping to the shores; in order to decide the disputed point, whether any river rises in the Chōōmorēēree, and also to obtain a tolerably correct notion of the circumference of the lake. The Gopa says it is too far for me to manage in one day, as the distance is considered *six* days' marching for laden sheep or goats. These animals are taken, when laden, from five to six miles a day, which would make the distance from thirty to six-and-thirty miles. It does not look nearly so far, but the outline is, in reality, from all accounts, very much more irregular than it appears from this point.

I do not see a single bird in the lake this year. The weather continues very cloudy, and hail fell to-day. The water was frozen in a pitcher inside my tent this morning. There was a heavy fall of snow on the snow-capped summits of the high mountains above Kōōrzuk, in the afternoon. I saw a white hare this evening on the plain which extends beyond this end of the lake.

KOORZUK. (Oojar.) District Roopshoo.

18*th August*, 1851. *Monday.*—This has been a most fatiguing day, and I am utterly worn out.

I left Th'hūttah at daybreak, and did not reach Chângdoom till past four o'clock, p.m., being about eleven hours on the road. I had no time for a regular breakfast, and indeed, I found no tent pitched. However, my servant produced a cold fowl, and, with the addition of a good glass of ale, I was tolerably recruited. I then sent my people in advance the next march, and cantered back here, arriving before dark. I rigidly followed the banks of the lake, and find there is *no* river, large or small, which rises in the Chōōmorēēree. Two fall *into* it, also five or six streams, but none rise anywhere near. High hills surround on every side, and the banks are all more or less sloping. There is no possibility of *any* efflux from this lake, and the sole way of accounting for the waters being kept at their level, is by the manifest theory of evaporation. Not only have they been kept from rising higher and higher, but it is plain that once the lake was, at least, twice its present size. The banks, whether high or receding, betray the unmistakeable lake-formation, and many signs of having once, though centuries ago, been covered by the waters of the Chōōmorēēree. The natives assert that this lake in fact extended as far as the Tchōō-Soowūrrh, including the little lake in its broad bosom. This theory requires immense capacities of belief, but I do credit about one half. I also believe that these mountains were submerged by the sea, and upheaved by some fearful convulsion of nature. Not that I profess to be competent to discuss such mighty questions, so I will hold my tongue with due modesty!

After leaving Th'hūttah, the way along the shore of the lake traversed a sandy plain, about three miles long and one broad, taking the utmost points of length and breadth. Then came a bad, stony, rocky quarter of a mile, where riding was impossible, followed by sandy plains, the most extensive being five miles long, and half a mile broad. The rest of the way along this side of the lake was rocky and bad.

I saw the road to Rodōkh, on this side of the Chōōmorēēree, but as long as it follows the neighbourhood of the lake, it rarely keeps to its shore, on account of the badness of the ground, and its heart-breaking windings.

I will describe the Chōōmorēēree as consisting of four irregular sides. The sun sets behind Kōōrzuk, so I will designate that side (roughly) the western. One breadth I will distinguish as the northern, and the opposite the southern. The side I went down at first to-day, I will call the eastern shore. My idea of the distance is this:—

1. The Eastern shore . 16 or 17 miles
2. „ Southern „   . . 2 „
3. „ Western „   . . 12 „
4. „ Northern „   . . 3 „

This estimate is taking the circumference of the lake along its actual shores, counting every *bay* and *gulph*, (if I may use the terms, which are not strictly applicable to a lake, I know.) The eastern shore is very irregular, the numberless projecting rocks, and the numerous *bays* one has to travel round, making two and four miles instead of probably one-eighth of that distance, if the outline were at all straight.

The hills are undulating all round, and some of the Heights are covered with snow on the summits. But on the southern extremity, beyond an extensive plain, rise very lofty mountains of icy whiteness, the snow appearing deep and unbroken. The white peaks of the elevated Pârung Range* rise in chilly grandeur and stern beauty far behind. The plain which extends beyond this end of the lake is slightly sloping. It is cut up near the shore by vast ravines, through which lie the numerous channels of a river, which rises in the snowy mountains beyond. I have not yet heard an authentic name for this river, but I

* The Pârung *Pass* is not at all visible.

fancy it is the "*Pára*," rising on the Pârung Pass or Range, which has been by some people absolutely represented as flowing *from* (and not into) the Chōōmorēēree. The Gopa calls the river the *Chōōmeeschurtze*, and says that it is a "brother of the Sutledge," (or Sutluj,) which peculiar term he explained by saying that it issued *from* the Sutluj. I cannot vouch for all this, but hope to have *ocular* and personal information soon.

This plain is, for a couple of miles, full of quick-sands and bogs,—dangerous to traverse near the shore of the lake. The river is not everywhere fordable nor passable, for a mile (or more) beyond the limits of the Chōōmorēēree. Higher up the plain the ground is pebbly, and the numerous channels of the river are quite shallow. These channels intersect the plain, which is at the broadest point (two miles above the lake) not less than half a mile wide.

Chângdoom is, by the path, about eight miles from this; good level road. This is a much easier side of the lake, and far less irregular in outline. The *boná fide* "Kōōrzuk" which I visited last year, is a mile from this plain by the bank of the Chōōmorēēree, and as I previously mentioned, a hill separates it from the lake itself.

I saw many traces of the Kiâng, or Wild-Horse, all along the unfrequented eastern shores, and hundreds probably go down to drink water along that bank, for I saw the print of many hoofs in the wet sand. There are one or two patches of grass, and the banks and rocks are covered with aromatic plants of two kinds, names unknown. I do not think the length of the Chōōmorēēree is more than nine or ten miles from end to end, as the crow flies.

I saw no birds but seven small ducks floating on the water near Chângdoom, and two black-billed crows on the encamping ground, where the road to Rodōkh turns off.

The thermometer gave the Chōōmorēēree (on the north-western point) an elevation of fourteen thousand seven hundred and ninety-four feet above the level of the sea.

CHOOMEESCHURTZEY. (Oojar.)

District Roopshoo.

Distance, twelve miles.

19*th August,* 1851. *Tuesday.*—I spent a most miserable night, and feel ill and exhausted to day. I sat up half the night, totally unable to breathe in a recumbent position, and my heart beat with hurried and distressing palpitations. I became so alarmed that the very darkness of the tent inspired me with a feeling of pain and horror, and I called for a light, that I might at least not die in the dark! But my sensations of misery were no laughing matter, and I feel that they cannot be free from danger.

This march is an easy one, the road good. It is sometimes made into two marches, making Chângdoom (which was passed *en route*) into one, and then the traveller proceeds to Noorbogō, two miles further, instead of halting here. The road from Chângdoom to this is across the plain, or rather pebbly bed of the river which flows into the Choōmoreēree on the southern side. I before remarked that the utmost breadth of this stream, (or rather the bed, for the river, though divided into numerous channels, by no means fills the wide "bed,") is about half a mile. The road keeps to the right of the swamps, bogs, and deep ravines,* which I had to circumvent yesterday, in my circuits round the lake. There is a great deal of grass surrounding our tents, and the encamping ground is by the river-side. The valley

* These ravines are formed by the river, and are from ten to forty feet deep.

is contracted now into fifty paces in breadth. Notwithstanding this narrowing of the channel, the river makes no show as to size, considering the numerous streams which here flow in one body.

The hills are barren, and even the Tartar furze is scarce and distant, though it abounds in the neighbourhood of Chângdoom, and all over the southern side of the lake. There is a bleak wind blowing, and I can hardly hold my pen. I have been a couple of hours writing these few lines,—my fingers are absolutely benumbed with the bitter cold. Nearly all my large goats are dead, in consequence of the very rigorous climate; I was less unfortunate last year.

The height of this encamping ground is about fifteen thousand feet above the level of the sea. I have the greatest difficulty in breathing, and my chest feels weighed down by a painful and indescribable oppression. These distressing sensations always become aggravated after nightfall.

TATUNG. (OOJAR.) DISTRICT ROOPSHOO. FOOT OF PARUNG PASS.

Distance, about eighteen miles.

21st *August*, 1851. *Thursday.* — I arrived here yesterday evening, at seven o'clock, p. m., but felt too ill to write. The march was a most weary one, and the road very rugged. It may be converted into two marches, making Phâlung-Palrâh (or Fâlung-Pâlrak) one stage. This encamping ground is about eight miles from Chōōmeeschūrtzey, and was formerly a spot of great importance. "Phâlung" means large rocks, and "Palrâh" is expressive of the meeting of the different traders who formerly congregated here, from distant districts and countries, for the purposes of barter and traffic. The spot is now nothing more than a halting-place, but it retains its name of importance. I did not halt there, as there was scarcely a square yard of grass visible, and having a dozen ponies with me, their starvation was to be avoided. There is not a blade even here, and the poor weary animals will, in reality, run some risk of being famished, as I hear that fodder can nowhere be obtained, even in the most moderate quantity, for the next fifteen or twenty miles; in fact, not till we reach Keebur, the first village in S'piti (also called Piti.) The unfortunate yâks, sheep, and goats will also suffer. From Noorbogō to Keebur, a distance of some five-and-thirty miles, this dearth of fodder prevails, and the road is bad into the bargain, laming all unshod cattle which traverse it. After passing Noorbogō, the stones, sharp and pointed, were destruction to the feet of every animal, and all have suffered severely. I am detained here much against my will, on account of the non-appearance of my rear-camp.

From Chōōmeeschūrtzey to Noorbogō, the path lay across tolerably level ground for two miles. I observed a stream (or river) falling into the one whose course we were pursuing, to the left or east of our road, a little on this side of Noorbogō. At the junction, our route turned abruptly to the right, following the bed of the latter river. A hundred paces further on we forded the wide channel, crossing over to the right bank. The valley consisted of the pebbly bed, flanked by barren hills of no great elevation above the river. Where we forded, the bed was not less than a hundred and fifty yards broad, and more than half of it was quite dry,—the space actually occupied by the stream being divided into several channels. The greatest depth of the ford was not more than two and a half feet, but though the inclination of the valley was very gradual, the current was extremely powerful, and the river rolled on with great velocity. Not a single rock obstructs the swift but placid flow of this stream, and the valley it waters being nearly level, there is no tumult or uproar in its course. The pebbly bed is broad, and intersected by numerous channels, and in many places quite unfordable.

Our route continued along the right bank, sometimes rising far above, and sometimes following the very bed itself. Sharp stones, pointed and searching, or innumerable pebbles, were the agreeable varieties of the rude and narrow path. I breakfasted half-way, and whether from exposure to the sun, or from the rarity of the air, I have had a most distressing head-ache from two o'clock, p.m.

Several rivers fall into the main stream we have followed, and it is worthy of remark, that the beds of all these are of the same description—broad, nearly level, pebbly, and divided into many shallow channels. This is a very different style of river from the ordinary streams, whether large or small, which rise on mountain Passes.

This encamping ground is a small piece of level, close to the right shore of the river, all pebbles and Tartar furze; no grass. The Pass is plainly visible, about a couple of miles off, as the crow flies. There are several snowy summits all around, and the latter half of yesterday's march disclosed many mountains whose hoary summits were dazzlingly white with perpetual snow. The elevation of this spot must be fully seventeen thousand feet above the sea; a cruel height at which to spend a night in a tent, for those who suffer as I do from the rarity of the air. Oppression on the chest, extreme difficulty of respiration, and frequent blood-spitting, have distracted me for the last sixteen hours. In addition to these miseries, my old cough has returned, from exposure last night to the icy air, for my tent was not finally pitched till ten o'clock, p.m. It was pitched before, but being blown down by a violent gust of wintry wind, I had to practise patience till all was put to rights again. The cold was intense indeed, and the furze would not burn. My bedding, at least my numerous rezâïs, were all behind; the only bed which had come up was broken to pieces, and but for forty Ladâk Numdahs, my situation would have been hopeless indeed. Accustomed to a great deal of clothing at night, I suffer most bitterly from a short allowance, and though the many Numdahs might have been sufficient for most people, I shivered till morning. I wear several furs and shawls, besides the covering of blankets and four rezâïs, yet I seldom feel sufficient warmth at night, in these elevated regions. As for lying down, it is vanity and vexation of spirit, and I have ceased to attempt it. My position at night is almost sitting up, propped up, as I am forced to be, by eight or ten pillows.

I had a bad attack of ague at midnight, and on the whole passed a night of extra misery. In the day-time, I feel comparatively happy, for though I cannot breathe freely, and the slightest exertion is beyond measure distressing, still I am accustomed to these disagreeable sensations, and can bear them with a good deal of philosophy, when not visited by them in their most aggravated forms, as always happens after nightfall. My head has nearly recovered its ache, though I passed such a bad night, and now that my things have all come up, I shall proceed up the Pass, late as it is (two o'clock, p.m.) The whole baggage is carried on yâks, and I find it impossible to muster men for my dhoolie. Riding up the Pass is pronounced impossible, and *walking* is utterly so. I am therefore reduced to a yâk; this will be the first time I ever tried the shaggy steed. The baggage becomes wofully ruined on these animals. I do not like the men of Rōōpshoo; they are dishonest, idle, and turbulent. The Gopa left me yesterday; and since his departure, the men will not obey a single order, and are ceaselessly squabbling with my people. Though there is abundance of wood (for firing) in this spot, I had the greatest difficulty in making the Rōōpshoo Yâk-men get me some last night, when I was perishing with cold, and ill.

I have picked up enough of the Thibetan tongue, to ask for the ordinary things I require. I will subjoin a short list of words, which will be useful to travellers. I shall follow the dialect used in Ladâk and Rōōpshoo. That of Bultistân or Little Thibet is in many words different. I must also premise that I have spelt the words, as my ear picked up the pronunciation, and if I am not strictly correct in my ideas of the proper sounds, at all events, I find I am understood. I may here and there have mixed up a word or two of the Bultistân dialect, in the vocabulary appended, and where I have given two words, generally one is of Little Thibet's peculiar tongue.

English.	Thibetan.
Rope	T'hâkpah
Horse	Tâh
Wild-Horse	Kiâng
Milk	Omāh
Butter	Murr
Ghee (or clarified butter)	Murr
Wheat-*ottah* (or coarse flour)	Bukpeh
Water	Chōō or Tchōō*
Wood	Shing
Fire	Mēh
Grass	Chooâh

* The "Ch" in Thibetan is always pronounced as if it were "Tch," an almost imperceptible sound of "T" being introduced.

English.	Thibetan.
Barley	Nuss
Sugar	Khâra
Goor (*i.e.*, Molasses)	Ghōt
Apples	Khōōshoo
Apricots	Choolie
Carpet	Churra
Egg	Biâbjōōn, or Dōhloo
Salt	Ehgoo
Milch Goat	Râhma
Sheep	Loogoo, or Khulwa
Cow	Pālung
Yâk	Yâk
Woman	Anneh
Man	Mēēnh*
Masōōr Dál†	Trunjoo
Peas	Poostrun
Rice	Dâss
Dog	Khee
Fowl	Zēhroo
Village	Yule
Cloth	Râï
House	Kungpa
Ass	Bŏmboo
Mule	Tēēoo
He-Goat	Rubbuk
Wheat	Trawh
Puttoo (or Woollen Cloth)	Numboo
Kilta (Hill Basket)	Tchēyboo
Load	Khoorroo
Paper	Shōōgoo

* Nasal sound to the "n."
† A Pulse common in India.

TATUNG.

English.	Thibetan.
Bed	Mâzok
Crockery	Kuriul
Tent	Koorrh
Red	Mârpo
White	Kârpo
Black	Nâgpo
Green	Junghoo
Yellow	Surboh
Blue	Hōnpoh
Big	Chunmoo
Little	Chhoongseh, or Choogun
Quickly	Looggur, or Ghiōkhpah
Chain	Chuktukh
River	Tōkpoh
Name	Meen
Come here	Dirionh*
Come quickly	Ghiōkhpa Shōkh, or Looggur
Go	Sōnh* [Shōkh
Come	Shōkh
Bring	Khéōnh*
Give	Tōnh or Tōnhg*
Book	Boyih
Ear	Numchōkh
Eye	Mikh
Did you see?	Tōnhga mat'hōng?
Bone	Roospa, or Roopah
Foot	Kungpa
Hand	Lukpah
Short	Toogun
Tall, High	Ringmoh
Long	Ringmoh

* Nasal sound to the "n" in all these words.

English.	Thibetan.
Mountain	Rigāh
Pass	La
To cross a Pass	La gapchyah
Valley	Lōōngpa
To go with	Niâmpoh châcheh
Sit down	Datcheh
(To) Open, (imp. mood)	Trōll
(To) Shut, (imp. mood)	Dumcheh
(To) Load, (imp. mood)	Gulcalcheh
(To) Mount or Ride, (imp. mood)	Zōhâncheh
Thief	Koonmah
To lie	Zōōnchen
Honest, Good	Ghyēhla
Is	Yōth
Yes	Hēēn
No	Mēhth
Broken	Châtpoh
Cooking Utensil	Nōth
Ink	Nâkcha
Pen	Dihnyoo
Pen-box	Nyōōkdoh
Ink-holder	Nâkōngh*
Spoon	T'hoormung
Knife	T'hee
To write	T'heecheh
One	Chick
Two	Neess
Three	Soom
Four	Jhee
Five	Kuhnâh* or Schnâchh*

* Nasal sound to the "n" in all these words.

English.	Thibetan.
Six	Troōk
Seven	Doōn
Eight	Gheütt
Nine	Ghoo or Oorghoō
Ten	Chheoōh*
Eleven	Chheoōhkchick
Twelve	Choogneēss
Thirteen	Chooksoōm
Fourteen	Choobjhee
Fifteen	Chongāh†
Sixteen	Chooroōkh
Seventeen	Choobdoōn
Eighteen	Choobgheütt
Nineteen	Choorghoo
Twenty	Nissoo
Thirty	Soomchoo
Forty	Jhibjoo
Fifty	Nūpchoo
Sixty	Troōkjoo
Seventy	Doōnchoo
Eighty	Ghiâchoo
Ninety	Goōpchoo
Hundred	Ghiâ
One Thousand	Tōnhg† Chick
Two Thousand	Tōnhg† Neess

The Roōpshoo people are Hindoos. They are a different race from the Bhōts, and winter

* These words beginning with "Ch" are pronounced with the sound of "Tch" always.

† Nasal sound to the letter "n," in all these words.

VOL. III.   C

and summer live in their black tents, with their flocks and herds of sheep, goats, and yâks. They make most wretched porters. Having described them last year, I may spare my remarks now. They are very ugly, with Tartar faces, and the men with their coarse black hair hanging in one pigtail behind, are not very pleasant to the eye, and still less so to sensitive olfactory organs!

KEEBUR. (First Village in S'piti or Piti.) Over the Parung Pass, twenty thousand feet above the level of the Sea.

Distance, about twenty miles.

23rd August, 1851. *Saturday.*—Arrived here late yesterday afternoon, too unwell to write; the effects of the sun, however, and not of the Pass. Though the most elevated of the many Passes I have crossed, I suffered but little. No sickness, and but a slight headache. I left Tâtung on Thursday about three o'clock, p.m., and reached the summit of the Pass at sunset exactly. Though I hurried down as fast as my guides would go, we were all benighted, and after groping in the dark for a couple of hours, halted on the first level spot near water, which happened to be by the side of a hill-stream, the situation anything but eligible—all stones, no grass, no wood. The cattle looked most miserable next morning, and indeed half the Camp had not come up, which delayed me in that rugged spot till the afternoon of yesterday, so that I did not arrive here till sunset. I am halting a few hours, to give my baggage time to reach Khâjeh, where I mean to dine this evening, going on to Dunkir early to-morrow.

The Pârung Pass is given an elevation of nineteen thousand feet above the level of the sea, in Moorcroft's Work, but I estimate it at twenty thousand feet.* Mr. Trebeck ascended it, and calls it the most difficult Pass he had ever crossed. I will here quote verbatim his account, to show how different the Passes are in June and August, and then I will describe the Pass as I found it. Let no cynic † assert that either is incorrect, because the difference is so great in the two descriptions. The actual difference, in fact, solely consists in the time of the year. Mr. Trebeck travelled over the Pârung Pass in June, and my transit has been in August, twenty years later.

* By measurement with the thermometer.
† That is, a "Cockney traveller" *disguised* as a "cynic."

Mr. Trebeck's Account of the Parung Pass.

"On the 9th of June, we crossed the Pârung La. The ascent, though not of the most abrupt description, occupied us from daybreak till noon. In the lower part, the snow lay in lines, with edges sufficiently frozen to bear our weight, and we stepped along as if we had been walking upon boards placed on their edges. Higher up it was softened by the sun, and we had the agreeable variety of sinking into it knee-deep. My horse was so utterly incapable of proceeding, long before reaching the summit, that it was necessary to dismount and leave him to his fate. I should have put an end to his sufferings, but was persuaded that some men might be sent back for him with food from Kiwâr,* though I had little expectation of this being effected in time.

The height of this Pass above the level of the sea, was not less than nineteen thousand feet. To the south, and south-west, a confused succession of snowy peaks presented itself, none of which were much higher than the Pârung La, though some loftier peaks appeared to the south-west. The crest of the Pârung La, and the descent on the southern face, were free from snow. The mountain on each side of the Pass was not more than one hundred and fifty feet above us; the descent was very steep. The Pass was, upon the whole, one of the most difficult we had encountered: we encamped in a gorge not exceeding twenty-five paces in breadth.

The road on the 20th commenced in the defile, through which, as usual, flowed a rivulet intersecting the path, but we crossed upon natural bridges of snow. This opened into a valley where the villages of Kikiem and Kiwâr, and their cultivated lands were met with. Short grass and furze covered

* I have never heard this village called "Kiwâr," but "*Keebur*."

the less abrupt slopes of the mountains, and a few stunted willows adorned the edges of the rivulets. Although much less fertile than Lahoul, the country surpassed that to the north of the Pârung La."

Mr. Trebeck returned by the Pârung Pass the following August, going over it almost the same day of the month as I did so many years after him. I need not copy the account he gives. Beyond the description of a storm he encountered, he says but little of the Pârung. I will now dismiss his account from my mind, and proceed in my own way to give my idea of the Pass, the road, the country, &c.

We did not leave Tâtung till three o'clock (or even later) on the afternoon of the 21st, and I fully expected that we should all be benighted in the midst of snow. Every one tried to dissuade me from going that day, and represented the dangers I should run, when night came on, at such a great height, and on very bad road. But I was " deaf to the voice of all the charmers," an laughed at them and their fears. The steeds on which I and all my servants were mounted, consisted of yâks—great shaggy males with large horns. The girths of my saddle did not, of course, attempt to meet, and yâk-hair ropes tied the saddle to its place;—a couple of the same kind of ropes did duty for reins, being fastened to both horns. A man led the animal by a third rope, passed through the cartilage of the nose. A second man accompanied me, to flog the yâk, and take care of me. I found the eccentric steed very easy and sure-footed, but slow. Moreover he had two very disagreeable habits, which I trust are not inherent in the whole race, viz., grinding his teeth in the most painful manner, and lying down with me on his back, without the slightest warning— up hill, down hill, in snow or mud alike. I rode every inch of the way from Tâtung to this place, ascent and descent, over steep and rugged paths; and considering it was my first attempt at this peculiar yâk-manship, I flatter myself I did something rather brave. Whoever saw this road would be forced to allow that it was, on the whole, a feat. The road was in many places so very bad that riding a horse would have been impossible, even to the best and boldest equestrian, and yet my gallant yâk carried me safely over everything. Frequently in the descent, a pathway, about eight inches wide, was flanked by fearful precipices, and the soil was crumbling and uncertain.

After leaving Tâtung, the road follows the ascending course of the river, which is called the Chōōmee-schūrtze by the Gopa of Rōōpshoo. The bed was broad and stony, and the water flowed in several channels very peacefully, as the inclination was gradual, and no stones impeded its course. The valley was almost entirely confined to the bed of the river, which, however, did not fill one half of the broad space. After some two or three miles of this sort of road, we came to the ascent of the Pass. There was a great deal of snow, but the ascent was not steep. After one or two snow-bridges and masses of snow, the stream which rises on the Pass and flows into the Chōōmee-schūrtze,* about half or a quarter of a mile from the *bonâ fide* ascent, was buried under snow and no longer seen. This snow rose abruptly in a wall (where the ascent was fairly commenced) about fifty or sixty feet high, and continued to the top of the Pass, deep and unbroken. The extent of this spotless expanse was from two to three miles. We avoided walking over it as long as we could, because the ground looked unsound, the snow appearing undermined by the force of water rushing through. Our path lay along a rugged side of the mountain, and was diversified by beds of snow.

* I see that the Chōōmee-schūrtze does not rise on the Pârung Pass; one branch has its source there, as mentioned in the text, but the longest arm comes from the left of the Pass. The natives declare that it issues from the Sutluj, far higher up, but this seems improbable; of course, it *may* be true, and on this point the natives are uniform in their assertions.

The last mile was a gentle ascent of deep snow; —the hills surrounding, about two hundred feet higher than the ground we trod, were covered with snow, not a rock marring the icy purity of its glittering surface.

The cold was intense, and the declining rays of the setting sun sunk below the horizon before we reached the actual summit of the Pass. I was so benumbed with cold that I anticipated unpleasant results; but I had no nausea, no headache of consequence, and altogether, I consider the Pârung Pass far easier than the Bara Lâcha, the Brârmoorj, and the Hânnoo Passes, though from two to four thousand feet higher than any of these. My servant brought me a glass of Port wine, and perhaps saved me from ague thereby, when I was chilled to death by the icy cold wind on the snowy summit of the Pârung.

The view commanded from the crest of this Pass is not striking. I turned to gaze on the side I had just come from, and I saw only harsh and barren mountains scarcely as high as the Pass, and a few snow-capped peaks. I turned my eyes to the view before me, and a line of snowy Heights in a regular range, with angular crests, bounded the vision, after the eye passed over the first and nearer barren mountains which formed and encompassed the descent.

I saw but few mountains higher than the Pârung range anywhere near. I before mentioned that this Pass is given an elevation of nineteen thousand feet above the level of the sea, and that I considered its altitude fully twenty thousand. The highest points of the range were not more than twenty-one thousand feet.

It is curious to observe the different effect on different Passes. Though the painful sensations experienced do most undoubtedly result from the rarity of the air, still, it is equally certain that in this Pass, illness is by no means experienced in the ratio of the elevation attained. For instance, on the Bara Lâcha and Hânnoo Passes, I was most miserably and inexpressibly ill, and on this Pârung Pass, though three or four thousand feet higher than either, I suffered no nausea, scarcely a headache. I had difficulty of respiration, but that is a symptom peculiarly incidental to me. I should very much like to hear a satisfactory reason given for the inconsistency above adverted to. I have been over so many Passes, that I have had ample opportunities of remarking how little the Pass-sickness is regulated by the height ascended, after an elevation of thirteen or fourteen thousand feet above the level of the sea. The "Bischk-ke-Bōottie," or poisonous plant, covers the ground for miles about

Tâtung. I observe that in Moorcroft's Work, that ōōjâr encamping ground is called "Trattung;" this must be a misprint or an error.

The descent of the Pârung Pass was very steep and rugged, and ruin to horses' feet. Every one of my ponies have suffered, and some are dead lame. There is very little snow anywhere on this face of the mountain, or on the actual crest. This is the southern face, and the Bara Lâcha lies to the south-west of the Pârung, at no great distance, as the crow flies.

No river rises on the descent or southern side, and not a blade of grass or even stunted Tartar furze is met with for many weary miles. At one spot called Parōchin, where some people halt, there is a patch (a few feet only in extent) of miserable-looking grass,—no wood, and water distant. This is at the foot of the first steep descent, or about a couple of miles from the crest.

The next level ground is two or three miles further on; it is covered with furze, but there is neither water nor grass. It was intensely dark when we arrived here, but I was forced to proceed, though the road was very rugged and very steep. A mile or less occupied a century of time in the darkness of the night, and when we did reach a small piece of level, large enough for my camp, where water was nigh, I saw that no wood or grass was in sight. The former I sent for from above, but the cattle starved, poor creatures. This river, by which we encamped, flows (I was told) from the Bara Lâcha. It is not nearly so quiet as the Chōōmeeschūrtze, but the bed is narrow and fordable as far as this. I asked the name, but it was such a heathen and difficult one that it soon escaped my memory. The stream is crossed at least twenty times between our night's encamping ground and this village. In some places it is rapid and three feet deep;—as I was riding a yâk, however, I felt no fear, for the animal seemed strong under me, and never gave way with the current, after the fashion of ponies and horses. The road is shocking—narrow and rugged, or leading through water and over large stones. About three miles from Keebur, the path leaves the left bank of the stream, and a steep ascent up a high mountain is succeeded by a long tract across the summit of the height, and then a descent leads to this village. To the west, on the opposite bank of the stream, which flows some distance below Keebur, stands the village of Kikiem, about three hundred feet above the little river which meanders through its narrow valley.

After leaving the night's encamping ground by

the side of the stream, we had to pass through a regular gorge, in the middle of which the river flowed. I was much struck by the Heights which formed this gorge:—about seven or eight hundred feet in elevation, rising perpendicularly above the stream, there was no mistaking that they had been riven asunder by some mighty power, probably a volcanic convulsion. So perfectly alike were these perpendicular Heights, (though severed,) that were they to be brought together now, they would amalgamate exactly, and the union would leave no unnatural points whatever. I observed this even still more when I reached the summit of the mountain, which rises gradually above the perpendicular Height, flanking the left bank of the stream. The exact resemblance of these severed hills, in altitude and every particular, must strike any observing person. They would beautifully dove-tail if brought together as they stand.

I observed many pretty wild-flowers, two of a new species,—new at least to me, along and above the banks of the stream, as we followed its course. These mountains are much more pleasing than the harsh and arid Heights of Bultistân and Ladâk. Grass and wild-flowers cover the majority of them, and stunted willows, gooseberry bushes, wild-roses, and many bright flowers fringe the banks of the Bara Lâcha stream. The mountains are well watered by numerous streamlets, and after the countries I have lately traversed, there is a delicious verdure refreshing to wearied eyes. Not a single tree, however, flourishes either here or at Kikiem. The elevation of both these villages must be about thirteen thousand feet,* above which elevation no grain will grow, and trees will scarcely thrive. The fields look well, though they are not yet ripe.

The houses are built on a rock, which expands, however, into the arable land that extends several hundred paces beyond. They are constructed of unhewn stones below; and unburnt bricks and mud, covered with a slight coating of whitewash, form the upper portion. They are flat-roofed, and a layer of dried furze lies on the tops of all. This Tartar furze still prevails, and is the only firewood procurable. I observed that it has all gone to seed; which seed hangs in long, thin pods. There is a great abundance of wild peas on the mountain side, which lies on the road to Keebur. The Coolies eat them raw in large quantities. I also observed a few rhubarb plants, very poor in

* I observe that Moorcroft's Work also gives Keebur an elevation above the level of the sea of thirteen thousand feet.

appearance, and some fine onion and garlic, in full flower.

S'piti or Piti is peopled by a race of Tartar origin. They are very ugly, but *seem** a simpler and better people than those of Rōōpshoo. The dress is very similar. The men here also wear the single pigtail hanging down behind, and the women plait their hair in at least one hundred and seventeen (more or less,) long thin plaits, which often depend to the waist. They wear a great many ornaments; large, discoloured turquoises being the favourite stone. These ornaments are very similar to those I described in the Ladâk attire.

The Rōōpshoo people are a bad set; dishonest, and really wicked. The Gopa of Rōōpshoo voluntarily exchanged three ponies with me, at Tōōgjeh Chumboo, and but for mine being footsore, he had the best of the bargain. Well! what did these honest Rōōpshoo people do to-day? They coolly walked off with the very ponies I had received in exchange, thus doubling their original number! They did this in open daylight; and when my servants tried to rescue my property, they threw large stones at them, and I preferred the loss o

* I soon found out that this judgment was by many degrees too favourable.

the ponies to a dangerous fray. I do not suppose I shall have any redress.

Besides this, they stole many articles, even some clothes belonging to my servants. And as for the provisions, butter, rice, flour, spices, sugar, &c., which I had in *kiltas*,* as kitchen store, they have devoured nearly the whole. They ended their last day's work, by killing two promising foals. This they managed by tying them in a sort of Gordian-knot on one of the mares, to save the trouble of carrying them up and down the Pass! What a pleasant kind of people, to travel through lonely desert mountains with! The Gopa gave me two men when he left, as "Zima-wallahs," or responsible parties. These very men were the first to hurl down stones, (at me as well as my servants,) when I naturally sought to recover the abducted nags.

Yâks are common here, and as I hear the road is very bad, I mean to ride one again.

I was delighted, on arrival at this village, to find a servant with letters from the Plains, the first for many weary days. This man had been waiting for me a fortnight, and thought I must have come to grief in the reported disturbances in Kashmir; for in the Plains, people seem to think

Or hill-baskets.

that Goolâb Singh has been murdered by his nephew, and that the Europeans in the Valley are all confined, and the Passes all closed! What can have given rise to such groundless and improbable rumours?

We have had clear weather and cloudless skies. How different from the tropical rains which are now deluging the burning plains of Hindostan. *Dieu soit béni*, that I am where I happen to be!

KAJEH. (DISTRICT OF S'PITI OR PITI.)

Distance, eight miles.

Same day.—We arrived here just as the day closed. The road is steep in parts, and in others very good. At first it follows the course of the Bara Lâcha stream, some distance above the bank. This stream empties itself into the river of S'piti, this branch of which is termed the Losar,—I suppose because it comes from the neighbourhood of the village of that name. Our route then lay along the left bank of the Losar, frequently close to the shore. This river flows along a broad bed, and is not fordable, though divided into several separate channels. Tamarisk grows along the shores, and several bushes, sweet-brier and goose-

Fort of Dankir in Spiti: Ladakh-Tartary.

berry among others. I also noticed some currant-bushes, the fruit small and sour, and of a yellowish white in colour. About a couple of miles from this village, a peculiarly unsafe-looking sanga spans the Losar over a part of the river where the channel rapidly contracts from fifty or sixty yards to scarcely twenty; almost opposite stands the village of Rērik.

We also passed the hamlet of Khee; and nearly on the opposite bank I noticed the village called Koorik. The hills are frequently quite barren, and the summits of the surrounding mountains are occasionally found capped with snow.

Llâmaism manifestly prevails in S'piti, to judge from the numerous *Mánies* we passed before reaching Khâjeh. Not a soul in this place can speak Hindostanee, and the Keebur Gopa has not yet arrived. I have been obliged to leave a horse behind, as he is too foot-sore to move further at present. Those marches between Noorbogō and Keebur have ruined all my stud.

DUNKIR. (District of S'piti or Piti.)

Distance, twelve miles.

24*th August,* 1851. *Sunday.*—I breakfasted

at the small village of Lâra, about five miles from Kâjeh, riding on here in the afternoon. The road to Lâra is very good on the whole, and follows the left bank of the Losar. This river is joined by the Lingti and the Pin, the former flowing into it on the right bank, and the latter a couple or so of miles higher up, on the left shore. I was quite surprised to see how the Lingti is changed since its course through Lahoūl, and that part of Ladâk below the Bara Lâcha Pass. There it is so still; —here, a perfect torrent, rushing madly through a confined channel, between high and perpendicular rocks. I know of no other "Lingti," so I suppose it must be the same. There is a route to Kōōloo, *via* the Kunzum* La, (or Pass,) from Dunkir, distant eight days' journey, so say the zemindârs (farmers). There is another route by the Bhubbeh Jōth or Pass, which is a very short road to Simla, as near again as the one I am taking.

The Pin flows from a direction south-westerly, and is as large a body of water as the one it forms a junction with. The united rivers are indifferently called the Pin, the Losar, and the S'piti river, by the natives of the country. The road is in parts good, and in others very steep and rugged. The last three miles consist of (principally) a long

* Called in Moorcroft's Work, the "Kulzum La."

"Goompha," or Buddhist Temple of Heemboorkzhun in Ladak, Thibet.

London, Hope & C.º Great Marlborough Street.

and steep ascent to the ruined fortress and small village of Dunkir. I observed near the western base of the high rock on which Dunkir is built, the evident ruins of extensive constructions, though not a brick was actually visible. But in all the neighbourhood of what is now Dunkir, below and around, the crumbling rocks still retain the form which they bore when crested by buildings.

How very different is the Dunkir of 1851 to that of 1821, judging from the drawing in the second volume of Moorcroft's Travels. In fact from that drawing it would seem that an entire " change had come over the spirit of the "—scene.

The Tartar furze is no longer seen, and the majority of the hills are nearly as bare as in Ladâk. Up to this, not a tree have I seen in S'piti, except the few stunted willows by the banks of the stream, when I first entered the district. Not a single tree has even been planted near the villages, as is the case in Ladâk and Lahoūl, near hamlets on the most desert mountains. Dunkir is a mere village now, the houses and Gōōmpa being scattered on a mountain, which appeared to me to be of peculiarly crumbling soil. A single bastion is built against the base of the eastern side; what it may be meant for, or was once intended for, I have not the ghost of an idea. The Fort is on the top of the hill, and is in ruins. There are traces of buildings on the southern continuation of the mountain, the soil being crumbling, and disposed in fanciful shapes. These once bore the weight of many Tartar houses, for I particularly remarked the disposition of the soil which supported the existing houses of Dunkir, and it was just the same, or rather would be just the same, were the buildings taken off.

I hardly know what I am writing, for a Babel of tongues is half distracting me; moreover, a mob of men, women, and children are ranged all round, and I am disturbed by being stared at. How many of the motley group have never seen a lady before! Their curiosity is absolutely insatiable.

There is not a single tree in or near Dunkir. In Mr. Trebeck's drawing,* there is one represented,—of good size too. I verily believe its only existence was in the draughtsman's fertile imagination. And yet it is a most strange mistake to make. An imaginary tree, where there are several would be a trifle,—I have inserted such myself(!); but where trees are positively *unknown*, it seems absurd and unpardonable.

* Given in the frontispiece to the first volume of Moorcroft's Works.

My camp is pitched on a small piece of grassy level, separated from Dunkir Hill by a khud. The only water which flows near, is far below the village, and I perceive that it is carried up in wooden barrels by men and women. Dunkir Hill stands out (if I may use the expression) beyond the general line of the adjacent range of mountains—more to the south. The face presented to the river is perpendicular and inaccessible, and the western side is likewise very precipitous. The northern connects the Hill with the neighbouring Heights, and I observed many snowy peaks beyond. With the exception of one woman, not a living soul now in Dunkir, can speak any language but Thibetan.

The principal crops are wheat and barley, which are still green. There seems but a poor show of fields altogether. The elevation of Dunkir is given at thirteen thousand feet above the level of the sea, in the Journal of Captain Gerrard, published by Colebrooke, in his " Remarks on the Sutluj River."—*See* "*Trans. Asiatic Society,*" *Vol.* 1.

POH. (DISTRICT OF S'PITI or PITI.)
Distance, about eight miles.
25*th August*, 1851. *Monday.*—This is a short

march, the road generally running along some little distance from the left bank of the river, and on the whole tolerably good. There were some precipitous and bad places, impossible for a mounted horse, but I was on a yâk, and never required to dismount. In fact, I am becoming a capital yâk-rider, and can manage the shaggy steed as well as a horse! The one I rode to-day, went at a good seven miles trot in the hour, where the road was at all tolerable.

I observed a half dried up tank to the right of the road. The hills continue savagely barren, and no village intervenes between Dunkir and Poh, on this bank of the river. I noticed one on the opposite shore, about three miles before reaching this village, and on inquiry, found that it was called Mânee.

How the S'piti river is changed in its appearance since we first saw it near Keebur! There it was very quiet, flowing in several channels, the bed broad and pebbly, like the Chōōmeeschūrtze, on the other side of the Pârung Pass. Now its bed is from twenty to forty yards broad, and the inclination much greater; it is generally confined by nearly perpendicular rocks, the waters flowing in a rapid and turbid flood.

About a mile before reaching Poh, I saw the first tree in the inhabited parts of S'piti. It was growing by itself, away from all vegetation. On approaching it, I perceived it was a pencil-cedar, in size and general luxuriance far inferior to those which grow in Lahoūl. In and about the immediate vicinity of Poh, there are several trees—pencil-cedars, willows, and one or two poplars, the latter very inferior in size and beauty to the famous Kashmir species.

We did not arrive here till dark, though the sun had not set when the village first appeared in sight from the top of a hill which we had to descend before we came to the stony level ground which precedes the point on which the village stands. The river takes a sweep close by, and the width of the valley in the neighbourhood may be nearly half a mile. There are no intelligent Tartars in Poh.

The difference of climate is quite striking. Instead of the ponderous bedding before requisite, I find two rezâïs quite sufficient at night. And yet Poh cannot be *less* than eleven thousand feet in altitude; probably it is at least three hundred more. Except between Parōchin and Keebur, I have seen no wild-flowers worth preserving in S'piti. The sweet-brier and wild-rose abound, but the flowers are all past. I have noticed wild-currant and gooseberry bushes, the fruit quite worthless.

LARI, or LURREE. (District of S'piti or Piti.)

Distance, seven or eight miles.

26th August, 1851. *Tuesday*.—This is the last village in S'piti, along the left bank of the river, and I hear that three days of Oōjâr interpose between Lâri and Châng, the first village in Busēhr. Hélas! hélas! I thought I had no more "Oōjâr" marching before me.

This is a very small village. It stands a little more than 400 feet above the river-bed, where the stream is not very full. The elevation of the hamlet is 11,515 feet above the level of the sea, measuring by the thermometer, and correcting the elevation by observations of the temperature of the air. At Lâri the thermometer boils at 194°.; and the temperature of the air in autumn is 39°.

The Coolies and yâks, &c. for the Oōjâr journey, come from the district of Pin, I believe. It is odd that it should be requisite to send so far, and I do not understand why the present set are not made to go on instead, for Poh is decidedly nearer than Pin. I had no intention of halting here, but I cannot induce the Pin people to move, though they are all on the spot. Bribes and threats have alike proved unavailing.

The people inhabiting the last twenty miles, seem a turbulent, disorderly, quarrelsome set. If a word is said to them, or if they are told to do what they do not like, they all talk at once in the most threatening manner, with raised voices and frantic gestures. Anything like coercion is out of the question, as they seem only too ready for blows, and glad of an excuse for violence. My servants tried to prevent their gathering round the spot where I was seated, and though nothing like force was used, the mob began to clamour, and to make the most alarming uproar. They painfully remind me of the Rōōpshoo people, and seem equally dishonest too. My sheep have been abstracted—the blankets covering the young calves, stolen—and a puttoo of very large size, belonging to Ghaussie, has mysteriously disappeared from his saddled yâk. I made over a pony to the Gopa of a village, and desired him to send it to Kōōloo as soon as its feet were recovered. He not only evaded giving me a receipt for the animal, but said, " what should he do if the animal *died?*" This was an odd speech to make, considering that the little nag was in perfect health, and merely foot-sore ! I strongly suspect he *will die* —an imaginary death at least. Poor me, ever victimized. I have again been necessitated to leave another pony behind, as he has only just arrived here, (four o'clock, p.m.,) also a Bultistân cow and calf. I have, however, been fortunate enough in being able to give them over to a gentleman who is surveying the district, and marches far more slowly than I do. I would recommend no one to take ponies the route I have gone, or any long distance in the hills, over roads unmade. Shoes would not for a week stand the cruel trial of ceaseless rocks and sharp stones, and a farrier is but rarely to be met with in the benighted districts of the Himalayas. I have lately had my ponies shod, but could only get enough of shoes for the fore-feet, and the business was but indifferently managed. Though they are all hill-ponies, have been rarely ridden, and never laden, they are all knocked up and foot-sore, and I do not expect one to reach Simla. It is always possible to hire ponies or yâks, through the less travelled districts of the hills, and the hire is so trifling, and so much trouble is saved, that it is by far the best plan. The animals I have were expressly purchased for carrying loads on the made roads, as I experienced so much delay last year from the lack of Coolies in the Simla district. I reckoned without my host, and I must put up with the consequences.

The houses in S'piti seem all built after the

same model; flat-roofed, bi-storied or poly-storied; the upper portion of unburnt bricks and mud, the lower generally of unhewn stones, and a slight coating of whitewash over the whole. They are all huddled close together. Thick layers of firewood are piled on the flat roofs of the houses, as an almost invariable rule.

The people are evidently Tartars, though they call themselves "Bhōts." I see a good many Lâmbas or Llâmas (priests). Some wear red, others yellow or black robes. The hair of some of these holy men is disgustingly matted and horrible-looking, long and filthy. I mentioned before that the women wore theirs in innumerable long thin plaits, which hang frequently below the waist. These are gathered together by turquoises, amber, and coral ornaments. The wife of the head-man of this village told me in reply to an inquiry on the subject, that these numerous plaits were opened once in *six weeks*, (*O mores!*) and then the head was washed and re-plaited for a similar interval;—*mon Dieu*, she made my flesh creep at the idea, and I instinctively moved further off.

Both sexes wear the Tartar boots, gartered generally by yâk-hair ropes below the knee. The women wear principally black woollen attire, with coloured trowsers, and no covering for the head. I observe among other ornaments, armlets of *China ware!* Beauty is totally unknown in S'piti.

I forgot to describe the march from Poh to Lâri. The only village passed *en route*, is Tâbo, about five miles from Poh. It is small, and appeared to consist principally of sacred edifices. I saw a long line of conical affairs, upwards of a hundred in number, rising from a base two feet elevated from the ground, which I was told were as sacred as the Mânies. Not a drop of milk to be obtained here, and my goats had not arrived at breakfast-time. I warn all travellers to make arrangements for this requisite, if they ever halt at this place. There are a few trees here, principally willows and poplars. The road from Poh to Tâbo is very bad, unfit for riding a horse. In many places the path is about eight inches wide, crumbling and unsafe, and flanked by nearly perpendicular precipices of loose and uncertain soil, terminating in the vortex of waters below.

I have lately ridden a *Zho*, (that is the hybrid between the bull-yâk and common cow,) and I think I prefer the zho to the yâk as a *steed*. It answers to the whip or spur much more like a horse, and I can ride it in the most dangerous and precipitous places with safety. My servants are not so brave, and while they dismount, wonder at my mad temerity. Not that *I* see any madness in it, and I feel no fear,—looking aside calmly at the abyss below, when not one inch intervenes between me and Eternity. I say this advisedly, for the path is often but *half a foot wide;* were it once lost, no human power could save man or beast. The soil in such places is of crumbling slate or limestone, such as I felt so terrific last year, and described in one Lahoūl march. I am daily accustomed to it now, and to tell the truth, I am much more frightened to go over such paths *on my feet*, however odd this assertion may seem. I shall never forget one night we were benighted in Bultistân, and came to a piece of this dangerous style of mountain. At each step I took I heard the ground under me rolling down the nearly perpendicular side of the mountain into the river below. I could *see* nothing, but I could hear the roaring Indus, and the crumbling of the soil, till at last I stopped still and fairly cried like a child! The Coolies carried me, but in the dark it was a service fraught with peril and real danger.

The S'piti people call me "Beebee"—a rather childish title for so sedate a personage. One man told me I was pretty, and about a dozen echoed the compliment. I did not feel much overpowered, and could not help laughing at them;—when I looked at their hideous faces, I really entirely agreed that the comparison *must* be in my favour, and did not wonder at their finding beauty in the contrast! (Oh dear, how vain I am, *n'est-ce-pas?*) I showed a looking-glass to a woman yesterday, and though she was painfully ugly, I protest she seemed to delight in her image, for she never ceased looking at it, for a good hour. This is the only glass I have left, and it was two-thirds broken yesterday. So much for vanity!

JEEOOMDOH. (Country of China.)
Oojar.

Distance, ten miles.

27*th August*, 1851. *Wednesday*.—My baggage started yesterday from Lâri, about three o'clock, p.m., with strict orders to proceed to this halting place. I arrived at a spot by the river side, guiltless of grass or wood, and found the camp coolly settled in this desert place. I was very angry, but I only wasted my wrath, for nothing would induce the S'piti people to move; so my ponies starved all night, and the only way I got tea, was by my Khidmutgar burning his walking-stick this morning, to light a fire. Two of the ponies walked back to Lâri in an independent manner, not liking (I suppose) the starving system, and the rest looked miserable this morning.

About a mile from the village, as I went along yesterday evening, I suddenly spied my bed lying by the road-side, two of my servants sitting by it, and the man whose business it was to carry "Squire," together with another Coolie, looking on in despair. I could not make out at first what had happened. The servants, however, explained that the Coolies belonging to the bed had thrown down their burthen and "bhâgeea," (run away,) and that it was too heavy for the single porter that remained to lift it. I must say I felt sufficiently annoyed at this *contretemps;*—this was the sole "Charpoy" remaining to me, all the spare ones I had brought in case of accidents, having gone to pieces, one after another, during my travels. Night was stealing on apace, and I could not go back to the village I had just left, as the whole of my Camp, (with the exception of the fragmentary portion I have just alluded to,) had gone on to the encamping ground in advance. While we were waiting in an apparently hopeless condition at this desert spot, quite at a loss what to do next, and I was on the point of abandoning the luckless bed to its fate, Providence came to our aid in an unexpected manner. All at once we observed jauntily trotting towards us on horseback, a Chinaman, whose red and yellow robes betokened his sacerdotal character, while other distinctive marks pointed him out as a Llâma of high degree, or Chief among the priests. The two Coolies suggested that we might enlist him temporarily, *vi et armis*, as a porter; but on my ordering them to seize him for the purpose, they hastily declined, and humbly supplicated me not to involve them in a deadly feud with the sacred Llâmas. Being thus forced to take the matter into my own hands, I at once resolved how to act. I waited till the man was within a hundred yards, and then sauntered carelessly towards him;—the slow, ambling pace of the Ghōōnt on which he was mounted, allowing me a good view of the horseman as he approached. His worldly goods, clothes, and cooking utensils were strapped behind his saddle, the high-peaked holsters of which, in front, were bristling with fire-arms. He was armed to the teeth besides, and his jewelled sword glittered even in the fading light. His steed was richly caparisoned; the saddle-cloth bright and gaudy. Quite coolly and undauntedly I approached the august traveller, and taking hold of his bridle, led him silently up to where lay the prostrate bedstead. He made no resistance, surprise appearing completely to overpower his faculties! Mustering the little Thibetan I knew, I then ordered him in a firm and resolute, but calm tone, to deliver up to me on the spot, his arms of every kind. Again he obeyed my cool command in speechless bewilderment, and even dismounted at my request, without attempting any remonstrance. I then proceeded to possess myself of all his weapons, intending to restore them in due time. I slung his magnificent sword by the strap attached to its gilded hilt across my own shoulders, and grasped his fire-arms in my hands, giving his Ghōōnt in charge to my servants. I observed that his ponderous saddle was all of wrought *steel*, a pad serving to prevent its galling his steed.

Preserving the same unconcerned manner, I next commanded the terror-stricken priest to "take up my bed and walk,"—or rather to assist the Coolies in so doing. And then the tongue was loosened, and the dumb man spake! He volubly asserted that he was a high-priest, one of the holy among the tribes,—a visitor, or rather an ambassador from China to S'piti, and that it was impossible he could demean himself by doing my bidding. My only reply to his rhetoric was an an imperative reiteration of my *hōōkm* (order). The strong man quailed before a woman's voice! I do believe he was in doubt as to my identity, regarding me, perchance, as a visitant from another world! At all events, he refused no longer, but tremblingly obeyed my directions, by lifting up the bed, and proceeding straightway with it to my camp. But for this, I should now be lying on the cold hard ground, instead of reposing on this comfortable couch.

It is impossible to resist making use of the *prestige* of one's appearance under such circumstances,—so novel and absolutely unearthly in the eyes of these ignorant dwellers in the wilds does a "Feringhee"* face appear. Resolution and intrepidity go a long way in terrifying them into abject obedience; indeed, I always found them more afraid of my simplest word, than of all the "*striking*" proofs given them of my servants' wrath.†

* European.

† I may here just add, that on reaching my camp, I found the bedstead faithfully delivered indeed, but that its unwilling bearer, after depositing it, had vanished on the instant. Alarmed, doubtless, at the idea of his further services being compulsorily required, the bird had flown! He did not even wait my arrival to redeem his weapons, &c., which of course

This is the usual halting place after Lâri, but as I accomplished three miles yesterday evening, I have resolved to proceed to Shoogoor, an encamping ground some five miles distant, also in the country of China.

The road from Lâri to Jeeoomdoh is very bad, rocky and crumbling alternately, averaging six inches of width. I infinitely prefer the yâk or zho to a pony or horse on such barbarous roads, as I have never to dismount from the former. I noticed a pencil-cedar growing in melancholy solitude far below the road, by the river's edge. Low shrubs abound on the hills all round, principally sweet-brier, wild-rose, a species of thorny ziziphus, and a variety of furze. No grass and no trees, till this spot is reached, where a small patch of the former and a few of the latter are found, near a very black torrent. This mountain Rapid sepa-

---

I purposed restoring to him; so I did the only thing which was left in my power by way of restitution. I took care of the property thus strangely acquired, until I had an opportunity of delivering it safely into the hands of the nearest public official, to be held in charge for its owner, should he ever appear to claim it. It is needless to say I never heard of its subsequent fate. The Ghōōnt was mysteriously spirited away during the same night the priestly impressment occurred;—of course the Llâma was lurking in the neighbourhood, and when all was still in the camp, mounted his nag and rode away!

rates S'piti from China, and is crossed by a frail bridge. The breadth is not more than ten yards, but the current is violent, wildly dashing over huge rocks, and terminating its impetuous course in the River of S'piti, not far below this. The extreme blackness of the hue of the water is very easily accounted for by the vicinity of soil as dark as coal, over which its course also lies.

I observed some gypsum rocks on the road to-day, but the general formation appeared to be of limestone or slate. No wild-flowers worth preserving; whether the season is past, or whether this country is deficient in that respect, is "beyond my poor divining," and I will not hazard an opinion.

There is a second road to Busēhr from Tâbo, along the right bank of the river, *viâ* Soomrah and Shealkur. The latter is in Kanâwr, (or Busēhr,) and is scarcely known by the above name in S'piti, being called instead, "Kiâkurr," or "Kâkhurr."

This road must be much shorter than the one I am following, for in order to circumvent a mountain torrent which is un-bridged and unfordable, we have to make a heart-rending *détour*, going direct east, when Busēhr lies immediately to the south.*

* And Chângo, the village we are bound for, lies to the direct west, which is in the diametrically opposite direction from Shoogoor, where my camp pitches this evening.

There is a marked path down to the river, about two miles from this, (I mean the tributary and not the main river,) and at certain seasons of the year, it is possible to cross the torrent, thereby saving a day's circuit. This river is called the Châla-Dōkpo; perpendicular cliffs of granite and mica slate confine its wild waters, in many places. The average breadth of this torrent is not more than twenty-five or thirty feet.

SHOOGOOR. OOJAR. (COUNTRY OF CHINA.)

Distance, five miles.

Same day.—Arrived here at sunset. On the whole a tolerable march, though as usual the narrow path and crumbling soil were not forgotten by the Genii of the road altogether. A few plants, but no grass on the hills. The ponies are absolutely exhausted from starvation, and the cattle in general have suffered greatly from the total lack of fodder.

First we had an ascent, very steep, then after a piece of indifferent road, alternately ascending and descending, we came to the descent which finished the march.

This ground belongs to China, and opposite, at

the distance of less than half a mile, stands the hamlet of Choorih, (or Keeorih,) the first in China, with its few fields of cultivation surrounding it. There is a second violent torrent, which is also of a deep black colour, and flows a little distance below this encamping ground. This torrent is the boundary between China and Busēhr. It is called the Zângcham or Pârati, and is about 100 feet in breadth. It falls into the S'piti river, about two miles south of Jeeoomdoh.* It is very rapid and violent, flowing at a great inclination, and with inconceivable velocity. Large stones block its course, and create the usual spray and uproar. There is neither bridge nor ford,—at least not at present. It appears to flow from the north-east.

I observe several mountains capped deeply with snow, beyond the immediate inner barren range. Heavy rain fell to-day in the direction of Busēhr, and snow whitened the more elevated Heights. A few drops of the distant deluge slightly sprinkled me on my way to this. It is more cool than cold at night under anything like shelter. The height of this spot cannot much exceed 11,500 feet above the level of the sea.

* The elevation of the spot where the confluence occurs, is 10,200 feet above the level of the sea.

There is one single tree visible in the village opposite. I should like to explore China, but any attempt to do so would be inevitably foiled, and I should feel painfully like a fool, were I forced, *vi et armis*, to return. The Chinese keep all visitors off by hurling stones at them, and in the mountains this method is most effectual. The Coolies wish to send my ponies round by a path leading directly through the Chinese village, as the direct route is reported dangerous for them. I said that if the ponies went, I should go too, and as they decline this responsibility, I suppose all will go by the break-neck path, *viâ* the torrent immediately below our camp.

Me voici in China! I purpose talking importantly of my visit to the land of pigtails, mysteriously concealing the immense extent of my travels in that inhospitable land—I mean to astonish by my audacious visit to regions where ordinary mortals are stoned to death! Oh! I will not say that I merely gazed at the first Chinese village at a respectful distance! But seriously, could I persuade my camp to invade the forbidden land, I should like of all things to make the experiment, and though I have no absolute proof that I bear a charmed life, I should be fearless as to the result. I cannot see what object they could have in impeding one of my gentle sex.

CHANGREYZING. (Illaka of Busehr.*)
Distance, about eight miles.

28*th August,* 1851. *Thursday.*—Most shocking road, steep and rocky, and at the very outset passing over a break-neck place. Instead of a reasonable bridge, the torrent was spanned by a huge slanting rock, and the luckless horses having been taken with ropes along this dangerous place, where man or beast might slide into Eternity in the twinkling of an eye, or in the rapid transit of a falling star,—the poor trembling animals first stumbled and fell along a stony, rocky sort of cave, below which the torrent roared in fury, and then followed a long rocky ascent, by way of an apology for a road. The ponies were cut se-

* This is the commencement of "*Chinese Tartary,*" which will now be traversed in my daily marches for several days. The intelligent reader will observe that the *names* are completely Chinese. When the Messrs. Gerrard visited Busehr, about thirty years ago, they were not allowed to go beyond Changreyzing; and when they attempted to reach Lâri *viâ* this route, they were effectually stopped by a large band of armed men. Bribes and threats proved alike unavailing, so they were forced to return to Busehr.

verely, and I fear all hope of their reaching Simla must now be abandoned, or at all events of their accompanying my Camp. During the rugged ascent, though the zho I was riding fell repeatedly, I was not converted into a "field-marshal," but sat quietly on the saddle till I could raise the animal. In fact, all the cattle in camp are weak and exhausted from want of fodder, and have scarcely the spirit to move one foot before the other.

I noticed again several rocks of gypsum, and for a mile of the way, mica glittered in large quantities in some of the pale blue rocks we passed. The sun was shining brightly, and the radiation was terrible to the eyes. Pencil-cedar grows on the hills, and I observed willows lower down. There is scarcely a blade of grass on these mountains; several shrubs and plants,—the wild-rose and sweet-brier, gooseberry and currant bushes, a variety of furze different from the Tartar species, (but equally fit for firewood,) and an aromatic plant,—are the principal products of the hills we passed.

This spot has an elevation of 12,500 feet above the level of the sea. It is the usual encamping ground after Jeeoomdoh, but as I halted at Shoogoor, I mean to proceed to the first village in Busēhr, on this side of the S'piti river. Since leaving Jeeoomdoh, I have not seen this stream, and this is accounted for by the fact of the *détour* we were forced to make in order to circumvent the torrent, which most officiously, and in the most *mal-apropos* manner, thrusts itself in the way. Changrēyzing is a scrap of a hamlet; only one family lives in this wilderness. A few small fields and two stone huts of rude construction constitute the whole place. There is some grass here, and if the ponies had only arrived, they might have a little of their staff of life. Before we reached this spot, I noticed about a dozen yâks and zhōs, being loaded by people from Chângo in Busēhr, with firewood. I observed plenty of pencil-cedar in the assorted bundles, from which I conclude that it makes a good wood for burning. When polished, it has a very pretty grain, and if fresh, a faint but pleasant smell;—it is not a *strong* kind of timber, however. The rocks in the neighbourhood of Changrēyzing are of granite, gneiss, and mica formation; limestone and clay-slate are also met with. I was much struck by observing pebbles embedded in clay, and numerous small round stones in the soil: all having the unmistakeable appearance of having been acted upon by water, though the river S'piti is upwards of 2,000 feet below this level, and there is no rivulet near.

CHÁNGO.* (Busehr.)
Distance, six miles.

29th August, 1851. *Friday.*—Reached this village at sunset yesterday. The road from Changrēyzing consists first of a steep and bad descent to the bed of a very violent Rapid, which pours vehemently down at a great inclination from massive large rocks, with terrific uproar and wild foam. The channel is extremely narrow, and a very frail bridge is thrown across this torrent at some distance above the wild waters. A long ascent follows, turning gradually from north to due west. A part of the road is very steep and rocky, but the latter portion is broad and good. There is a pile of stones at the top of the Height, on which flags, horns, and painted pieces of cloth, bits of wool, ribands of cloth, &c., were fastened. This, and one or two Mánies I observed during the march, evince the prevalence of Llâmaism in these parts likewise. A long descent, steep and bad, leads to Chângo, which is a large village, surrounded by fields, on the left bank of the S'piti river.

* Called by the people of S'piti, "Châng."

Opposite, on the right shore, I see a few fields and trees, but no village. The river is narrow and rapid, averaging about twenty-five yards in breadth.

Sheâlkur, called by the people of S'piti, Kâkhurr and Kiâkurr indifferently, is about three miles higher up, on the right bank of the river. I saw it as I descended to Chângo. There is a ruined fort there, and a small village which is situated fifty or sixty feet above the river. A sanga spans the flood, I am told, though I could not see any. The height of Sheâlkur is given at 10,998 feet above the level of the sea;—Chângo may be two or three hundred feet lower.

One of my ponies is *non inventus* to-day, and I am waiting to see if the Coolies of S'piti will bring it to me. It is now noon,—oppressively hot in tents. The price of Ghōōnts here is from eighty to one hundred and fifty rupees:—very different from Kashmir prices, or even the market value in Ladâk or Bultistân.

The surrounding hills continue barren, and devoid of even grass. The breadth of the valley may be from two hundred yards to half a mile. Though the elevation of this village is ten thousand four hundred and seventy-nine feet above the level of the sea, (by measurement of the thermometer; for water boils at 196° Fâhrenheit,) the summers here are sultry. In this month, the thermometer averages 80° in the shade at noon. The village is situated in a plain, lying east and west, in a dell watered by two streams, which no sooner escape from their dark and tortuous channel, through lofty and inaccessible crags and nearly perpendicular Heights, than they are turned into conduits by the mountaineers, and made to irrigate the fields laid out in terraces, one below the other. The crops principally consist of wheat, barley, millet, *ogal, phâphur*, turnips, peas, beans, &c., and are very luxuriant. The situation of Chângo pleasantly contrasts with the sterile and rugged character of the surrounding country. The picturesque glen terminates to the north and south in bare ridges, on which nothing animate is seen. On the west is the S'piti river, flowing very tranquilly, considering the rapidity of the current, and the great inclination at which it flows. On the east, at the head of the Plain, is a high peak, the crest white and hoary with eternal snows. The seasons at Chângo are a month earlier than at Nâko. Seed-time begins in March, and the harvest is ready in July and August. Snow falls continuously from November to March, but is seldom more than a foot deep in the vicinity of the village. In April and May there is rain occasionally.

LEO, or LEE. (Busehr.)

Distance, ten miles.

Same day.—I rode here on an impetuous little Ghōōnt, quite unattended, having distanced all my escorts, and arrived in the village at sunset. However, it was nearly dark before I found my Camp; and I was weary of wandering through the cultivated and scattered portions of the village, which is an extensive one for the Hills. The numerous fruit-trees which stud the ground almost concealed my little Camp. It was some time before I could dislodge a guide, and at first I only secured a woman, old and stupid. Verily, these women are scarcely human, with far less intelligence and sense than apes and baboons.

After leaving Chângo, our road ascended some two thousand feet in four miles. Here the path divided, the upper leading to Nâko, the lower being the direct route to Leo.

Nâko is situated at an elevation of more than twelve thousand feet above the level of the sea. The cultivation is luxuriant, and fields of barley, wheat, phaphur and turnips, produce plentiful crops. These fields are generally partitioned by dikes of granite, instead of—as in the neighbouring villages—barberry and gooseberry bushes.

Grain is sown at Nâko in March and April, and is reaped in August and September. Towards the end of October snow generally falls, but seldom exceeds two feet in depth in the neighbourhood of the village. It lies, however, for nearly six months. Some authors attribute the fact of its not falling sooner than it does, to moisture in the air; for winter may indeed be said to begin in the first week of October under a clear sky. The thermometer during that month is seldom above 20° Fâhrenheit at sunrise. In this month the average height of the temperature at noon is 75°.

The cattle at Nâko are fed principally upon the leaves of poplar. The only other trees at this elevation, or anywhere near, are junipers and a few stunted willows, which have been planted.

Most people are deluded into going by Nâko, which is out of the road, merely to suit the convenience of the Coolies, who like to be changed as soon as possible. Having expressed my positive determination *not* to go *viâ* Nâko, I found the substitutes for the yâks and men of Chângo ready at a village called Leerik, three or four miles distant from this. I observed Nâko higher up on the same hill as the one on which Leerik is situated,—perhaps six hundred feet almost directly above. Nâko seemed to consist of three nearly distinct villages on the slope of a mountain, whose summit cannot be less than sixteen thousand feet. The elevation of Nâko is given at twelve thousand feet above the level of the sea.

The road from Chângo to Leo is decidedly bad, steep and stony, but I did not once dismount from the fiery little pony I rode, though perchance I showed in my persistence as much recklessness as skill! The natives stared at the risks I laughingly ran, and tried to persuade me to dismount.

There are a great many apricot trees about Leerik, and a few willows;—the village itself is small. From Leerik to Leo the road is a steep and rugged descent to the bed of the river of S'piti. A very formidable wooden bridge, of most peculiar build, spans the violent waters at an elevation of some twenty feet. A flight of stone steps conducts from the bridge to the road above, which is on a level with this village, and not more than three or four hundred yards distant.

Leo or Lee is a large, straggling village, situated immediately above the right bank of the river. The cultivation is extensive and promising, and the trees are numerous, principally fine specimens of apricot. The traveller is ushered into Leo by a long line of Mânies, and many Llâmaic edifices are seen about the precincts of the place. The hills are nearly bare, and to me very uninteresting, for (at this season at least,) no pretty wild-flowers enamelled the ground, and the wild-roses were all faded and gone.

As I rode through Leerik, I saw the apricots drying on the tops of the houses, as in Ladâk, so I suppose the dried fruit called "Komânies" is also common in Busēhr. I have seen no vineyards as yet, but I believe this part of Busēhr is *not* called Kanâwr.* The Kanâwr grapes are deservedly famous.

I have only six ponies left out of the twelve I had not a month ago. The Siâna or head-man of Chângo refused to give a receipt for the two little nags I was forced to leave in his village, so I mean to keep the pony I rode to-day as a hostage. I would recommend no one to bring either horses or ponies this route. The road through Busēhr is supposed to be "*made*,"— Heaven save the mark! and yet they are many

* An error. The whole of Upper Busēhr is also called Kanâwr, but not by the people of the country.

D *

degrees better than the S'piti roads, which are a disgrace to civilization. Pardon, dear rulers of that ungodly country, pray pardon my candour, for the truth, however unpalatable, *must* be told. I find that the honest Coolies of Lâri have stolen the following articles—one of my saddle-girths, one spit, one china jar, a blanket, and two sheep.

HANGO. (Busehr.)

Distance, seven and a half miles.

30*th August*, 1851. *Saturday.*—Breakfasted here, but purpose dining at Soongnum, the next ordinary march. The Coolies insist upon being changed at this place, which is invariably a source of delay and trouble.

This march goes over a high mountain, about the elevation of Nâko, some twelve thousand feet above the level of the sea. The first half of the way is a very steep ascent. The gallant little Ghōōnt, in his fretful impatience, exhausted his strength, and one-third of the distance I was forced to ride the yâk which had accompanied me as the steed of my escort. As I was too lazy to change the saddle, I found a single puttoo (blanket), rather a precarious seat on the back of the bull in steep or rugged parts.

There was a mile or so of good and nearly level ground, and a steep but short descent led to the streamlet on which Hângo is situated. This stream falls into the S'piti river nearly a mile from this; and the united rivers soon after form a junction with the Sutluj. We almost entirely left the course of the S'piti to-day, but I could occasionally see it far below, its banks generally perpendicular, and the average breadth varying from ten to twenty yards. The mountain which rises above Nâko is fully sixteen thousand feet in altitude, rising in gradual and undulating slopes above the village. The summit is partially covered with snow, and many of the surrounding Heights are similarly capped.

I noticed a very white mountain to the left, which my guide told me was called the "*Poo*." He spoke such questionable Oordoo, that I could not understand the other items of information he gave me regarding it.

Hângo is eleven thousand eight hundred and twelve feet above the level of the sea. It is situated at the head of a dell, in the peaceful bosom of cultivation. There are a few poplars here, but no fruit-trees. The glen lies East and West, and has a tolerably level surface. As a stream flows on each side of this glen, and a third through the centre thereof, the supply of water is always abundant. The Siberian barley is very luxuriant here, and the ear of this grain is so large and full, that the average of some ten, casually picked, was *ninety-eight fold*. All the crops are very fine.

The surrounding mountains are limestone. Those on the north are precipitous and sterile; those on the south are less steep, and are pleasingly verdant in comparison, being covered with grass and furze.

The thermometer exhibits the boiling point of water at 193°; and when the "corrected" elevation was estimated by Captain J. D. Hebbert, the temperature of the air was 35°. The estimate of altitude I have given above is taken from Captain Hebbert's journal. Captain Gerrard estimates the elevation at about four hundred feet less.

The hills are more or less covered with a few plants, some strongly aromatic, which, in the almost total absence of grass, are cut and dried. They are heaped on the roofs of the houses as fodder. We saw a sort of broom, yellow flowered, and a variety of furze also, on the hills to-day. No trees; only a few rose-bushes.

Hângo is a large place, apparently consisting of

two or three villages in the valley. There are many trees also, mostly apricot and apple varieties. The people here seem to speak the Thibetan language; most certainly their dialect resembles the peculiar one used in Ladâk. They are much better-looking as a race, and are good-humoured. I will not yet vouch for their honesty, till I have tried it thoroughly.

Yâks and zhos still prevail. I have been trying to purchase some beasts of burthen; but mules appear unknown; ponies scarce and dear, and "bōmboos" (donkeys) no one appears willing to sell. I am told that the price current of the latter is from twelve to sixteen rupees, which is treble the value of those animals in the plains of Hindostan, and yet even at this high rate, no one hitherto has agreed to sell the few I require.

So far, I observe that the houses in Busēhr are constructed generally of stone and mud, flat-roofed, and one storied. I am writing in a temple, the walls glaringly painted with hideous images, and the altar adorned with painted gods, of sorts and sizes. The building is about twelve feet square, four pillars forming a second square in the centre, and about fifteen feet high. There are flags on the altar and pillars—painted gods flaring in red and yellow, stamped on the cloth—and sundry holy books are placed on the altar.

SOONGNUM. (District of Busehr.) Over Hungrung Pass, 14,837 Feet in elevation above the level of the sea.

Distance, nine and a half miles.

31st August, 1851. *Sunday.*—I was detained so long at Hângo for the last six Coolies requisite, that the sun set long before I reached half-way. The first four miles is a steep ascent to the summit of the Hungrung Pass, the elevation of which above the level of the sea, is estimated at fourteen thousand eight hundred and thirty-seven feet. The road to the summit is broad and good, though very steep. A pile of Llâmaic stones, adorned by flags and horns, marks the crest of the Pass.

The mountain is of limestone formation, and is broken by the action of the weather into a gravelly surface, thickly covered in places with furze, juniper, and coarse short grass, which afford pasturage for cattle.

There is a little snow on a hill to the left of the Pass, about fifty feet above. The view from the summit is rather confined:—on each side, one very snowy mountain is visible, and to the

North, I observed a black pyramidal peak. A little above the summit of the Pass to the left hand, I saw a flock of ten or twelve wild sheep, called by the natives "Meerig," or some such vague attempt at a name. It was a little past sunset, and though they were not fifty yards off, I could not see them clearly enough to describe them faithfully. I am safe, however, in saying that the colour of the animal is light, something of a squirrel-hue. I have five skins of this wild sheep, and the fur is soft as the marmot's, but the hairs are shorter.

The descent of Hungrung Pass is very steep and bad. The path goes down to the bed of a rivulet which is crossed and re-crossed repeatedly, and an ascent leads to this village. Night fell almost immediately after I had passed the first part of the descent, and beyond the badness of the pathway, I cannot safely vouch for anything. Long before reaching this village, I could see the dark shade of trees, the outline distinct against the starry sky. There was a very juvenile moon, but even this faint light soon sunk to sleep. I was much exhausted when I arrived here, as I had to walk a great part of the descent, and the sharp stones cut open my slight boots, severely wounding my feet. Once when I was riding, the pony stumbled against a rock, but

I still kept my seat, though he went over on his side. I was not at all hurt.

Soongnum is a large village,—plenty of trees: vineyards and apricots abound, and Llâmas are innumerable. The village is situated on the left bank of the Durbung, a considerable stream, spanned by a sanga in the commencement of to-morrow's march. The houses appear almost entirely made of wood, and are very numerous, built close to one another on the slope of the hill. There is a house here which is reserved for the accommodation of strangers, and saves the trouble of pitching tents. To the right of the road to Simla, a path leads to S'piti, through a rather difficult pass.

The elevation of Soongnum is 9,691 feet above the level of the sea, by thermometrical observations.*

KANUM. (DISTRICT OF BUSEHR.) OVER THE ROONUNG PASS, 14,508 FEET ABOVE THE LEVEL OF THE SEA.

Distance, about eleven miles.

1st September, 1851. *Monday.*—Arrived here late last night, wearied beyond measure. I had a very bad zho to ride, and this animal infinitely preferred going over the khud during the descent,

* Water boils here at 197° Fâhrenheit.

to keeping to the pathway like most civilized steeds. The consequence was, that after running many hair-breadth escapes, I was forced to walk when it became dark, till weariness compelled me to seek a *porter*.* The latter part of the march was very rugged, while the ascent, (though steep,) was excellent—a good broad road the whole way. A pile of stones, with the ordinary accompaniment of flags, horns, and pieces of cloth stamped with religious sentences, marked the crest of the Pass. When we reached that spot, a fine range of snow-clad Heights burst on the view. The hills were principally of clay-slate formation, and less bare. Creeping juniper is found on the Pass, and trees are more frequent. Near the summit, on the descending face of the Roonung Pass, there are three paths. The first, which branches off mostly to the left, is the direct route to Kânum, a rather rugged *pugdundie*, or footpath. The second, or middle road, is the one we took;—steep and bad enough in all conscience, besides being somewhat of a *détour*. The third route was

* Who carried me on his back! I have been reduced to this mode of conveyance for many long miles in the Himalayas, where riding and the dhoolie were both impracticable. Considering the *hydrophobia* with which these mountaineers are afflicted, the horrors of the alternative can be imagined!

the most to the right, and led direct to Leepee, the march beyond this. There is no village on the road, and thefore the wretched Coolies bring unwary travellers to Lubrung or Kânum, merely to suit their own convenience, the direct road to Leepee being also the continuation of the regular "made" route through Busēhr. The way I was taken passes below Lubrung, the path steep and bad, repeatedly crossing the rivulet called Zoong.

This is a very large village, the fields of cultivation stretching over an extensive portion of the slope of a hill. The elevation of Kânum is 9,060 feet above the level of the sea, by thermometrical observations. Water boils here at 198° Fâhrenheit. Lubrung is perched right opposite, the Zoong flowing between. The Sutluj is quite close to Kânum, and visible from my camp. There are a great many trees about this village—firs, willows, poplars, and numerous fruit-trees and vines, laden principally with unripe fruit. Apples, apricots, and pears are nearly fit for eating, but very inferior to the fruit in Kashmir. The head-man, (called in Busēhr "the Mookeea,") brought me a *dâlly* of apples, and at Soongnum, a similar functionary gave me a large quantity of excellent raisins. Grapes were not ripe, either there or at Leo.

After leaving Soongnum, the road led to the bed of the Durbung stream. We crossed by a rude sanga, and immediately after that, the ascent began, from first to last very steep. At a mile, we passed the village of Tâhling, a small wood-built hamlet; there I saw one of my Ghōōnts. Poor wearied animal, he was totally unable to proceed! I occasionally wonder if the organ of acquisitiveness be equally developed in the people of Busēhr, S'piti, and Rōōpshoo, and if I shall ever be fortunate enough to see my ponies again. The Firs were very numerous about and above Tâhling, and the sight of my old friends plunged me into a sentimental mood. However absurd it may seem, I have a positive and doting fondness for this dear tree. A strange feeling of pain and pleasure, curiously mingled, passes across my heart, and I never see any one of the genus " Fir," without that peculiar sentiment, expressively termed by the French, " resserrement de cœur,"—alas! why does "happiness thus glide away?" Dear tree, "I love thee not wisely, but too well!" though it sounds odd to say this in grave earnestness, as I really do. Not that I am given to the sentimental mood, but there are times when thoughts cannot be chained, and memory wings her flight to that past, which is gone and can never return. How can I help being sad when I recall happier days, and feel

> "The mortal coldness of the soul,
>   Like death itself come down;
> It cannot feel for others' woes,
>   It dare not dream its own;
> A heavy chill has frozen o'er
>   The fountain of my tears,
> And though the eye may sparkle still,
>   'Tis where the *ice* appears."

Ah! I have had sufferings enough to make me sadder than I often am, but—

> "The tree will wither long before it fall;
> The hull drives on, though mast and sail be torn;
> The roof-tree sinks, but moulders on the hall
> In massy hoariness; the ruin'd wall
> Stands when its wind-worn battlements are gone;
> The bars survive the captive they enthral;
> The day drags through though storms keep out the sun;
> And thus the heart will break, yet *brokenly live on:*
> Even as a broken mirror, which the glass
> In every fragment multiplies; and makes
> A thousand images of one that was,
> The same, and still the more, the more it breaks;
> And thus the heart will do which not forsakes,
> Living in shatter'd guise, and still, and cold,
> And bloodless, with its sleepless sorrow aches,
> Yet withers on till all without is old,
> *Showing no visible sign*, for such things are untold."

Those who know what sorrow is, will feel how

true are these lines, and that yet it is possible to conquer one's-self so far as to brood but seldom over lost happiness, or past trials.

> "Have I not had to wrestle with my lot?
> Have I not suffered things to be forgiven?
> Have I not had my brain sear'd, my heart riven,
> Hopes sapp'd, name blighted, *Life's life lied away?*
> And only not to desperation driven,
> Because not altogether of such clay
> As rots into the souls of those whom I survey.
> From mighty wrongs to petty perfidy
> Have I not seen what human things could do?
> From the loud roar of foaming calumny
> To the small whisper of the as paltry few,
> And subtler venom of the reptile crew,
> The Janus glance of whose significant eye,
> Learning *to lie with silence,* would *seem* true,
> And without utterance, save the shrug or sigh,
> Deal round to happy fools its speechless obloquy.
> But I have lived, and have not lived in vain:
> My mind may lose its force, my blood its fire,
> And my frame perish even in *conquering* pain;
> But there is that within me which shall tire
> Torture and time, and breathe when I expire."

Thus is it that I can laugh now, where once I would have "wept tears of blood," and it is but seldom that the dark shadows of bitter memories cloud my heart. When happier hours are recalled, something trifling in itself rouses the phantoms of the past, and then, though "I am not of the plaintive mood," yet, very occasionally, "I feel an ebb in my philosophy, and the tide rising in my altered eye." *Dieu soit béni*, this is soon dispelled, and even when totally alone, the transition from the deepest melancholy, and most hopeless despondency, to the most reckless or childish mirth, is as rapid as it may appear unnatural. As mere nothings suddenly touch some chord in the heart, and bring on a long train of memories,—sad, whether those memories be bright or dark, for past happiness is as painful to dwell upon, as past sorrow, nay, to me, far more so;—as mere trifles in themselves thus recall past scenes, so do mere nothings, mere trifles, equally banish those phantoms of the past.

" And slight withal may be the things which bring
  Back on the heart the weight which it would fling
  Aside for ever; *it may be a sound—*
  A tone of music—summer's eve—or spring—
  A flower—the wind—the ocean—which shall wound,
  Striking the electric chain wherewith we are darkly bound;
  And how and why we know not, nor can trace
  Home to its cloud this lightning of the mind,
  But feel the shock renew'd, nor can efface
  The blight and blackening which it leaves behind,
  Which out of things familiar, undesign'd,
  When least we deem of such, calls up to view
  The spectres whom no exorcism can bind,
  The cold—the chang'd—perchance the dead—anew,

The mourn'd, the lov'd, the lost—too many!—yet how few!"

And this strange "lightning of the mind" can replace dark and gloomy thoughts, by brighter hopes and anticipations. The sanguine live on "*hope*," and though it may, like the Ignis Fatuus, lead on deludingly,—what would life be without its light, when no positive and tangible happiness gilds one's lot? Many pass through their career in this world in a stupid sameness, knowing no extremes of bliss or woe; the petty concerns of life form their only care; their minds too narrow, and their objects too confined, to have higher or wilder thoughts. And yet they are happy enough, in their own stupid, plodding way. Such a life would fret me to madness! for though what is vulgarly called solitude, is never wearisome to me, I am fond of danger and the excitement of travel. "Quiet to quick bosoms is a hell." And this, perchance, has "been my bane;" there is a fire—

"And motion of the soul which will not dwell
In its own narrow being, but aspire
Beyond the ordinary medium of desire;
And, but once kindled, quenchless evermore,
Preys upon high adventure, nor can tire
Of aught but *rest;* a fever at the core,
Fatal to him who bears, to all who ever bore."

LEEPEE. (DISTRICT OF BUSEHR.)

Distance, seven and a half miles.

Same day.—The Kirmanung Ghât is ascended in this march, and the summit is called half-way. The path is steep and stony in parts, but I rode the whole distance on a Kânum Ghōōnt. The way was wooded with Pines, and as these beautiful trees cover all the hills in the vicinity, the burning sun was less overpoweringly felt. How pleasing a difference from the barren and treeless deserts of Thibet! A little before reaching this village, we came into the "made" road, which goes straight from Soongnum to Leepee. It did not seem a very brilliant one, from the specimen I had of it.

Leepee is a village of considerable size, situated on the left bank of a large stream, called the Teetee. A sanga (wooden bridge) spans this body of water, at the commencement of to-morrow's march. The houses are all made of wood. Cultivation is extensive, and the trees numerous. Several varieties of fir, willows, poplars, &c. form the principal timber of the district, and a good many fruit-trees are also found. Vineyards are numerous, but the grapes are still unripe. I also observe numbers of walnut trees, heavily laden with half-ripe nuts,—very fine specimens. There is a house here for travellers, which is far better than a small tent, being cooler by many degrees. The people of this place are very civil; but no Coolies are ready, and I cannot go on to the next march, as I had hoped to do.

The mountains in this neighbourhood are of clay-slate, gneiss, granite and mica slate. The bottom of the dell in which Leepee is situated, is 8,700 feet in elevation above the sea-level.

PUNGHEE. (DISTRICT OF BUSEHR.) OVER THE OORUNG OR WERANG PASS, 13,000 FEET IN ELEVATION ABOVE THE SEA.

Distance, thirteen miles.

2nd September, 1851. *Tuesday*.—After leaving Leepee, the road ascended the Oorung or Werang Pass, by a steep, but good path;—a great part of the way deliciously wooded. I should say that the elevation of this Ghât or Pass must be more than thirteen thousand feet above the level of the sea. The crest is some distance above the forest line, and pencil-cedars are found in the vicinity, but firs continue the prevailing timber. The descent is steep, and in parts rocky and bad. This village is attained by several descents, intermingled with a few short ascents here and there, very prettily wooded. A torrent, forming a series of cascades, is crossed by a wooden bridge, between Gungâra and Punghee; it is called the Késhang. The former is a village some distance below the road, and the Coolies were waiting by the wayside, to change, according to the disagreeable custom prevalent in Busēhr, at every available spot. This peculiarity causes great delay to those who are unwilling to halt at or near every village, however short the march.

This village is like the rest I have stopped at in Busēhr, a motley assemblage of wooden houses, crowded together, plenty of trees, and a few fields of cultivation; very little level ground. Vineyards and walnut trees abound. The grapes are nearly ripe here, if I am to judge from the dâlly presented by the Mookeea of the village on my arrival.

I observed quantities of micaceous rock throughout this march, and I picked up numerous pieces of mica on the path. I also noticed ore of various sorts, glittering in the fragments of rock by the wayside. I feel the heat most oppressive after the cold climates I have so long wandered in.

I am told that Kanâwr is only another name for Busēhr, and is not confined to any particular part of the district.* Llâmaism still prevails. The men wear their hair differently in Busēhr from Thibet, as, instead of the long side-locks of Bultistân, or the pigtails of Rōōpshoo and S'piti, they cut their hair short. They are a much better looking race altogether, and the young women are mostly pretty, or at least nice looking. They have classical features, and many boast of that great beauty, the short upper lip. They seem a merry, good-tempered people. The majority of the men understand the language of the Plains, but very few of the fairer sex either speak or understand any tongue but the dialect peculiar to Busēhr. It seems no longer to resemble the varieties of Thibetan, as I observed that it did in the upper parts of the country. I could see Cheenee, (the Governor-General's place of residence last year, and the march succeeding this,) almost immediately after descending the Oorung Ghât.

* It is certainly confined to the *Upper* Section of Busēhr, as I found out subsequently, on arrival, at Rampore, the Capital of Busēhr.

Punghee is 9,200 feet above the level of the sea, and 2,500 feet above the Sutluj at this part of its course.

CHEENEE. (District of Busehr.)

Distance, eight miles.

3rd September, 1851. *Wednesday.*—This march consists of a descent, and the rest a tolerably level road—sometimes good, sometimes bad; nearly the whole way prettily wooded with firs. There is an eccentric Fort close by, made, as is usual in Busēhr, of alternate layers of wood and stone, high and narrow, the four sides of equal breadth. The Governor-General's large house stands here, and a few tents (occupied by "Cockneys" I suppose) vary the scene. There is a good deal of forest, principally of firs, all about Cheenee, and a great many vineyards, and walnut trees.

The grapes of Kanâwr are deservedly famed for size and flavour. They are largely exported, and are sent to the Plains as well as Simla. The best way of carrying them is in small baskets, placing the fruit in layers singly, between layers of cotton. In this way they travel great distances safe and uninjured, but they are also taken in kiltas, (hill-baskets,) placed in bunches, and the tops of these long baskets merely covered, as a protection from sun or rain. Of course one-third are ruined before they thus reach even Simla. The Sutluj is some two miles below this, and very plainly visible. The breadth of the channel averages thirty or forty yards, and is confined generally by nearly precipitous banks, above which rise wooded or cultivated slopes, and several small villages are dotted over the neighbouring mountains. The Malgoon, a rapid torrent, is crossed in this march; —it passes on to the Sutluj.

As I am going to the Borenda Pass, Cheenee is some four miles out of my way; I have come here to make my horses over in charge to the Vakeel of the Busēhr Râjah, as they are unable to proceed at present, and moreover the route I am going is totally impracticable for ponies or horses.

The road to Simla from Rampore, is by this village. The marches are—

From Cheenee to

1. Rogee . . . 8 miles.
2. Meeroo . . . $8\frac{1}{2}$,,
3. Cheergâon, also called
   Tholong . . . 5 ,,
4. Nachâr . . . 11 ,,
5. Turanda . . 8 ,,

6. Surâhn . . . 13 miles.
7. Gourakotee . . 9¾ ,,
8. Rampore . . . 8 ,,
9. Nirt . . . 12 ,,
10. Kotgurh . . 8¾ ,,
11. Nâgkanda . . 10¼ ,,
12. Matteâna . . 13 ,,
13. Fâgoo . . . 15 ,,
14. Simla . . . 14 ,,

There are halting places between Mutteâna and Fâgoo, and Fâgoo and Simla. Theog is half-way between the two former, and Muhâsoo about eight miles from Fâgoo. Indifferent road as far as Rampore;—thence to Simla, excellent made road. Dâk-Bungalows, (minus servants,) from Kotgurh to Muhâsoo.

Cheenee is 10,200 feet above the level of the sea. The Sutluj is 400 feet below. The surrounding rocks are of granite and gneiss.

NEAR THE VILLAGE OF POOAREE.

(DISTRICT OF BUSEHR.) BY THE LEFT BANK OF THE RIVER SUTLUJ.

Distance, about three miles.

4*th September*, 1851. *Thursday.* The patch

from Cheenee to this encamping ground, (a small level spot, a little above the left bank of the Sutluj,) is a steep descent, the road a mere footpath. We passed several vineyards, and two small hamlets. It was night, for I did not start till late, but the pine-torches lighted us on our way, eclipsing the faint radiance of the young moon. A "Cheēka," or bridge of ropes, spans the Sutluj, immediately below this spot. This bridge is on the same principle as the one at Nâssbun, between Bunhâl and Jummoo, which I described in a former part of this Journal, except that it is slighter, the ropes being fewer. Those which waft the traveller across, consist solely of two yâk-hair ropes, and a feeling of insecurity stole unpleasantly over me, as I looked on the slight protection between me and the wild river below, a certain grave to all who might fall into it. The people tried to persuade me not to tempt fate at the late hour I arrived, but I resolved to go across, dark and horrible though the passage appeared in the blackness of night. There was no moon, and torches could not be taken across.

I was bound by ropes, and pulled very rapidly over to the left bank. I felt very little nervousness after all, and the passage was rapidly effected. I infinitely prefer this kind of mountain-bridge to the Zampa, or twig-construction. Across the latter it is utterly impossible to take ponies, but, (as I mentioned at Nâssbun,) I saw one dragged across the Chundra-Bhâga, over a Chēēka bridge, well bound by ropes. As the road I am now about to follow is impassable for horses, there are no preparations for the transit of such bulky animals at this Chēēka over the Sutluj.

The village of Pooâree is one or two miles out of the way, some distance above this spot, and not in sight. I saw it as I was riding from Punghee to Cheenee. It seems a village of some size, and belongs to the Wuzeer Monsookh-Dass, the Prime Minister of the Râjah of Busēhr. There are numerous vineyards on the opposite bank of the Sutluj. I sent my servant over this morning with two kiltas, (or hill-baskets of goodly size,) to have have them filled with grapes. He effected the purchase of that quantity for *one Rupee!* The grapes are purple or yellow, fine large specimens, of excellent flavour, and quite ripe. The Mookeea of Pooâree is a disagreeable, disobliging man, and I have great difficulty in getting away. The heat is very oppressive in a small tent, as the sun is blazing, not a cloud obscuring its painful splendour. The greater part of Busēhr is not subject to the periodical rains, and a heavy shower is a rare visitant in the upper sections of the district.

On arrival in my camp last night, I ordered my Dhobie to do some work for me before he went to sleep, and to my astonishment, he coolly declined obedience. Unaccustomed to such mutinous conduct, I desired the recreant to be dismissed my service on the spot, and my Sirdâr was directed to see the delinquent across the foaming Sutluj. In vain the man wept and prayed,—in vain he deprecated the extreme step of so sudden a "rookhsut,"* as he weepingly pointed to the cataract he was to cross in the deep blackness of the midnight hour. His pusillanimity and womanly tears only excited my derision; and as I had but recently trusted my equally valuable life to the tender mercies of the frail suspension-bridge of yâk-hair ropes, I could find no sympathy for this great he-thing, sobbing and screaming like an overgrown baby;—he was, therefore, *vi et armis*, put into the halter of ropes, and launched across the wild vortex. I stood on the bank of the river, laughing at his abject terror, but when this amusement was over, I continued to gaze on the surging waters, rushing so madly on.

"Lo! where it comes like an Eternity,
　As if to sweep down all things in its track

* Dismissal.

Charming the eye with dread,—a matchless cataract,
Horribly beautiful!—"

I gazed on the turmoil of waters, and as I sadly thought on the Past, and the dim uncertain Future, I forgot the very existence of my offending retainer. And what time or place so fitted for such reveries, as the hour and scene I unconsciously chose,—the dark and gloomy night adding to the charms of savage scenery.

" 'Tis night, when meditation bids us feel
We once have lov'd, though love is at an end:
The heart, lone mourner of its baffled zeal,
Though friendless now, will *dream* it had a friend."

Extreme fatigue at last roused me from my sad contemplations, and I retraced my steps slowly to my solitary camp, feeling how mournfully true are those warning words of Manfred,—

"There are shades which *will not* vanish,
There are thoughts we *cannot* banish."

This morning while I was indolently strolling in front of my little encampment, I spied my late slave, the Ex-Dhobie, on the opposite bank of the Sutluj, extended on a rock, in a piteous state of despair. Putting some money and a branch of luscious grapes into a bag, I fastened it to the halter used for passengers.

My present was pulled across with the rapidity of lightning, and given by the opposite ferrymen to my miserable attendant. I also called out out to him as loud as I could in the hopes of being heard above the "din of waters," the favorite salutation of the Hindoos,—"Râm-Râm-Jee,"— and my facetious politeness touched him to tears! But looking upon the male-Niobe as a *numuk-hurâm*, an ungrateful servant to an indulgent mistress, I have not taken him back into my service, thereby producing a salutary discipline in the small remainder of my once numerous retinue, which effect I hope will last till I reach the terminus of my wanderings. There is no chance of the man coming to any harm, as the village of Cheenee is so close, and there are plenty of his tribe there at present.

It is a great mistake pitching a Camp so far from any village;—we have had the greatest trouble in getting anything we want, even in the shape of supplies. Though the sun has long since risen, not a Coolie has condescended as yet to make his appearance. I am so anxious to reach my journey's end, having been a long time now without intelligence from those dear to me, that I shall hurry on, leaving all my baggage behind, should that in the end prove my sole mode or hope of progression.

Pooâree is 7,033 feet above the level of the sea. The thermometer boils at 202° of Fâhrenheit.

RALHA. (District of Busēhr.)
Distance, about six miles.

5th September, 1851. *Friday.*—Most shocking road, rocky and rugged beyond measure, running along the left bank of the Sutluj,—frequently dangerous and precipitous. Even the Dandy, an affair carried by two men at a time, and consisting merely of a Durry* slung on a pole,—even this conveyance was soon out of the question, and the last three miles I was carried by three or four men alternately. At Bârung, a small village of many orchards, I found all my baggage lying about, the Coolies flown, and two goats and three fowls reported stolen. I only got on here by dint of a great deal of positiveness and resolution; but I was forced to leave behind the majority of my baggage, the tiny village only producing five-and-twenty men, ten of whom were reserved for the Dandy.

* A sort of drugget or carpet.

I reached this place at ten o'clock, p.m., and was not sorry to find dinner ready. I see no village here, merely a great many vineyards of very excellent grapes, and one or two paltry huts. We have had a little rain this morning, and the skies are still clouded. The entire march was well wooded, and the trees were very fine specimens of fir and walnut. The flora of these hills now assimilates to that on the slopes of the higher mountains and Passes of Budrawâr and Kishtawâr. Balsam begins to be the predominant flower here, as there; the underwood, too, is very dense, another point of resemblance. The Sutluj is very rapid, and the mountains rising above the opposite bank are generally precipitous and perpendicular; the average breadth of the bed continues the same. We crossed two considerable streams, which flow into the Sutluj, in to-day's march.

BROANG. (DISTRICT OF BUSEHR.) NEAR THE FOOT OF THE BROANG OR BORENDA PASS.

Distance, four or five miles.

6*th September,* 1851. *Saturday.*—I arrived here yesterday afternoon. The Coolies at Râlha tried to make me halt, and even **unconditionally** declined to move; so I called to my servants, and walked off philosophically, knowing that they would not dare to choose but to follow me. I was right in my conjecture, though I had to walk the whole way, the road was so horribly bad. The route-book says of the march from Pooâree to Broâng, "No great ascent or descent in this stage," &c. What a deceiver—what a shocking romancer! There is *nothing but* "ascent and descent," and very steep too;—not a consecutive five hundred yards of anything like level in the entire march. The path often lies along the naked face of the rock, at a cruel angle, abruptly terminating in a precipice overhanging the river, or in the river itself. For the last two miles, the road forsakes the bank of the Sutluj, and turning to the left, descends to the bed of the Bupsa, a rapid and unfordable stream of considerable size, which falls into the Sutluj. When we crossed the sanga which spans this river, we followed the left bank, and a long and steep ascent, refreshingly wooded, led to this Satanic village. And I have every reason to call it names:—no wood, no Coolies, "no nothing!" No one knows where the Mookeea is, and I feel as if it will prove a sort of "Bussmun Fort" prison to me. At the bridge over the Bupsa, there are two roads. Some of my people lost their way at that spot, and have only just arrived in camp. So let me advertise, for the benefit of all guideless travellers, that the right and best path leads back to the Sutluj, and along its left bank to a village, one march from Nachâr, or four days' easy journeying from Rampore.

This is a small village, in sight of the Pass I am going to cross, (sometime before Christmas I trust,) and there are three or four other villages near, so there ought to be no excuse for Coolies. The Roopin Pass is to the north-west, and reported an easy one,—at present free from snow, or at all events nearly so. A traveller going from this place over the Roopin Pass, would go to Sungla,—a village some four or five coss distant,—but the direct road from Cheenee to the Roopin Pass is by Meybur. This route joins the one I am going, at the village of Janleg, twenty-three and a half miles distant from Broâng. There is another road from the Roopin Pass, which does not join this one till the village of Rooroo is attained, twenty-five miles beyond Janleg. From Rooroo there are three roads; first to Rampore, second to Nâgkunda, (between Kotgurh and Simla,) third to Simla, *viâ* Kotkâï and Fâgoo. No vineyards in Broâng.

8th September, 1851. *Monday.*—Still here, alas, my evil fate! The village is gone mad after some festival the last three days, and the idiotical inhabitants do nothing but carry about in procession, *kiltas* of unleavened bread, headed by a hideous god of theirs carried by a priest. And this procession is accompanied by the unearthly music of discordant instruments, depriving me of my seventeen senses all at once, the miserable thieves! I made every preparation to start this afternoon, without a single Coolie, or even guide, so desperate I felt. I took my servants merely, and three goats lightly laden with some blankets and a few clothes, leaving my valuable baggage all behind. And yet I knew that a Pass of peculiar difficulty lay before me, and some four-and-twenty miles of Oōjâr! In fact, nothing but a solemn assurance that I should get twelve Coolies to-morrow morning, prevented my actually starting off almost unattended, not an hour ago. I mean to go, however, to-morrow morning, leaving all the baggage, for which I cannot get porters by that time, to reach Rampore as it best may, though I have no doubt I shall lose one half.

The heat here is really trying to people coming from the icy climates of the North. I expire during the day, and at night mosquitoes and sand-flies devour me. But my curtains have arrived, and I hope to sleep undisturbed to-night at least. The hills around are covered with trees and thick underwood. I observe some very fine horse-chesnuts.

Oh, ye people of circumscribed patience or choleric temperaments! do not come to Broâng, as ye value your peace of mind.

There is a temple (as I know to my sorrow) close to the small encamping ground here. It is built with a Chinese roof, and body of wood and stone, in regular layers. All the houses are principally constructed of wood. And though wood is so plentiful, these children of Satan will not bring a load for my kitchen, but go dancing and howling after their insensate Deity.

KILVAH. (DISTRICT OF BUSEHR.)
Distance, about five miles.

10*th September*, 1851. *Wednesday.*—Here am I, journeying to Rampore, having for once in my life giving up a plan of march I had determined fixedly upon. And this is how it came to pass. Yesterday, about two o'clock in the afternoon, nine Coolies were given to me:—with this woful number I prepared, late as it was, to start for the formidable Pass of Borenda; "formidable," according to native report, at any rate. I could not take half the things I look upon as absolute necessaries, and anything like a *conveyance* was out of the question. I thought with despair of the reputed height (between fifteen and sixteen thousand feet above the sea) of the Pass I was to climb myself, and of the painful difficulty of breathing I experience at all great elevations. However, I was determined to go, though, as my untoward destiny would have it, I was very ill all day. I sat on the steps of the temple, waiting for a guide:—the sun was very hot, and I was not sorry for the delay. My servants and the nine Coolies had started. Just as I was moving, (having bribed a man to be my cicerone,) I received intelligence that half the porters had left their loads on the road, and decamped. I was in despair, and recalled the few remaining at their post, giving orders for a march to Rampore direct. Even for this I was obliged to wait till this morning, and the Satanic men and women of Broâng only brought the luggage two miles, then and there leaving it to its fate.

The road follows the Râlha route as far as the sanga over the Bupsa afore-mentioned, and then turns to the Sutluj, following the left bank of that river the rest of the way. The path is very bad, rocky, and heathenish to the last degree; even a Dandy is out of the question. I walked almost the whole way, and feel very tired. The heat was great, and the sharp, burning stones have wounded my feet; so I consider myself very much a victim. There is no one to pity me, therefore I do not see why I should not compassionate my own sufferings most heartily, as in fact, believe me, I do!

I hear that eight loads of mine are lying at Râlha still, and there being no village at that vine-growing spot, I have no hopes of seeing my baggage, unless filthy lucre can induce the Mookeea of this place to send his own Coolies for it. The Broâng-ites have coolly appropriated my tent-poles. Everything else has come up except one fine milch-goat, the third stolen since I crossed the Sutluj, not a week ago.

There are a great many vineyards here, and the hills are thickly wooded, principally with firs. I observed many pretty wild-flowers as I slowly walked along; but the fate of my principal flower-press, drowned near Tâtung by the Rōōpshoo Coolies, quite disheartened me from a once favourite pursuit, and I did not gather a single specimen. Holly abounds all over these hills, and some of the trees are very large. The underwood is generally luxuriant, and water abundant. There is no village between Broâng and Kilvah; only a few scanty fields and one hut passed on the way.

JANEE. (District of Busehr.)

Distance, six or eight miles.

11*th September*, 1851. *Thursday.*—Most horrible road and the heat very great. Though I had the Dandy with me, I was forced to walk two-thirds of the march, and my feet are blistered, and my knees ache from the steepness of the way. The path generally keeps to the left bank of the Sutluj, and is often very dangerous. The least carelessness, the slightest inadvertence, and the hapless traveller would solve, in one moment, the great enigma of that unknown world beyond the grave. No human power could save him from finding a watery tomb in the foaming river below. Four or five inches alone were often all that intervened between the perpendicular hill to the left, and the precipitous bank which rose above the torrent that swept madly and unheedingly on. How regardless were the wild waters of the pigmy mortals risking a grave in their stormy embrace!

The Sutluj is very violent throughout this march, and the bed—blocked up by huge rocks—is white with countless breakers. In several places the channel is much confined by perpendicular bold rocks, and the restrained flood dashes downward with double vehemence, as if chafing at and defying all control.

"———————— How profound
The gulph! and how the giant element
  From rock to rock leaps with delirious bound;
Crushing the cliffs, which downward worn and rent
With his fierce footsteps, yield in chasms a fearful vent,
To the broad column which rolls on, and shows
  More like the fountain of an infant sea,
Torn from the womb of mountains by the throes
  Of a new world, than only thus to be
Parent of rivers which flow gushingly
With many windings through the vale."

The latter two miles to this village of Jânee, consist of a steep ascent, partially wooded. The actual village is half a mile still higher up the mountain, but as soon as it comes in sight there are two paths, and travellers wishing to avoid a useless ascent must take the lower one, leading to a "Dogrie," or sort of temple, where the Mookeea is in attendance, and all requisite supplies are easily sent for.

I am distressed beyond measure at the non-appearance of my poor little pet "Squire." It appears that he remained behind with two or three loads between Broâng and the bridge. The Coolies said that he flew at them, and they were afraid to bring him on. I have sent Ghaussie back to search for him, with strict orders not to show his face in Camp without the poor animal. All my servants are useless from sickness;—one I left behind at Chângo, unable to procure "carriage" of any sort for him. A second became so incapacitated from rheumatism that I discharged him at Cheenee, and even my factotum, Ghaussie, is quite useless, from something of the same nature. In fact the Khidmutgar and Bhishtee are now the only servants "fit for duty," and I am inconvenienced beyond measure.

Vines do not grow here: fir and holly thickly wood the hills surrounding. I noticed several villages high up on the opposite mountains environed by a good many fields of cultivation. The houses are principally made of wood, and have a picturesque appearance from a little distance.

A pretty face is a rarity now. The only beauty I have lately seen is a daughter of the Mookeea of Kilvah. She is in my camp now, and is most certainly a very handsome girl. Her complexion is clear, and comparatively fair; features faultless, and eyes of beautiful shape and fascinating sweetness. The expression of her face is one of peculiar softness, modesty, and gentleness. Her figure, graceful and symmetrical, is tall beyond her compeers. The round and perfectly shaped arm is striking in its delicate contour. Were she but *fair*, the *toute ensemble* might form the model of a high-born English beauty.

NACHAR. (District of Busehr.)
ELEVATION, 6,774 FEET ABOVE THE LEVEL OF THE SEA.*

Distance, nine miles.

13*th September*, 1851. *Saturday.*—I did not arrive here till a couple of hours before sunset yesterday, consuming *ten hours* in accomplishing a short march of nine miles. The road was bad beyond compare, rugged and dangerous to the last degree. Ascent and descent were ceaseless, and often the path lay along the naked face of the bare, bold rock, inclined to the river at a terrific angle. In other parts, rude notches cut in a plank of wood, led from one impossible rock to another, the chasm beyond being unpleasant to delicate nerves.

I was worn out with fatigue, when we reached

* According to "Hebbert's Heights."

the sanga which spans the Sutluj, on the road between Tholong and Nachâr. Fortunately, here we came to the main road, and I was carried up the two miles' ascent which leads from the sanga to this village. My dhoolie was *non inventus*, but I was too tired to despise the Dandy.

This is a large village, but I am told not a Coolie will be procurable for days! Some people lately gone on have taken two hundred and twenty Coolies (!) and depopulated the land *pro tempore*. I suspect this party will haunt me like the magnificent Mr. Bayley last year.

This "New Road," so eternally talked of, so incessantly vaunted in 1850, and which I, in my simplicity, absolutely believed to be no fable, I find has turned out a very "Mrs. Harris!" Lives lost, labour and money squandered,—and lo! whole miles of this wonderful road have crumbled into the Sutluj. The natives of this country talk of the Busēhr section of the vaunted route, (or rather, *route to be*,) with mingled horror and contempt. The forced (and in this district, totally unpaid) labour for months, has been a severe and tyrannical imposition on the unwilling peasants, while the loss of limb, and even life, has been cruel indeed.

The peasants themselves are my informants,

and high and low in every village bitterly complain of the celebrated "New Road," which is (or *was?*) supposed to be such an incalculable blessing. I myself have met with several of the victims of tyranny, maimed and crippled, being carried to their homes, to be replaced by others who may share the same untimely fate. Even if the "New Road" eventually succeeds, surely this is very like "doing evil, that good may come,"— and very wrong too.

Oh! ye just and matchless rulers of British India!

TURANDA. (District of Busehr.)
ELEVATION ABOVE THE LEVEL OF THE SEA, 7,200 FEET.*

Distance, eight miles.

14*th September*, 1851. *Sunday.*—I walked the whole way here, and feel so tired, and absolutely ill in consequence, that it is a painful effort to sit up at all. A few words and I will dismiss the march, and indulge once more in—what is but rarely a pleasure to me,—the *dolce far niente*.

The pathway I followed, after leaving Turanda, was through a tangled, wooded lane, the highway

* According to "Hebbert's Heights."

being some distance above. When we entered the made road, I was delighted with its celestial shade of firs, some most magnificent ancestral trees. Throughout the first half of the march, scarcely a ray of sun pierced through the refreshing shelter of mount and tree. Ascents and descents were ceaseless, till we reached the bed of a torrent, which flows into the Sutluj, and is spanned at this spot by a sanga. A long, steep ascent, hot and scarcely shaded by a single tree, followed by a pretty wooded road, led to this village. That weary ascent has nearly been the death of me. Frequently, I lay down beneath any projecting rock, sick unto death,—overpowered by the burning sun, and the hurried and almost convulsive beatings of my heart, from the effort of ascending that unfeeling, remorseless mountain.

The cause of this unwonted walk, was not *my* sovereign will and pleasure, I can conscientiously "affirm on oath." The fact is, that the obliging Mate of Nachâr brought me a dozen old women this morning, as the sole porters available for the next century to come, on account of the depopulating party ahead. I had not even the satisfaction of seeing a pretty face among my lady-Coolies, all toothless—wrinkled—witches of ugliness. I sorrowed for the Mookeea of Kilvah's lovely Peri, for a pretty female face is a refreshing sight, strangely so to me. I remember in Calcutta, being fascinated by a beautiful face, and having great difficulty in forbearing to gaze too fixedly at the Venus in church, evidently to her no small amusement. But I am becoming discursive, wandering parenthetically from my subject.

Revenons à nos moutons. And the "sheep" I left so rudely, were those twelve or fifteen old women, my Nachâr porters. As I said, these women were all the "carriage" brought me by the intelligent Mate, after forcing me to halt so long. Half a dozen loads lay on the ground, and the Dhoolie and Dandy looked equally hopeless, so I called philosophy to my aid, and walked away without further parley. Half my baggage is still behind, and Ghaussie has just come up *without* poor little Squire. It appears that he followed some itinerant musical Fakir to Pooâree, (the road he knew,) and it is by no means certain, that I ever shall see him again. "I never loved a dear Gazelle," &c., but I must not sentimentalise, while I ought to be making an effort to have him searched for without delay.[*]

---

[*] Nearly two months subsequently, hearing that the young Râjah of Busēhr had my dog in his possession, I had him restored after a great deal of trouble. I was first forced to pay thirty-six rupees, (nearly £4,) on various pretences, before I could get

I found that the old women of Nachâr deposited my loads at a small village, about a third of the proper march; all my persuasions, though urged by the eloquence of double hire, *prepaid*, were totally unavailing, and they fled—pathetically talking of young children left at home: but excuse me, beldames, those same small babes must—oh! those toothless young mammas! —*must* have been fabulous. Taking three Coolies for the breakfast things, I came wearily on here with my servants, leaving the baggage to follow, as it best might, feeling on the whole, desperate.

This spot is beautifully wooded, and a cool wind

my favourite out of the rapacious clutches of this scion of kings. The young Râjah was equally dishonest about a bedstead of mine, which was accidentally left behind in his territories. I had actually sent him in a letter the requisite Coolie hire, for the carriage of my property to Simla, that there might be no excuse for appropriation; and I have now still in my possession, an *autograph* letter of His Highness', in which he tells me, "he has found my bed, and four of my stray ponies," adding "that he will bring them to Simla, where he is going for the Governor-General's Durbar." I had left Simla by that time, but deputed a friend to take charge of my property. However, the honest Râjah denied all knowledge of the said property, though reminded of his own written assurance of its safety. So it all ended by my being regularly robbed by him and his myrmidons. So much for *Royalty* in the East!

is blowing. The Sutluj flows many, many hundred feet below; indeed we had very few glimpses of the river, during to-day's march. The mountains surrounding Turanda exhibit but little granite; gneiss and mica-slate are the predominant formation.

The encamping ground here is considerably above the village, and in the absence of my tents, a *vague* house is my shelter, fortunately well-stocked with wood. I must note a sagacious remark of mine here, which will demonstrate perfectly how our rule puffs up the hill-people, till this *mental obesity* (figurative) renders them highly disagreeable to travellers: ecce sig.—In Thibet where trees are scarce indeed, wood is supplied freely by the villagers,—as freely as the water from the mountain stream. In these hills, so thickly wooded, it is difficult, even through their loved "pisa,"* to procure a sufficiency of firewood, and the villagers are generally a disobliging set of people, always declining to perform the very simplest offices, even when they see that the majority of the servants have not arrived in camp. In Thibet, the villagers good-humouredly busy themselves in affording every assistance to the wearied servants, and while they rarely dream of

* *Pisa* means *coppers*, or copper currency.

asking for "buckshish," are pleased and grateful when the most trifling gratuity is proffered. At Nachâr, I offered the Jânee Coolies, (only about five-and-twenty in number,) twenty Co.'s rupees, if they would go on to Surâhn, two marches, when I found that there appeared a likelihood of my being detained for want of Coolies. But though I proffered pre-payment to the amount of nearly treble the regulated hire, the wretches would not oblige me. And yet,—(such, my Posterity, is the justice prevalent in the year of our Lord, eighteen hundred and fifty-one!)—and yet, allow me to remark, that the "depopulating party" before alluded to, *coerced*, by the aid of the strong arm of authority, the Coolies of a dozen villages, to go three marches consecutively! They perchance had the same sort of *prescriptive* right to the Coolies of the country, as the Governor-General's Secretary last year, seriously oppressing the people thereby, and most seriously inconveniencing and delaying all peaceful travellers, who paid probably twice as much in consequence, to be able to accomplish a couple of marches in a week! But this is the justice prevalent all over the British Himalayas, and I have become quite used to bearing it philosophically.

SURAHN. (District of Busehr.)
ELEVATION, 7,246 FEET ABOVE THE LEVEL OF THE SEA.*

Distance, thirteen miles.

16th September, 1851. *Tuesday.*—I arrived here this morning, crippled and utterly knocked up, having absolutely walked the whole distance. After waiting all day for Coolies, I started towards evening, accompanied merely by two of my people, leaving Dandy and baggage hopelessly behind. Nothing has yet arrived, and I need hardly say that I am not very comfortable. I am endeavouring to recruit my fatigues, but as yet my wearied frame and blistered feet sorely remind me of my horrid walk.

The march is a very pretty one, wooded and shaded by forests of innumerable pine, oak and holly trees. The wild-flowers and underwood closely assimilate to those which cover the hills of Kishtawâr and Bhudurwâr, (or Puddurrooa,) balsam and fox-glove being the most luxuriant of all.

There was no village actually passed by the road-side, but I observed several above and below;

* According to "Hebbert's Heights."

the fields of cultivation were ripe and promising: buckwheat is largely grown, and in full flower. The road was a good made one, but the ascents and descents were steep and ceaseless.

The night fell when we reached about half-way, and the darkness of a moonless night and thick forests, was by no means encouraging, especially when I remembered that bears and leopards were said to abound. Indeed, I shudderingly recalled the fate of a man, only two days ago, cruelly mangled by a bear on this road, when quietly pursuing his way by night.

The very darkness prevented my halting, *en chemin,* for I dreaded to find a devouring beast in ambush, as I passed each spreading tree. I could not rest my weary feet, and slowly I walked on. My servants led the way, *feeling* for the road by means of poles, and when very doubtful, *rolling stones* down the khuds, to discover the depth and direction of the precipices. I heard the rustling of wild beasts in the long grass below the pathway, and but for very shame, I could have heartily wept. At last, fairly worn out, I lay down on the ground, resigning myself to any fate in store for me! It began to rain, by way of adding another misery, and I soon became thoroughly chilled. Even in this miserable position, I could not help sleeping, so tired was I. At moon-rise I got up, and we resolutely proceeded on our way, my servants kindly trying to rouse me to exertion, and even offering to carry me. I thought my handkerchief looked ominously dark, after a fit of coughing on the road, and when the moonbeams broke from their cloudy prison, they disclosed the truth—the white cambric was deeply dyed in the crimson stain of the vital stream, from my lungs, I suppose. I soon felt very ill, and once more lay down, a deadly faintness palsying every limb, and a black darkness passing over my eyes. I thus passed several hours in a state of unconsciousness. The day was breaking when I recovered a little; I then forced myself to rise, and slowly, wearily, at last arrived here, after many lengthened pauses by the wayside.

It is now evening, and yet I feel the prostrating effects of over-exertion and exposure to wet and cold.

We crossed a large and impetuous torrent, called the Chaundé, between Turanda and this: a bridge spanned it.

Surâhn is the usual summer residence of the Râjah of Busēhr, boasting, as it does, of the cool airs which never visit his capital (Rampore) for six or eight months of the year. He has a palace here, and the village seems of some size, while minor hamlets are scattered all over the mountain.

The Sutluj flows far below, in a rapid and angry flood. In some places the bed is so much confined by rocks, and the current so impeded by huge blocks of stone, that the river becomes a foaming torrent. How very different from the placid Sutluj of the plains of Hindostan. There are hot Springs three miles distant from Suráhn, near the Sutluj.

Formerly human victims used to be sacrificed regularly at a temple in this village—a remarkable edifice, sacred to Bheema Káli, the patroness of Busēhr.

There is a Bazaar here, and supplies are procurable, even sugar and soap;—such *extensive* Bunniahs have been rare on the heathen roads I have come.

GOURA. (District of Busehr.)

Distance, nine and a half miles.

17*th September*, 1851. *Wednesday.*—This march consists principally of a long descent, followed by a similar ascent. I came in the Dandy, or I am certain I should not be alive now to tell the tale. The ascent is succeeded by a long piece of tolerably level ground, beautifully shaded.

I breakfasted at a village half-way up the ascent, called Muzowlie, if my ear did not deceive me. This seems a straggling sort of place, houses and fields scattered over a large extent of ground. I find the heat very great here, though the site of the village is far elevated above the Sutluj, and look forward with considerable dread to the day (or days) I must spend at Rampore, where the temperature is close and hot beyond measure.

The march to-day must have been planned by some genius escaped from Bedlam. In the most senseless manner imaginable, at least five miles is added to the distance, by a very unnecessary *détour*. The violent torrent, called the Manglad, is crossed after passing Surân, and is a frightfully rapid stream.

The costume of the women has greatly changed since we reached Turanda. The head-dress no longer consists of the small man's cap, which was very becoming to a pretty face. A dirty white or coloured handkerchief is now bound round the head tightly, concealing all the hair, except the bunch which hangs behind:—this is interlaced with so much coloured worsted, that it is difficult to say how much hair the fair ones possess, but a heterogeneous mass is partially disclosed below the handkerchief. The attire rarely consists of more than one blanket, generally of the coloured stripes made in Kanâwr above Cheenee, and largely sold at the Rampore Fairs twice a year. This blanket is fastened by pins or skewers, as in Lahoūl, and is the prevalent costume all about Broâng and Kilvah, as well as here. It always makes me nervous to contemplate this fragile dress, or rather its slight support—frequently a single skewer! The costume of the men has not varied; woollen trowsers, and woollen jacket with a short, full skirt attached. The puttoo cap, white, black or coloured, with a padded, round rim, is the head-dress; the hair cut short, and the crowns generally shaven. A ragged woollen *cummer-bund*, or waist-band, girdles the dress,—and there a Busēhri stands in full costume before the reader. Let him look well!

Beauty has vanished, and there is no "Peri"* among the women now. They no longer act as porters. Since reaching Surâhn, the custom seems to be forgotten.

I mean to travel by night to Rampore, on account of the heat. I have not slept for two nights, but I am anxious to reach Rampore, hoping to receive letters on arrival. The young Râjah of

* The correct orthography (and pronunciation likewise) of this word is *Purrie,* and its literal meaning "a fairy." It has been corrupted by poetical license into "Peri," and is used generally to represent a transcendent beauty, simply.

Busēhr is there, business having detained him below, and as yet prevented him from paying the usual summer visit to Surâhn.

RAMPORE. (Capital of Busehr.)
ELEVATION ABOVE THE LEVEL OF THE SEA, 3,373 FEET.
Distance, eight miles.

19*th September*, 1851. *Friday*.—I reached this fiery "Tartarus" yesterday, before daybreak, and could not get anything in the shape of a house in which to pass the heat of the day. The Wuzeer pitched a tent for me, but the high temperature was terrible to a traveller fresh from the icy Regions of Thibet. I languished all day, and anything like exertion was a moral impossibility. I am detained here by the absence of my baggage, as only twenty Coolies, including the dhoolie-men, arrived yesterday. I should go on to Kotgurh, and await my baggage in that more genial clime, but the box containing the "sinews" of travel, —money,—is still behind, and I have not enough left in my desk to pay the Coolies another march. I am endeavouring to find a good pony to purchase, as I hate the Dandy and dhoolie very heartily, and I do not know when I shall see **my** horses again. I tried two ponies, one a Ghōōnt, and the other a Yârkhundi, this evening. The owner asks one hundred and twenty rupees for the former, and sixty for the latter. I have not decided about the purchase.

The march from Goura is chiefly a descent, a good made road. I came by torch-light, and insecure though my position was in the Dandy, I slept a great part of the way from sheer exhaustion. The Coolies at last *tied* me to the Dandy-pole, seeing that I *could not* keep my eyes from closing in slumber!

My arrival here was greeted by two packets of letters from the Plains, which had been brought by some servants, who for ten days had waited my coming. After long silence from those we love, how dearly welcome are any tidings of their welfare, especially when the long interval has been passed in lone wanderings through strange countries.

"The parted bosom clings to wonted home,
If aught that's kindred cheer the welcome hearth."

There is but little to say of Rampore :—it is a small city, on the left bank of the Sutluj. The Râjah's palace stands at one extremity, and is not a very imposing structure. The houses are principally built of stone, with slated pent-roofs. The heat is intolerable, hemmed in as the city is by mountains all round. There is a *Jhōōla* across the Sutluj, (made of ropes on the "Chēēkha" model,) below Rampore, and a made road to Kōōloo beyond. The marches to Sooltânpore, the capital of Kōōloo, are seven in number; viz.,

1. Ursoo . . . 6 miles.
2. Serân . . . 7 ,,
3. Butthâr . . 8 ,,
4. Plâch . . . 13 ,,
5. Larjee . . . 12 ,,
6. Bijoūra . . 12 ,,
7. Sooltânpore . . 9 ,,

There are two roads hence to Nâgkunda; one viâ Kotgurh, and the other by a new route.

The form of government is most strange, and quite beyond my comprehension. There is a young Râjah of thirteen, the nominal prince of Busēhr. Wuzeer Munsookh Dâss, who held the reins of government (*de facto*) during the old Râjah's lifetime, is a mere cypher now, superseded by some emissary of the Simla or Lahore authorities, a quondam *Bunniah*,* (or grain-seller,) a one-eyed native of Agra, who writes a very bad hand in very indifferent English. No one knows to whom or to what he owes his present promotion. He is hated by high and low alike, whereas the superseded Wuzeer is beloved and reverenced by all

* !

the natives of the Râj of Busēhr. It is said that the Rânee, on the decease of her spouse last year, complained against the Wuzeer, wishing to have the government of the district in her own hands, during the minority of her son. Her ambition was not gratified; and the one-eyed Bunniah has all the power vested in his hated person—the great men of the Râj being all subject to his authority, and the young Râjah having to pay, out of his small revenue, the salary of his enforced master—three hundred rupees a month, besides the cost of his myrmidons. The elevated Bunniah is vaguely styled the "Deputy *Sâhib!*" Upstart insolence,—"*Sâhib*," forsooth! The little Râjah has been taught English, and his master, (a Baboo from the Plains,) says that he can both speak and write the foreign tongue with ease and fluency.

I had some conversation with a Busēhr trader, regarding Mr. Strachey and the frays and disputes he was so seriously involved in at Lēh, with Busty Râm and his people. This trader was at Lēh the whole time of these frays. He showed me a certificate from Mr. Strachey, which was penned in terms of high commendation. According to the Busēhri's account, Mr. Strachey behaved with moderation and temper; and but for this discreet conduct, the results to himself and his small band of followers and adherents might have been fatal indeed. The traders from Busēhr to Thibet all complain bitterly of the "zōōlm" (oppression) practised by Busty Râm at Lēh, thereby greatly repressing the free course of trade. They say that when Sir Henry Lawrence was at Lēh, the greatest precautions were taken to prevent any access to him, or anything like free communication or a plain exposition of real facts.

A man brought me two sable skins, and an immense bright yellow cap of Lahâssa, worn by the men in authority at Rodōkh. The price of each small skin of sable was twenty-two rupees. The only manufacture of any consequence, at Rampore, is the Chuddur, or Shawl, made of fine wool, value from sixteen to twenty-one Company's rupees. They are more expensive at Simla, as a matter of course. Two great fairs are held twice a year here; one in November and one in April. Traders flock to these fairs from distant districts, and woollen manufactures, in particular, are largely sold.

It is now noon, and really it is impossible to describe the frightful heat in this small tent. The elevation of Rampore above the average level of the plains of the Punjâb cannot be more than one thousand feet, or at most, fifteen hundred.

The Valley is scarcely a gun-shot wide, and the hills (barren of trees) which confine the spot radiate extra heat. The caloric thus multiplied makes an annihilating sum total, as I know to my cost. Plaintains flourish here, which alone argues the trifling altitude of the city of Rampore. The Kotwâl sent me a basket of that Plains' fruit yesterday, and they were quite ripe. I was as weary of the beautiful Kanâwr grapes, a few days ago, as of the most luscious apricots of Bultistân; but now, when expiring with heat, what would I not give for a fine bunch or two! I remember, with repentance, how I lavishly squandered those delicious grapes when I had them in plenty, and how it is entirely owing to my carelessness that the kiltas bought at the bridge below Pooâree, are long since ruined.

NACHAR. (District of Busehr.)

Distance, thirty-eight and a half miles (or four marches) from Rampore.

26*th September*, 1851. *Friday.*—I *think* this is the twenty-sixth day in the month, and Friday the day of the week, but I am by no means certain of the important fact. In sooth, were it not for some sort of diary, it would be impossible for any finite memory to keep a register of weeks and days passed in countries where no English reckoning is kept. I am now on my way to Cheenee, and perhaps Punghee. Having fruitlessly despatched three servants, with money, Sepoys and Purwânnahs, and in the same unprofitable manner wasted a week in heat and inaction down at Rampore, and neither baggage nor ponies arriving, I found my only plan remaining was to make up my mind to start myself. My servants returned, some malingering, and all with their mouths full of falsehoods, which I instinctively discovered to be such. So, on the evening of the 23rd, I left Rampore, being most kindly accommodated with the loan of a pony from the Wuzeer, and thus freed from the harassing annoyances ever, in my opinion, attendant on any conveyance requiring such foreign aid as that of Coolies. It soon became too dark to proceed, and I halted about half-way from Gaura, at a small village, name unknown. In the early morning we proceeded to Muzowlie, about six miles from Surâhn, and there I breakfasted, not reaching Surâhn till sunset. Before daylight we continued our course; but though we went on steadily, the few loads I had with me did not reach Turanda till near sunset yesterday. I was most disagreeably employed in the hot sun, searching for baggage of mine, which I heard was lying in some "Dogri"* off the road. I took a Coolie and my Bhishtie, and after a head-and-heart-breaking hunt, a mile down a hot khud, I discovered three loads lying in an out-of-the-way hut, in a rather eccentric style. I tried both remonstrances and bribes, but for a long time without effect. However, I trust the said baggage is now on its way to Rampore.

As I had promised not to take the pony too far, I was obliged to look for a Dandy and bearers at Turanda, and did not get off till near daylight this morning, arriving here to breakfast. I am only waiting for Coolies to proceed to Chirgâon, the next stage.

I have found the greater part of my baggage off the road, in wild places. A great portion has been destroyed, and (among other things) a trunk of some value is nowhere to be found. Ditto poor little Squire, of whom I can hear no tidings. I have despatched a good servant on the Broâng road, while I proceed to Cheenee. Having hired mules to go to Simla and Julundhur, before leaving Rampore, this Chevy-Chase is as expensive as it is *un*-amusing.

* Or Hill-Temple.

I described the road before as far as this, so I will spare my aching head much more writing. I may, however, say a few words generally, in repetition.

From Rampore to Surâhn, the marches consist principally of steep ascents, and two descents. From Surâhn to Turanda, a very fatiguing march of thirteen miles, nothing but ascent and descent hopelessly alternating, and very little level anywhere. As the crow flies, I am sure Turanda is scarcely four miles from Surâhn. The greater part of the way is prettily wooded. From Turanda to this, a long and bad descent is followed by an ascent, then a second ascent and short descent. The hills from Gaura upwards, are beautifully wooded, with firs of various kinds, oaks, rhododendrons, &c., &c. The underwood is dense, and balsam, foxglove, potentilla sanguinia, geranium, &c., cover the slopes, intermingled with the long rank grass. Bears, wolves and leopards are said to abound all over these mountains.

There is a bridge of some sort across the Sutluj, below Turanda, leading to the opposite Heights, and by a footpath to Kōōloo. From this village there is a road to Lahoūl, *viâ* the Bhubbeh Pass. There are twelve marches as far as Kōksur, the first village in Lahoūl, whence one route leads to

Ladâk, Triloknâth, and Chumba, and the other, crossing the Zampa, over the Chundra, below Kōksur, goes to Kōōloo and Mundy, or Kangra, thence by Nadaun or Jwâla Mookhi, to the plains of the Punjâb. I described several of these routes last year. The following is the route to Nachâr in Busēhr, from Kōksur in Lahoūl. The three first marches are in Oōjâr encamping grounds; no villages near.

4th march.	.	Lohsur (a small village).
5th ,,	.	Pâmo.
6th ,,	.	Kurjeh.
7th ,,	.	Kooling.
8th ,,	.	Moodh.
9th ,,	.	Bhubbeh Jōth, (Oōjâr.)
10th ,,	.	Other side of the above Pass, (Oōjâr.)
11th ,,	.	Ghâtgâon, (a village.)
12th ,,	.	Nachâr.

There is a road from this place (Nachâr) to S'piti direct, *viâ* the Bhubbeh Jōth, but I am told it is a somewhat rugged path.

CHEENEE.* (DISTRICT OF BUSEHR.)

Distance, thirty-two and a half miles, or three marches.

28*th September*, 1851. *Sunday.*—I arrived here in the dead of the night, enduring heat, cold and fatigue in painful extremes, during my Dandy-dâk from Nachâr. The distance is three marches,—Cheergâon, eleven miles from Nachâr; Meeroo, five miles; and from Meeroo to this, sixteen and a half miles. The latter long march is often divided into two, by making Rogee, (a village some distance off the road, down a khud,) one stage. I need not say much about the road, as it is sufficient to describe it in two words—very bad. It is a "made road" too, but "made" by some Bedlamite, I opine. Anything like level is unknown, and the ascents and descents are steep and ceaseless. In numberless places, great rocks impede the way, and many of the steepest places are regular *stairs*, constructed of wood and stone. I was speculating *en route*, how my ponies would surmount the difficulties of the way, and I have but faint hopes of their reaching Simla for the next twelve-month.

* In Chinese Tartary.

I left Nachâr about four o'clock, p.m., on Friday, and walked to the bridge over the Sutluj, described before. This little bit of exercise was by no means a pleasure, but a work of pain and difficulty, my feet having never recovered the blistering of former forced walks. The Dandy-Coolies had not arrived, so, after wasting the greater part of the day at Nachâr, I came on, as the only chance of extracting men from the lazy old Mate. My plan succeeded, for the Dandy and two necessary loads overtook us at the aforesaid bridge, about three miles from Nachâr. It was fortunate it did, for I was then so lame and wearied, that all prospects of reaching my destination were hopeless. We were benighted about half-way, and when the thick darkness rendered further progress dangerous, we halted on a small piece of level, near the right bank of the Sutluj, where a natural cave afforded me shelter from the heavy dews of night. We reached Meeroo at eight, a.m., and after breakfast and a bath, I proceeded to Cheergâon, the next march.

The Wuzeer's letter procured me Coolies at once, and after a half-hour's halt, I went on. I had only one servant left with me, and he bravely proceeded, though completely knocked up. This last march we accomplished principally by the light of pine torches, the infant moon being soon cradled to sleep in the giant mountains around. I found it very cold, and sleep impossible. The chill night-air has done me no good, and my old cough is again troubling me sadly.

What a difference between the temperature of Cheenee and Rampore! Though now mid-day, my hands are benumbed with cold, and the wind is blowing a very wintry blast. All the visitors have flown, and with them the Bunniahs, so supplies are with difficulty procured. Of the four ponies left here, one is dead, and the other three and my cow have but this moment arrived. This delay has made me lose many hours here. I am now going to return to Rampore, though I have caught a severe cold, and feel stupid and ill.

JUTOG. (Two miles from Simla-Ghat; the elevation the same as the average heights of Simla).

Distance, a hundred and forty-six miles from Cheenee.

9*th October*, 1851. *Thursday.*—I suppose I must say a few words, before I close my Journal of Hill-marching, and yet I feel in no humour to write at all.

I left Cheenee on Monday, the 29th, after seeing my ponies, or rather their miserable wrecks, shod by a Mogul *con amore*. The process was edifying; —not a scrap was pared off the horny parts, and the shoes I had fortunately brought, were hammered on in a very rude and unscientific manner. I went dâk to Cheergâon, and arrived there in the second watch of the night, lighted by many torches. I tried to proceed at once, but found no Coolies ready. In the morning I walked on, hopeless of any carriage being procurable, as long as I remained meekly quiescent. The sun was very hot, and I had a bad cold and cough, but I persevered as long as my aching feet could drag me on. I reached the spot where we had bivouacked in my upward journey, and under the shelter of the same rock, broke my fast by an attack on the well-packed kiltas of grapes. And this was my only breakfast. Feverish and exhausted, all grosser aliment was unpalatable.

As I was reading a letter brought by one of the Râjah's Mercuries, the Dandy arrived to my great relief. This letter came from the Plains, and was very welcome in the wild lands of Busēhr, where letters do not often wander. It was near sunset when I reached Nachâr, seriously ill:—during the night, fever came on, and I passed a miserable time, without medicine of any sort, and only a single attendant by me.

It was with pain and difficulty that I reached Turanda on the 1st of October. Though I gave more than treble the hire in advance, four of my ponies and my cow were left behind at Konghōs, a village about five miles from Turanda, and my bedding and clothes ditto. Bribing the Mate of Turanda, I managed to induce him to send two of his Coolies off to Konghōs; and in the meanwhile I shivered with cold, having nothing to defend me from the keen night-air and heavy nocturnal dews, but a light Kashmir scarf, besides the white clothes I wore during the hot noon-tide. The bundles did not arrive till three o'clock in the morning. At first, for the sake of a spring of water close by, I bivouacked below the house I formerly occupied, and I did this more for the relief of the only servant with me. It seemed, indeed, as if "misfortunes never come single," for this night, of all nights, when I had not a change of attire near, and no bed or bedding, I fell into the rocky basin of water in the dark. As it was three feet deep, I was wet to the skin from head to foot. I tried to restore warmth by crouching close to a large fire, after this untimely bath, and I told my servant to dry my shoes, (my only pair!) as speedily as possible, that I might walk up to the house, where I could make better arrangements for escaping "death from cold." *Hélas!* fate was not weary of troubling me,—my shoes were burnt to cinders, by the carelessness of my attendant; so that I had no means of moving to the only shelter in the neighbourhood, and even this was a quarter of a mile off, an ascent the whole way.

There was no use to rail or storm, so I only crouched closer to my fire, till a Coolie came from the somewhat distant village, and carried me up to the house before described. I found a large store of wood there, and lit two huge fires, lying down close to them. My servant had produced a thin rezâï, (or wadded quilt,) which I placed under me, and fell asleep. I was quite alone, far from the village, and might have been burnt to death as it happened. Several sparks fell on the rezâï, and the ignited cotton smouldered long before I awoke. In fact, the burning reached my arm, before the heavy slumber induced by cold and fever was dispelled, and consciousness restored. I sat up in alarm, and for some time every attempt I made to put out the fire in the cotton, seemed only to make it spread. There was no water near, and I did not know how to save the only thing I had in the shape of bedding that miserable night. At last, I resorted to the painful expedient of picking out each burning piece of cotton with my fingers, scorching myself most distressingly the while. It is so difficult to extinguish ignited cotton, that even after I had separated each burning piece, I felt far from comfortable when I lay down once more, being uncertain whether I had not still a smouldering fire beneath me, and that I might not sleep to wake no more, or at least wake too late. Fear, fever, and the bitter cold kept me awake till my bedding and clothes arrived near morning, and thought was busy throughout the live-long night,—rife with sad remembrances and mournful anticipations. For

"— ever and anon of griefs subdued
There comes a token like a scorpion's sting
Scarce seen, but with fresh bitterness embued."

When borne down with the iron hand of illness, the most buoyant heart will sink at last, and in moments of solitary suffering I have often felt quite despairing. *Mais revenons à nos moutons*, for I must not linger by the way.

I have said *supra* that my bedding and clothes arrived in the morning, but my ponies have apparently been appropriated by some cool individual who does not know how to distinguish between *meum* and *tuum*, as they have never come up to this day, nor do I dare longer to hope I shall ever see them again. If I thought they had broken their necks, I might learn resignedly to exclaim, "*Requiescat in pace!*"— but to be robbed in open day is rather temper-trying.

That delightful man, Mr. Edwardes, the "Superintendent of Hill-States, Simla," has ruined the districts under his charge, and rendered all travelling within his boundaries, far more a pain than a pleasure. No matter what articles of value are lost or stolen, he always arbitrarily takes the part of the Coolies; and whether they behave well or ill, advocates their cause, and teaches them to be insolent, disobliging, and subject to no rule of any sort. At Nâgkunda, I saw a formal "notice," signed by the name of that august official, informing all travellers that they were to obtain no Coolies at Simla, or in the Simla District, on any pretext whatsoever. To secure a single Coolie, I have paid eight annas or a rupee for one short march, after having to bribe the Mate first. Were all this *general*, it would be bad enough; but as it is merely confined to those who have not the awful honour of the great man's acquaintance, I cannot see by what laws of justice the gentleman legislates. His royal Purwânnah will summon at an hour's notice a hundred porters at every hill-Chowkie, at a regulated hire of three annas per man. Forsooth! and this is the *justice* practised by that item of humanity, the Superintendent of Hill-States, resident at Simla! The Governor-General is reckoned a clever man, and yet he allows himself to be fawned upon and flattered into a tolerance of this just and upright ruler.

I have not time to waste more words on him, so I shall return to my neglected tale. I left myself between Earth and Hades, and I was rude to myself thereby—consequently I apologize.

On the 2nd I reached Surâhn. My cold and cough, and many painful attendant symptoms, were frightfully aggravated; my voice had disappeared *in toto*, and speaking even in a whisper was "vanity and vexation of spirit,"—an inexpressibly painful effort. The one-eyed Bunniah Deputy expressed his utter inability to aid me in recovering property still wantonly scattered, though I represented to him, that a bed—the hire paid some days before by my Khidmutgâr *in advance*,—was at that moment lying in a Dogri below (and considerably off) the road, and that my ponies and cow were in the same pleasing manner left behind. The young Râjah promised to aid me, and sent some of his own people to collect my various missing property, live-stock included. This young boy is the only person worth his salt in the whole of Busēhr, whether private or public.

I received a letter written *in English* by himself —very creditable to him, considering that he has only studied the foreign tongue about a twelve-month.

I was very ill from fever at Gaura, the hoarseness seeming to become worse if possible, and many bad symptoms supervening. I proceeded by night to Rampore, and thence to Nirt, where I remained during the heat of the day, on the 4th. I never had a more trying journey than between Nirt and Kotgurh. The Coolies were the worst set that ever it was my evil fate to have *harnessed* to my Dandy, and I was very ill. However, after much suffering, I reached Kotgurh at last, where I found that my Camp had gone on that morning, and but one servant and a few things awaiting my arrival at the Dâk-Bungalow.

I was rejoiced by the sight of many letters, which contained no bad news of import.

Though the Mate received a rupee for his own particular self, merely for providing me with three Coolies, he was so dissatisfied, that he threatened insolently to recall the men! I laughed philosophically at his insolence, and was glad to find a pony to ride on in the evening to my Camp. The thirteen mules were tied in the middle of the road, about three miles from Nâgkunda. I subsequently found that my mule-drivers had a peculiar habit of encamping in the jungles, recklessly disregarding all "Chowkies."

On the 6th, I went to Nâgkunda, where I breakfasted, and in the afternoon proceeded towards Muttiâna. Of course, instead of reaching that place, I found my tent pitched at the foot of the last ascent, far from any village where people ordinarily encamp.

On the 7th, I reached Theog, on the 8th, my camp was pitched about a mile beyond Muhâsoo Proper, and to-day I have come on here, about two miles beyond the Simla Ghât.

I have discovered a thief in one of my servants, who was convicted of stealing money, absolutely within a couple of yards of me. He is evidently an experienced rogue. I did not alarm him, when he stood convicted in my very presence, hoping by my leniency to induce him to come on, and as soon as I arrived at a Thannah, I meant to have him apprehended. This, I hoped, would make him confess to many heavy charges I have against him of systematic robbery since last March, and perhaps lead to the recovery of many things I valued, which have disappeared this year. However, the thief, on some pretence, remained behind two days ago, between Theog and Fâgoo, and has not appeared since. All my servants say he has probably stolen something the last day he was in my Camp. I suppose I shall soon learn this to my sorrow.

I need say nothing of the road from Cheenee to Rampore, having fully expatiated on it before. From Rampore to Simla, the marches are—

1. Nirt, or Nirtnuggur 12 miles.
2. Kotgurh . 12 ,, (Dâk-Bungalow.)
3. Nâgkunda . 10 ,, ,,
4. Muttiâna . 13 ,, ,,
5. Theog . 8 ,, ,,
6. Fâgoo . 6 ,, ,,
7. Simla 12 or 14 ,, (No Dâk-Bungalow.)

Excellent made road the whole way.

From Rampore to Nirt, the road follows the left bank of the Sutluj; it is nearly level, and insufferably hot. From Nirt to Kotgurh, the made road goes by Kâpo, but there is a footpath which shortens the distance fully four miles:—it is not good for riding. Between Nirt and Kotgurh, there is an ascent of between three and four thousand feet. The elevation of Kotgurh is about a thousand feet less than the average altitude of Simla. From Kotgurh to Nâgkunda, there is some level, and a good deal of ascent, as the latter is upwards of nine thousand feet in elevation. A very prettily-wooded road.

I observed the Kōōloo route on the opposite bank of the Sutluj, by which I came last year, and Dilâss far above the river, was conspicuous in the distance. As I mentioned last year, a wooden bridge spans the Sutluj, about three miles below Komhârsin. A footpath leads from Kâpo to Mundy and Bilaspore, and thence to the Plains; but the road is rugged, and riding unpleasant, if not impossible. From Nâgkunda to Muttiâna, there is a footpath which leads over the hills, and is shorter than the main road by five miles; it is very tolerable, and many useless ascents and descents are spared. I need say nothing further of the route to Simla, as I think I described it before.

This place, Jutog, is a Hill-Cantonment. The Ghorkha corps, styled "the Nusseeree Battalion," is stationed here; and a few Bungalows, Lines, and a Parade-ground constitute the "Cantonment" of Jutog. Simla is in sight, its wooded beauties forming a great contrast to the bare ugliness of the spot chosen for this Cantonment.

I believe the "new road" (so often alluded to) between Simla and the Plains is open now, but my mule-drivers seeming averse to that route, I have given up the idea of following it. It goes *viâ* Dugshaï, a Hill-Cantonment not far beyond Subâthoo, and two Dâk-Bungalows are built at convenient halting-places:—the road is said to be good and level. I give this account entirely from hearsay; I hope it happens to be correct. The other parts of the "new road" between Rampore and Simla, in this district, are nearly as unfinished as the Busēhr section. It is quite impassable, and yet appears so deceptively good in the fragments which join the old road, that sign-posts are requisite to warn the unwary traveller. They were blasting rocks within a few feet of me, in the most reckless manner possible. I wonder that accidents are not even more frequent than they are, though, Heaven knows, life has been wantonly destroyed too much already, on this "Mrs. Harris" route to Thibet. It is a sort of soap-bubble of his "Most Noble"-ship—a monomania—a species of idiosyncracy fatal to all connected with its fabulous completion.

As I rode through Simla, I recognised each spot I passed; and the very trees, stones, and houses seemed well-remembered, and still well-loved friends. But all who made the haunts so dear, were far away, and Simla had no longer charms for me. I came on here to be *alone*; for, in the gay precincts of the modern Hill-Babylon, I should have been more than alone, and that is the " solitude" which oppresses me.

In a wild place, away from the small Cantonment, my miserable remnants of tents are pitched, and I do not give one sigh to the gay Simla far behind. Why did I not remain there to forget my lonely wanderings in social mirth, for I dare say I might soon find more than one familiar face in the throngs of that giddy mountain-capital? Let me reply in the beautiful,—and beautifully true,—words of the Pilgrim Childe :—

"To sit on rocks, to muse o'er flood and fell,
 To slowly trace the forest's shady scene,
 Where things that own not man's dominion dwell,
 And mortal foot hath ne'er or rarely been ;
 To climb the trackless mountain all unseen,
 With the wild flock that never needs a fold ;
 Alone o'er steeps and foaming falls to lean ;
 This is not solitude; 'tis but to hold
 Converse with nature's charms, and view her stores unroll'd.

"But 'midst the crowd, the hum, the shock of men,
 To hear, to see, to feel, and to possess,
 And roam along, the world's tired denizen,
 With none who bless us, none whom we can bless;

Minions of splendour shrinking from distress!
None that, with kindred consciousness endued,
If we were not, would seem to smile the less,
Of all that flatter'd, follow'd, sought, pursued;
This is to be alone; this, this is Solitude!"

KALKA. (FOOT OF THE SIMLA HILLS.)
Distance, forty-one miles.

15th October, 1851.—This is the foot of the Himalaya, and now my journey is nearly at its close. I go on this evening by palanquin-dâk to Julundhur, where I must commence preparations for my journey to Bombay *en route* to England. I need not here describe the road, &c., from Jutog, as the greater portion of it is sufficiently detailed in Vol. I. Nor have I tried the much-talked-of "New Road," to enable me to report on its advantages. I marched slowly down from Jutog, encamping every day just where fancy listed, and met with no stirring adventures to record.

The regular stages from Simla are

Syree . 10 miles. Hurreedpoor . 10 miles.
Kussowlie 12 ,, Kalka . . . 9 ,,

I bid adieu with regret to the beautiful mountains of the snowy Himalaya, for truly are

" —— The mountains, waves, and skies a part
Of me and of my soul, as I of them."

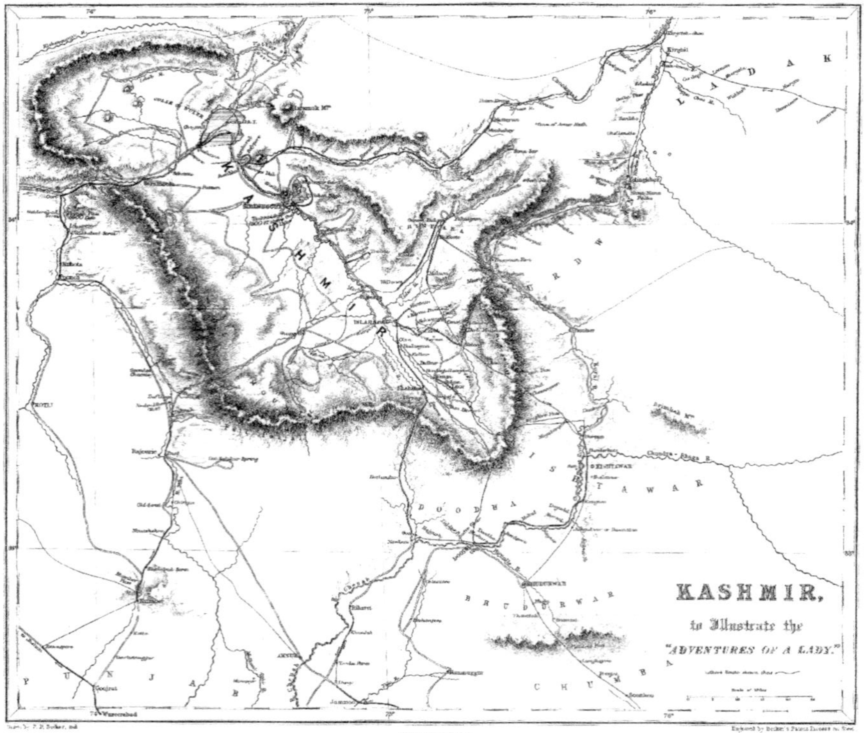

Engraved by Becker's Patent Process on Steel.

London, Hope & Cº.

A SHORT HISTORICAL SKETCH OF KASHMIR.

"As the active world is inferior to the rational soul, so Fiction gives to mankind what History denies, and in some measure satisfies the mind with shadows, when it cannot enjoy the substance."—LORD BACON.

IN quoting the above sentence from that profound observer, I would remark how apposite it is to the Hindoo histories in particular, though intended to apply to fiction generally. The history of the East is so clouded with mythology, trebly dim in the far ages of the past,—so overcast by time, and confused by the myriad legends and traditions, which are inextricably interwoven with the annals of the kingdoms,—that our efforts to separate fact from fiction are utterly vain. Therefore the mind, having little substantial gratification, must be permitted to indulge in phantoms, and to dwell with greater interest than the subject would otherwise create, on the mass of Hindoo fable, that must too frequently supply the deficiency of *sober* history, which all Oriental inquirers have so great cause to lament.

To those who take an interest in that land of poetry—beautiful Kashmir—it may prove interesting to learn a few particulars of its early history and legendary origin, without the trouble of consulting the *black classics*, or the erudite works of laborious historians. Space will not permit of any lengthened details, so I will only give a rapid sketch of the almost forgotten ages of the past, when the province was in its pristine glory, exercising a far more potent influence on the neighbouring principalities, and possessing more political importance, than in its now fallen state it can ever again hope to enjoy. And, passing on from these remote ages, I will endeavour to give a brief *résumé* of its history, up to the present period.

In a previous page I have mentioned that the Valley of Kashmir was once a vast lake, according to all the traditionary accounts of the province. The principal Sanscrit History of Kashmir is that entitled the "Râjah Tarangini," which was first introduced to the knowledge of the Mohammedan world by the minister of the great Akbâr, a man who has distinguished himself by his learned writings. The "Râjah Tarangini" is a series of compositions, indited by different authors at different periods, many of whom are, in fact, merely the chroniclers of their own particular eras. There are several ancient Persian writers, too, who have compiled Histories of Kashmir, but I will not take up the little space I have left in enumerating the names of these authors. Great discrepancies are found to exist on comparing the various accounts, but this is to be expected, especially where Orientals are the chroniclers.

But, that I may proceed *ab ovo usque ad mala*, let me go back some four thousand five hundred years, to the remote ages when Kashmir was a lake, called " Satísâras,"—from " Satí," a virtuous woman, and "Sâras," a lake. Abul Fâzl, the Mohammedan historian and minister of the Emperor Akbâr, alluded to above, makes the etymology of the lake " the Lake of Uma" (the wife of Maha-Déo); and he is so far borne out in his assertion, by the fact that one of the names of Maha-Déo's consort is "Satí," in the character of a faithful and loving wife.

The Pass of Baramoolla,—which is the only break in the mountainous confines of Kashmir, and through which the Jhelum now flows to the plain-lands of the Punjâb,—had no existence at the period I have referred to,

G * 2

i.e. when Kashmir was an extensive lake,—for the snow-capped Heights then completely encircled the pent-up waters of the mountain reservoir. According to one eminent authority,* Kashmir was inundated on account of the relapse of the inhabitants to idolatry, after having been taught the worship of the one true God by *Moses*, who died there, and whose tomb is by some said to be still pointed out. But this is merely a wild legend, and I shall proceed to more authentic accounts.

The draining of the lake ("Satísaras") is ascribed, by the Hindoo historians, to Kushup, or Kasyapa, the son of Marichi. According to some accounts, he was a Hindoo saint and seer; according to others, he is popularly represented as the grandson of the divine Brâhma, and a Déo or Genii—the servant of Solomon, by whose commands he effected the desiccation of the valley. The means he employed were of Herculean engineering skill,—for he is said to have cut through the snowy barrier, opening a passage for the superfluous waters at the spot now called the "Pass of Baramoolla," the break in the encircling mountains before alluded to. One legend goes on to state that a demon, an *Afrit*, yclept Jaladéo, used to dwell in the middle of the lake; and that this

* Bedia-ud-din, a Persian historian.

evil spirit seized and tormented all who came within his reach, preying on the *genus homo* in a most heterodox manner. Fortunately for mankind, Kushup, the grandson of Brâhma, visited these regions, and was struck by the desolated aspect of the locality. His heart was moved to pity, and he vowed to effect the deliverance of the neighbouring people from their persecutor, the *Afrit*. To carry out this object, Kushup devoted a thousand years to religious austerities in Noubadan, near Heerapore, until Maha-Déo at last appeared to him, and heard his prayers. Vishnoo and Brâhma were accordingly sent to expel the fiend, but a hundred years passed in hopeless conflict. Vishnoo at last perceiving that the lake afforded a secure retreat to the enemy, who was thus enabled to elude all his assaults, commanded the chasm of Baramoolla to be made, by which the valley was desiccated, the demon caught, and the country rendered habitable. From these incidents, the newly-redeemed valley was called " Kushup-Sar," or the " Lake of Kushup,"—now corrupted into Kashmir.

It is just possible that modern intellects may regard these traditions—so gravely narrated in Oriental histories as matters of notorious *fact*—in the light of mere fables! I will, therefore, suggest a very probable elucidation of the theory generally credited, that the Valley of Kashmir was, *ipso facto*, a lake in the olden time; shewing that so far the legends are corroborated by many presumptive proofs.

There are so many arguments which the geologist and philosopher can advance to support this theory, that it is folly to throw discredit on it, and the existence of the present Pass of Baramoola can easily be accounted for, by the supposition that some violent convulsion of nature rent asunder the confining mountains, and thereby opened an outlet for the waters of the lake. The terrible earthquakes which have convulsed Kashmir, and of which I have given a cursory account in Vol. I., add weight to the above supposition;— indeed, there are ample grounds for believing, that to this day volcanic action is going on beneath the peaceful and smiling Valley, which may at any period break out with irresistible and overwhelming force, changing *de novo* the face of nature.

But to return to my subject. The district so newly recovered by Kushup, owed its population to his skill in attracting inhabitants from the neighbouring countries. The religion of the province at this time was that of the *Nágas*, or Snake-gods, of which I will give a short description. I must premise that ancient authorities place the date of the desiccation of the valley as far back as B.C. 3714; but the "adjusted date" of Professor H. H. Wilson, in his able "Essay on the Hindoo History of Kashmir," makes it B.C. 2666.

Regarding the Ophite creed, or snake-worship, there is ample reason to believe that at one time it extended all over India; as, besides the numerous fables and traditions relating to the Snake-gods, which are found scattered all through the *Puránas*, (or Sacred Writings of the Hindoos,) there are palpable vestiges of the same, still to be traced in the existing religious observances of the Hindoos. In the holy books of this race, the destruction of the entire serpent-genus by the Rájah Janaméjaya, the son of Paricshit, is chronicled as a historical event, but probably it is merely a typical and emblematical shadowing forth of the actual fact—*i. e.*, that the faith of the Vedas was founded on the ruins of the original and local superstition of the *Nágas*, when Janaméjaya subverted the ancient Ophite worship. At all events, there is no doubt whatever that this singular superstition existed originally in Kashmir, as snakes and snake-deities play an important part in the legendary history of the Valley. Abul Fâzl mentions "that there are *seven hundred* places where carved snakes are worshipped in the Province." (This was alluding to an epoch about 350 or 400 years B.C.)

The first Prince whose name has been recorded in *authentic* ancient histories of Kashmir (after the first settlement of the Valley by Kushup, or Kasyapa,) is Gonerda,—the "adjusted date" of whose reign is fixed by Professor Wilson, 1400 years B.C. During the period which intervened between the desiccation of the valley and the accession of Gonerda—an interval extending over 1266 years—the country was governed by upwards of fifty kings in succession, of the Caurava family, who are, according to learned authors, of the same race as the "Pandoos," or five demigod heroes, famed in Hindoo epic verse, of whom I have given a short account elsewhere.*

These Caurava Princes are nameless in history,

---

* (See the appendix to Vol. II.) These five princely heroes were born in the Himalayan Mountains, according to the Pauranic writers, whither Pandoo, with his consort, Koonti, had accompanied the Rishis, and where the gods themselves descended to rear a princely race. To quote from the "Mahábhárat Adi Parva (ii. 64):—"Thus the five god-given sons of Pandoo grew up in the holy mountain of Himavat, endowed with divine force, and with the strength, the gait, and the prowess of lions, expert archers, lovely as the moon, renowned through the world, and honouring the race of Kooroo."

on account of their disregard of the holy precepts of the Vedas (says an author in the "Râjah Tarangini,") and their vicious and unholy lives in other respects. An odd reason, after all, for their names being forgotten or unrecorded!

After Gonerda I. follow fifty-three princes. Thirty-five of these are nameless; the cognomens of the rest I give in a note for the benefit of the curious.* The last of these reigns ended B.C. 388, according to the "adjusted dates," or, according to the ancient writers, 1182 B.C. Of these numerous princes, only two or three deserve any particular notice.

Jaloca, the son and successor of Asoca, was a brave and gallant prince, and devout withal. He overcame the Buddha heresies; and it is supposed that the Brahminical creed was at this time introduced by him into the kingdom in its genuine form.

Of Prince Damodara II. there is a legend which, to this day, is current in Kashmir, so I

* The names of the three first are, Gonerda I., Damodara I., Gonerda II. Then follow the thirty-five kings whose names are forgotten. The rest are: Lava, Cusésaya, Khagéndra, Soorenda, Godhara, Sooverna, Janaca, Sachinara, Asoca, Jaloca, Damodara II. Then come three Tartar princes consecutively:—by name, Hushca, Jushca, Canishca. The last of the fifty-three kings is Abhimanyoo.

will mention it. One day when he was travelling from his palace to the *Vitastá* (or Jhelum), where he performed his daily ablutions, some famishing Brahmins importuned him for food. The river was still at some distance, and he told them to wait till he had bathed. To hasten the moment of their relief, the holy men agreed to bring the stream up to the Prince; and *instanter* the water from the distant river bubbled up from different places near them, forming the identical springs which are still to be seen. The King persisted in bathing in the original stream, thereby incensing the Brahmins by his want of faith in their miraculous exhibition of power. Denouncing a malediction on his incredulous head, they transmogrified him into a snake, in which form, according to popular belief, he is frequently still to be seen, as it is said he pertinaciously continues to haunt the valley, about nine coss from the capital.

The next period is comprised within 378 years, according to Professor Wilson, though the Oriental writers give a range nearly three times as great, or 1013 years. Twenty-one princes reigned in this interval, which would make the average of each reign preposterous and impossible, if any one could be foolish enough to credit the chronology of the vague authors of the East.

This period, viz., the Gonerdiya Dynasty, extended from 388 B.C. to 28 B.C.* The first of the dynasty, Gonerda III., restored the Ophite worship, and the offering of sacrifices for the propitiation of the *Nágas*. Nára, another of these princes, came to his end through the treachery and vice of the priests. A Buddha ascetic having seduced one of the royal spouses from her allegiance to her lord, the incensed and outraged monarch committed a thousand *Vihárs* to the flames, and gave the land pertaining to them to the Brahmins. Subsequently, he fell a victim to the vengeance of the enraged priesthood, whom he had punished in this *wholesale* manner.

The next is the Aditya Dynasty, from 10 B.C. to 135 A.D.; during which six princes reigned, of whom there is not much to chronicle. †

Tunjina and his consort were a miraculously pious connubial pair; but space will not allow me to detail their history. There was a terrible famine in this reign.

* These twenty-one Princes were named as follows:— Gonerda II., Vibhishana, Indrajit, Rávana, Vibhishana II., Nara, Sidha, Utpalácsha, Hiranyácsha, Hiranyacula, Vamacula, Mihiracula, Vaca, Cshitinanda, Vasunanda, Nara II., Acsha, Gopaditya, Gokerna, Narendraditya, Yudhisht'hir.

† The names of these six Princes are—Pratapaditya, Jalaucas, Tunjina, Vijaya, Jayéndra, Arya.

After this, the Gonerdiya Dynasty again flourished, but the chronological data are quite inadmissible, since, even by the "adjusted dates," ten princes are made to reign 433 years.*
The Carota Dynasty began to reign A.D. 615. The chronology after this is found to be very correct in the "Râjah Tarangini." There were seventeen princes, whose reigns extended over 260 years and 5 months, bringing the date to 874 A.D.†
I will give a few particulars of these dynasties presently, but must first mention the names and duration of the two remaining Hindoo dynasties.
The Uptâla, or Vermá Dynasty, from A.D. 876 to A.D. 960 : twelve princes in about 84 years.‡

* These ten Princes are—Mégavâhana, Sreshtaséna, Hiranya, Matrigupta, Pravaraséna, Yudhisht'hir II., Nandravat, Ranâditya, Vicramâditya, Bâladitya.

† These seventeen Princes are—Durlabhaverdhana, Pratâpaditya, Chandrapéra, Târapéra, Lalitaditya, Cuvalayaditya, Vajraditya, Prithivyapéra, Sangramapéra, Jajja, Jayapéra, Lalitapira, Sangramapéra II., Vrihaspati, Ajitapéra, Anangapéra, Utpalapíra.

‡ These are—Avanti or Aditya-Vermâ, Sancra-Vermâ, Gopâla-Vermâ, Sancatâ, Soojândha-Rânee, Part'ha, Nirjita-Vermâ, (also called *Pángoo,* or the cripple,) Chacra-Vermâ, Soora-Vermâ, Part'ha (a second time), Chacra-Vermâ (ditto), Sancâra-Verdhâna, Chacra-Vermâ (a third time), Unmatti Vermâ, Soora-Vermâ II. ("Vermâ" is an adjunct, expressing a *Cshétrya,* or military descent.)

The last (mixed) dynasties, from A.D. 960 to A.D. 1024-5: nine princes reigned a little more than 64 years.*

Passing over the dry political details of each reign, I will merely select a few anecdotes regarding the more noted of the kingly rulers of Kashmir during the Hindoo dynasties, before I proceed to give a sketch of the comparatively modern rule of the Mohammedan conquerors, who invaded and finally subdued the beautiful vale.

In the Carcota Dynasty, I only find one king of any celebrity—Jayapéra. (See note containing names of the Carcota Princes, *supra*.) This sovereign was a mighty warrior, and many were his noble and valorous deeds during his prosperous reign of thirty-one years. His first expedition, however, proved disastrous to himself, as his kingdom was usurped, during his absence, by his brother-in-law, Jajja. His army deserted him in his misfortunes, so he retired to Pryâg (the ancient name of Allahabad). After performing sundry religious penances at the holy city, he determined to go forth and seek his fortune alone. He is supposed to have wandered as far as Behâr, where,

* These are—Yasascâra-Déva, Sangrâma-Déva, Pârvagupta, Cshémagupta, Abhimanyoo, Nandigupta, Tribhoovana, Bhimagupta, Didda-Ranee, Sangrâma-Déva.

despite his humble attire, a lovely female dancer was so struck with his kingly bearing, that she took him home, and tended him devotedly. Shortly after this, he killed a lion unaided, in a chance encounter, which wonderful feat was traced to him the next day through the entanglement of one of his bracelets in the monster's mane. The King of Behâr was so delighted with the bravery he had evinced, that he gave him his daughter in marriage, and furnished him with an army to recover his paternal dominions. He ultimately succeeded in this legitimate object, and the usurper was slain.

After devoting some years to literature and religion, he sallied forth once more on a warlike expedition, and having reduced some strong Forts *en route*, proceeded against Aramuri, king of Nepâl. When the rival forces met, Jayapéra is said to have become excited even to temerity, and rushing alone and unaided into the river which separated the armies, he was taken prisoner, and his panic-struck army fled. Shortly after this, a devoted follower of the captive monarch resolved to rescue him at the risk of his own life, and on various ingenious pretexts obtained access to his master, in the stronghold where the Nepalese had imprisoned him. Owing to the river that intervened between the fortress and the army which Déva-Serma, the faithful adherent, had collected for the king, great difficulties opposed the escape of the royal prisoner. All suggestions failing to convince his master of the practicability of escape, Déva-Serma retired into the adjoining chamber. When the king sought him, he found him lying on the floor strangled with his own turban; near the corpse lay a leaf on which these words were inscribed: "You must effect your escape by the open window; I die to enable you; my body inflated with your breath will serve you as a float, so tie yourself with my turban, and quickly cross the river." Thus, aided by this singular raft, the "hero of a hundred fights" escaped at last, and joining his army, he led them against his foes, whom he routed in their unprepared state. He killed their king out of revenge, and left the country a miserable waste.

Returning to his native valley, he was spending his time in feasting and revelry, in order to enjoy his lately acquired treasures, when an extraordinary occurrence changed his character, and rendered him oppressive and extortionate. A *Nága*, or serpent-deity, appeared to him in a dream, and implored his aid against a magician, who by his enchantments sought to overcome and carry him off. The Nâga promised to reward his royal protector, by revealing to him the existence of a gold mine, and then the vision disappeared. When the king awoke, he disbelieved what his slumbers had shadowed forth, but resolved to test the truth by ordering the magician alluded to, to show him the person of the snake-god. This the latter effected by making the waters of one of the lakes in Kashmir retire at his command, exposing to view the deity and his serpent-retinue. Jayapéra then, giving the magician a handsome gratuity, interposed his authority in behalf of the Nâga, and the waters were recalled. After this the serpent-god visited him once more in his slumbers, but to punish his want of faith, instead of a gold mine, he only revealed a copper one. In order to have this mine wrought, the king became oppressive and cruel to his people, and amassed wealth at the cost of many lives. He had a miserable end, dying of a painful disease, consequent, it was said, on a Brahmin's curse.

In the Aditya Dynasty, Jayendra was a sovereign noted for his long arms, the hands reaching below his knees. He was preceded by the sovereign Tunjina, in whose reign occurred the terrible famine I before mentioned, and he was succeeded by his own prime minister, Sandhimati. Tradition says, however, that the said Sandhimati was put to death by Jayendra, just before his own demise, in order to frustrate the prophecy which predicated the elevation of his quondam minister to the throne; and that the *Yoginis* restored animation to the impaled corpse of Sandhimati, who under the name of "Arga Râjah," was subsequently proclaimed king. After reigning forty-seven years, he voluntarily abdicated the throne, on finding that a true descendant of Yudhisht'hir still lived, and retired into seclusion, ending his holy life in ascetic mortification. His abdication in favour of the great-grandson of Yudhisht'hir, Méghavâhana, revived the Gonerda Dynasty.

The founder of the Uptala or Vermâ Dynasty was Avanti-Vermâ, who built the city of Avantipoora, and made it his capital. This once renowned city is now the ruined and desolate Wantipoor, which I described in Vol. II. during my wanderings in the Valley of Kashmir. A great many cities were founded by Avanti-Vermâ and his family;—his minister likewise followed his example, and was, moreover, a munificent patron of the learned.

The reign of this monarch was rendered still more remarkable by a famine, consequent on the rivers overflowing their banks and inundating the surrounding country, thus ruining the crops, and submerging numerous villages. The dearth became so dreadful at last, that the country was rapidly becoming depopulated. After ten years of suffering, the evil was remedied by the ingenuity of one Sujjya, whose birth was said to be very mysterious. Receiving several bags of specie from the royal treasury, he proceeded in a boat to all the places where the water was collected, and in each spot threw a bag of coin. The villagers, tempted by the money, combined to effect its recovery, for which purpose they blocked up the channel of the Vitastá (*i. e.* the Jhelum) where it issues from the mountains, the banks being there almost contiguous. They then drained the land, and the irregular passages being cleared, the dyke was broken down, when the river burst forth with an impetus proportioned to its long confinement, rushing into its old channel, and into various new ones, and fertilizing the country. To provide against the recurrence of the former calamity, dykes and canals were constructed, so that the waters were distributed equally and plentifully throughout the kingdom. Soojjya being abundantly recompensed for his labours, was enabled to perpetuate his honoured name by founding the city of Soojjyapoor, on the banks of the Vitastá, near the place where it first issues. Avanti-Vermâ commenced his reign A.D. 876, and ruled till his death, about twenty-eight years subsequent to his accession. I will not particularize any more of the Hindoo kings, but after dwelling a little on a few of the most important points connected with ancient Kashmir, I will proceed to the Mohammedan sovereigns.

There is no doubt that Kashmir was well known in the days of Herodotus and Alexander, under the names Kaspapyrus, and Abisarus, and it is very probable that the kingdom extended in those days beyond the confines of the mere valley, and its mountainous boundary. I will not enter into any disquisitions regarding the change of name, though it would be a very simple task to point out the striking affinities to be traced even in the nomenclature; nor will I dwell on its limits in the days of Herodotus and Alexander, since it would be necessary to devote a volume to the subject, if I hoped to do it justice in any way. I refer the reader for further particulars to Appendix VIII. of Professor Wilson's erudite essay, Vol. XV. "Asiatic Researches." I have myself repeatedly observed the references made by Herodotus to Kaspatyrus, and the various data of situation, &c., would be highly convincing to any reasonable mind, as to the striking analogy between the place of which he writes, and Kashmir. Strabo, Arrian, Quintus Curtius and Diodorus Siculus, evidently refer to Kashmir, or its immediately neighbouring districts, in their writings, which I will leave the reader to consult, and proceed to say a few words on the religion of the country in the olden time.

This was originally the Ophite, or snake-worship, but as I have before remarked, there is a striking analogy between this creed and the Hindoo, and the Nâgas are certainly included in the orthodox Hindoo Pantheon. At all events, in process of time the genuine religion of Siva was engrafted on the original ancient superstition, and the Buddhist religion preceded the full Brahminical faith, and the introduction of *castes*. About the period of Damodâra's reign, the creed of Buddha prevailed, and under the Tartar princes who subsequently reigned, Kashmir became a Buddha country. After the last of this race of Tartars, the throne was filled by one who inclined to the Brahminical tenets, and though for a long time the Buddhist faith was not extirpated, it declined rapidly, until at last the genuine Hindoo religion, or the exclusive worship of Siva and his *Sacti* (or consort) prevailed, and Buddhaism was at an end. After the Mohammedan conquest of Kashmir, the inhabitants became chiefly Mussulmans; and now the followers of Mahomet far out-number those of Brâhma, even since the Seikhs in their turn took possession of the province.

The exact date of the first subjugation of Kashmir by the Mohammedan power is uncertain, but the province was attacked and ravaged as early as A.D. 1012, by the great Sultan Mahmoud of Ghuzni. After this, a long succession of Tartar princes of the Chug, or Chagatay tribe, governed Kashmir till A.D. 1586, when it was subdued by the great Akbâr, and remained subject to the Moguls of Delhi until Ahmed Shah Abdâli, the sovereign of Kabool and founder of the Duranny Dynasty, conquered the whole province, and annexed it to the kingdom of Affghanistân, in the year A.D. 1754. During this dynasty, Kashmir was governed by viceroys, and when the Abdâli power began to totter, about the year 1809, the Governor of Kashmir was one of the first to claim the sovereignty of the beautiful valley, on the plea that he had long performed the functions, and held the power of an independent prince. The viceroy, or *Soubadár*, of the province in 1809 was one Mohammed Azim Khân, who seeing the power of his legitimate sovereign on the wane in Affghanistân, threw off the yoke altogether, and set his master at defiance in his mountain-râj. In 1816, a powerful force from Kabool attempted the recovery of Kashmir, but was compelled to retreat with disgrace and great loss—in consequence of treachery, according to most accounts.

In 1819, Runjeet Singh, Maha-Râjah of the Seikh nation, sent Dewân Chund with an army, which finally effected the conquest of Kashmir, and several portions of the country in its immediate vicinity. In 1820, Mohammed Azim Khân deputed two persons to Delhi, with overtures of alliance to the British Government, earnestly praying that the valley might be taken under its protection. This proposal was rejected by the Government, and the sovereign of Lahore kept undisturbed possession of Kashmir till the wars of the Punjâb terminated the Seikh power, and the Seikh nation and Seikh kingdom were vanquished by the British arms. The lovely valley, so famed as the earthly Paradise from the olden times of distant ages, was then sold for "filthy lucre," by the Honourable John Company, to its present rapacious master, Maha-Râjah Goolâb Singh.

I have but cursorily glanced, in the above historical sketch, at the comparatively modern history of the valley, because it is so much better known than the ancient Hindoo records of the province, and I have been forced to husband the little space I have to devote to this interesting topic. I could write pages on pages descriptive of the pomp and state of Kashmir, during the reigns of the Mogul princes,—the Adonis husband-lover, the gallant Jehânghir,* who succeeded the original conqueror, his father, the great Akbâr;†—Shah Jehân,‡ who improved and beautified the valley, adding magnificent palaces of architectural beauty to the natural loveliness of the lovely country; —and Aurungzēb,§ the mighty "Alumghir" of history, who followed the example of his ancestors in regarding Kashmir as a favourite summer

* Jehânghir sat on the throne of Delhi from 1605 to his death, in 1628.

† This prince, the greatest of all the sovereigns of Delhi, was born at Amerkōte, in 1542, proclaimed Emperor in 1556, and died at Agra in 1605.

‡ Shah Jehân ascended the throne of Delhi in 1628, and died in 1658.

§ Aurungzēb reigned almost half a century, dying the 21st February, 1707.

resort, which the haughty Mogul emperors might justly take a pride in adorning, though to a true lover of the picturesque such artificial embellishments could in no way add to the native beauty of this, the second Eden.

But I must not dwell on these later days, for they are doubtless familiar to the majority of readers,—and now having completed my proposed historical sketch to the best of my ability, I shall bid farewell for ever to the sweet Valley of Romance.

JOURNEY FROM THE PUNJAB TO BOMBAY,

OVERLAND,

Viâ the famous Caves of Ajunta and Ellora. Also a short account of the Mahablèshwur and Neilgherry Mountains,—the Sanataria of the Bombay and Madras Presidencies.

JOURNEY FROM THE PUNJAB TO BOMBAY.

CHAPTER I.

THOUGH the journey from the north of India to Bombay is over travelled ground, it may not be uninteresting to subjoin an account of the route, and to give a cursory description of the far-famed caves of Ellora and Ajunta. I kept a "Journal" during my long march from the north-west to the south-west of Hindostan; but as there may not be sufficient interest in the *details* of travelling through such well-known countries, I will merely draw up a short sketch of the said journey.

I left Julundhur, (*en route* for England,) about the 29th of January, 1852, and a *dák* of horses and palanquin carriages conveyed me expeditiously to Agra. "Probett and Company" have excellent travelling conveyances, and the speed on the grand trunk road now averages ten miles an hour; the luxurious traveller reclining (if he so wishes,) as comfortably as in a bed, the interior of the carriage being fitted up for the purpose.

I need not say anything of a city so well known as Agra, though its splendid edifices,—the Tâj Mâhal, the Fort, the Motee Musjid,* &c., &c., —scarcely deserve to be passed over in silence. I have no doubt, however, they are as familiar to the reader as myself.

On the 5th of February, I left Agra for Indore, the capital of Malwâ, and the residence of Maha-Râjah Hurry Râo Holkar, the sovereign of Malwâ. At Agra, the grand trunk road branches off to Calcutta, while the Indore route is rocky, sandy, and comparatively uncivilized. A great proportion of the road is across a country totally uninhabited, or infested with *dakoits.*† The people are Mahrattas, a wild and warlike race. The general aspect of the country between Agra and Gwalior, before entering the *bonâ fide* Mahratta districts, is bare and uninteresting, and several small hills stud the melancholy-looking wastes of land. Low shrubs dot the jungle here and there, but trees are scarce. Tigers, panthers, wolves, and bears, are said to roam at large throughout the entire district between Agra and Indore, and the *dákoitees* that occur are frequent. While travelling "Dâk," in the year 1848, I was myself robbed of several valuables;—two of my *pittárahs*

* The Pearl Mosque. † Gangs of robbers.

(boxes) were carried off by night, the cowardly bearers running away, and leaving the property under their charge to its fate. On account of the great scarcity of villages, it is impossible to post relays of bearers on this road, and the only way of travelling is to go from Dâk-Bungalow to Dâk-Bungalow, taking a set of bearers, (from thirty to fifty,) from Agra. Remembering all I had suffered on my last trip of this kind, I did my utmost to *circumvent* the road in some ingenious manner or other. I verily believe I wrote to every Post-Master in upper India, but found all my projected routes miserable failures. My only remaining resource was to purchase a carriage, fitted up for travelling, in which I could place my nightly couch when requisite;—sending this on to Agra, I overtook it there. My "camp" I despatched to Asseergurh, nearly a hundred miles beyond Indore; and as it left the Punjâb in November, I hoped to find my horses fresh and frisky, and my people prepared by their long rest, to encounter the "forced marching" in store for us, as soon as I should rejoin them. I reached Indore on the 17th of February, having performed the journey from Agra in twelve days, inclusive of three days' halt at the Gwalior Presidency, and three more at Seepree, where I had been kindly invited by

Captain M— and his wife to pass a few days. This rapid travelling—rapid indeed for these uncivilized regions—could not have been effected in the ordinary mode, or in any other than the one I adopted. Armed with magisterial Purwânnahs, I went as far as Goonah, about half-way from Agra to Indore, in my carriage drawn by bullocks, and from Goonah to Indore, I rode the horses of the Mahratta cavalry, which are stationed every five miles along the greater part of this road. Numerous were my accidents and misadventures, both in the carriage and on horseback; the bullocks were frequently wild and unaccustomed to harness, and the horses totally unused to a side-saddle, or a lady's habit, so that I had more than one narrow escape during the journey. Far from feeling nervous, however, after an equestrian wrestle, I only enjoyed the ride the more fully. The mornings as well as the nights were cool;— the moon shone brightly, and, escorted by several horsemen of the Irregular Cavalry, I rode daily from thirty to sixty miles, instead of confining myself to the Dâk-Bungalows along this road, eighteen of which are built at distances meant to constitute ordinary travelling stages.* I had three servants with me, who were always

* See Appendix.

mounted in the same manner as myself. My two carriage-horses I was forced to abandon *en route*, as they became galled and foot-sore, from the severe work they underwent.

Shortly after leaving Seepree, we narrowly escaped an awkward accident. The bullocks harnessed to my Equirotal were wild and unmanageable:—the country we were traversing was hilly, and the road, though broad, was rocky, and flanked by many ravines. In the middle of the night we came to a very bad part,—on the right there was a steep declivity, terminating in a horrible chasm. The headstrong kine, infinitely preferring in their wilfulness the wrong and dangerous path, rushed off the direct road, down this declivity, and had I not most providentially been awake, we should all have found ourselves buried under the fragments of the carriage, in the precipitous ravine which yawned below our feet. In less time than it has taken me to write these few words, I jumped out of the Equirotal, and hurried to the head of the bullocks,—thus at the critical moment, arresting their headlong career, until my servants (who were close behind) came up, and unyoked the unruly animals. The driver, inexperienced and cowardly, had dexterously fled from the danger at the very commencement. Every descent seemed alluring to these cross-grained, ill-bred creatures, who never saw a declivity, no matter how rocky or steep, but they incontinently went off at a wild, mad pace, recklessly perilling my neck and my carriage in the most unpleasant manner, as if both were not of inestimable value !

I was rejoiced to reach Goonah, where, through the assistance of Captain B——, who commands the Contingent stationed there, I made the arrangements already mentioned, and accomplished the last one hundred and eighty miles (much more to my satisfaction) on horseback. My carriage, which had been repeatedly overturned, was by this time broken, and unfit for further use until I could get it repaired by proper workmen at Indore; and as I had studiously avoided bringing a palanquin, it was fortunate that my *nerves* did not stand in the way of my mounting strange horses, unused to European riders.

I had one rather serious rencontre with a party of Mahratta Dakoits, on which occasion I think I may justly lay claim to having escaped solely by my fearless horsemanship and unwavering presence of mind. I was riding along, very early one morning, on a little Mahratta mare, about eighty miles from Indore, escorted by several troopers of the Cavalry Contingent, and two of my own servants. My body-guard were so arranged, that some rode before me, leading the way, and some behind. Just as the day broke, five Mahratta horsemen, armed to the teeth, with long spears in their hands, rode up to our party, and demanded in authoritative terms that the little mare I was riding should be delivered up to them upon the spot! My valiant escort fled at their approach, and I was left to settle accounts with these wild horsemen in the best way I could. Even had they been ambassadors from the owner of the steed, I could not have complied with their request, however politely urged, as I had no other available means of reaching the nearest halting-place. But as it was, these men,—so ferocious in aspect, so bellicose in word and gesture,—I had never beheld before! Their long sharp spears, pointed at me, threatened each moment death and destruction. Twice I manage to break through the lawless band, and manœuvre my horse through the ring they formed around me, and twice was I again surrounded, and nearly overcome by the overwhelming number of my enemies. I made my little steed lash out before and behind, to prevent the too near approach of the spears, and fortunately for me, the animal was too full of life and vice to require much prompting to rear, and plunge, and kick. Repeatedly the five spears narrowly grazed either me or my gallant grey, but after nearly ten minutes of desperate *Jung*,* I succeeded in dashing through the lists of wild horsemen, and with the aid of whip and spur, rode fairly away. My escort, who had so gallantly and courageously left me to my fate, slunk into camp long after I was safely housed. They had the grace to look heartily ashamed of themselves, and I humanely spared them the many sarcasms their pusillanimity deserved. I reported the whole affair to the proper authorities, and I sincerely trust the lawless miscreants were caught, and duly punished for such an unheard of attack in the protected States, where, though robberies are frequent, personal violence is rarely attempted.

I had another narrow escape on the following evening, my enemy on this occasion being a panther. It was just sunset, and having distanced my attendant troopers, by taking a longer and a harder gallop than their steeds or their nerves permitted, I was not at all charmed to see a huge panther, or some such wild beast, (a *bughurra* the natives called it subsequently,) ap-

* War—battle.

proaching me from the waste land to my left. For a long time he lay crouching behind a bush, apparently awaiting my coming up. My steed was exhausted by the long gallop he had had, and appeared a little lame. Neither persuasive nor coercive measures could at first induce him to accelerate his pace, so I turned my thoughts to the hope of escape offered by the jungly expanse on my right, purposing to strike off across country, and having circumvented the foe lying in wait, to return to the road a mile or so in advance. But my plans were frustrated almost as soon as formed, for not a hundred yards distant appeared a second wild animal, horribly like a tiger, which stood eyeing me steadfastly as I hesitated on the road! Despair made me bold,—with sudden energy I urged on my halting steed, and escaped both the wild denizens of the jungle at once, though *how* I was so fortunate as to accomplish this, I should find it impossible now to describe.*

The country between Gwalior and Indore wears the same desolate aspect as the tract between Agra and Gwalior. The landscape is studded with hills, as barren as the plain, and low shrubs are

* Probably the horse scented the tiger, and became as alarmed as his rider. He snorted in apparent terror when the enemy came in sight.

scattered here and there, without trees or grass to lend refreshing verdure to the scene.

Unless Euclid was all wrong, when he laboriously propounded that "any two sides of a triangle are greater than the third," I had no business at Gwalior, supposing I meant to reach Indore by the direct route from Agra. In fact, Seepree (as well as Gwalior,) is all out of the way, and there is little to be seen at either locality. For the benefit of those who may wish to travel from Agra to Indore, I have subjoined in the Appendix, the regular marches and Dâk-Bungalows, &c.

As I was detained a few days at Indore, in order to get my Equirotal repaired, I much regretted that illness prevented my paying a visit to my old haunts at Mhow, the neighbouring military station, where I spent one year not long ago. It was alas! a year of sorrow and sickness, and I sigh to recall that sad time, though its gloom may occasionally have been chequered with fitful gleams of sunshine;—transitory happiness, only to be succeeded by more terrible misery. I mournfully pondered on the many changes which had taken place since I last trod that very ground four long years ago;—my child taken from me, and I now alone in this weary world. "*Alone!*"—ah! how much of desolation there is in that word, when one's "household gods lie shivered around," and the halcyon days of youth are passing away in melancholy isolation from all that is dear and hallowed to the human breast, ere its feelings and sympathies have become cold and dead.

"There's not a joy the world can give, like that it takes away,
When the glow of early thought declines in feeling's dull decay;
'Tis not on youth's smooth cheek the blush alone which fades so fast,
But the tender bloom of heart is gone ere youth itself be past.
Then the few whose spirits float above the wreck of happiness
Are driven o'er the shoals of guilt or ocean of excess;
The magnet of their course is gone, or only points in vain
The shore to which their shiver'd sail shall never stretch again.
Though wit may flash from fluent lips, and mirth distract the breast,
Through midnight hours that yield no more their former hope of rest;
'Tis but as ivy leaves around the ruin'd turret wreath,
All green and wildly fresh without, but worn and grey beneath.
Oh! *could I feel as I have felt*, or be what I have been,
Or weep as I could once have wept, o'er many a vanish'd scene;
As springs, in deserts found, seem sweet, all brackish though they be,
So, midst the withered waste of life, those tears would flow to me."

Can there be anything in the English language more beautiful and more exquisitely *true* than these lines? They are true indeed, and those who have passed through the fiery ordeal of sorrow and trial must keenly appreciate all the melancholy fidelity of the utter desolation depicted in those touching stanzas, and feel that he who wrote them must have suffered, and suffered deeply. Would that *I* could "feel as I have felt, and be what I have been." *Hélas! hélas!* all retrospections are worse than vain;—better to "be that light, unmeaning thing, that smiles with all and weeps with none."

But my mournful reminiscences have induced me to treat Malwâ very unceremoniously, in breaking off my description of the country. There is, however, but little to add to the account, and I will wind up with a few words regarding the climate. According to my experience, Gwalior, Seepree and Goonah, with all the intermediate country, are very hot. The temperature was as high in February in those rocky tracts, as it is in the Punjâb six weeks *later*. But Mhow is certainly one of the coolest and pleasantest stations in India, for, though little of cold weather visits it, the great extreme of heat is almost equally unknown.

I observed very large herds of antelopes, ravine deer,* and the spotted deer, bounding along the

* The Gazelle species. These deer are smaller than ordi-

jungly wastes of the Gwalior and Mahratta districts, and often these beautiful and graceful creatures crossed my path within twenty yards of my horse.

Before proceeding to Ajunta, I will give a cursory account of the Mahrattas, once a formidable and warlike tribe.

The original Mahratta State comprehended a large tract of country, including Kandeish, Boglâna, and a part of Berâr, extending to the northwest as far as the Nerbudda. These were districts of great natural strength, being interspersed with strong-holds, mountain fastnesses, and deep defiles, admirably adapted to defensive warfare. But though the Mahrattas were a numerous nation, little mention is made of them in Indian History, till the reign of Aurungzēb, in the seventeenth century. Probably the country was divided into little principalities and chiefdoms, which, though never *subjugated* by the neighbouring Mohammedan sovereigns, were, in all probability, more or less controlled by, or dependent upon them. The Mussulman writers were notoriously jealous of every thing pertaining to the Hindoos, so probably avoided all mention of these tribes. The first

nary antelopes; the colour of the fur is much darker, brown instead of fawn-colour; the head is more beautiful, and the large black eyes more full and melting.

Mahratta chieftain, who formed the separate principalities into an empire, was Sevajee, who was born in A.D. 1628, and died in 1680. He extended his kingdom to the range of hills that form the boundary of the Concan, and from Surat along the sea-coast to the neighbourhood of Goa, which was then a Portuguese settlement of importance. He was succeeded by his son Sambajee, who still further increased his dominions, but falling into Aurungzēb's hands, he was killed only nine years subsequent to his father's death. It was the son of this potentate, by name Sâhoo, who originated the anomalous description of government which prevailed under the "Peshwâs." The Râjah Sâhoo, a weak-minded prince, on his accession, delegated the whole of his sovereign power to a Brahmin from the alien State of the Concan, who had been the Commandant of a large body of horse during the latter portion of his grandfather's reign. This man, Balâjee Bishnâth by name, was appointed Peshwâ, and all orders and details of government issued directly from him, as the chief of the kingdom. This priest militant possessed an unbounded ascendancy over the mind of the imbecile monarch, and from that time to the dismemberment of the empire, the Peshwâs were regularly installed by the Râjah, who became a sovereign only in name, being in point of fact detained a prisoner at Sattâra, a strong hill-fortress in the province of Beejapore. For more than a century, the descendants of Sevajee, the founder of the Mahratta empire, were successively imprisoned by their *soi-disant* deputies. The form of government was quite farcical, as far as the nominal sovereigns were concerned;—the Peshwâ, on succeeding to office, repaired to Sattâra, to receive from his powerless royal captive the robe of investiture, (the *khilaut*, or dress of honour,) nor did he ever take the field without seeking an audience of his enslaved *master*. There were some privileges still attached to the country surrounding the regal city of Sattâra, by way of royal immunities, and the prisoner-sovereign was lodged in the splendid misery of royal state and pomp.

The son of Balâjee Bishnâth, by name Balâjee Bajerow, usurped in his turn the whole authority without any difficulty, as Rane, Sâhoo Râjah's successor, was likewise an imbecile prince. The empire extended greatly during the Peshwâ dynasties, and from being a nation whose insignificant name and extent it is difficult to trace during the first century of its existence, it became so important and powerful, that it subjugated or laid under heavy tribute the whole of the Deccan and South of Hindostan. The sea bounded the empire to the east and west; the north of the dominions reached to Agra, while Cape Comorin was the southern limit. The Mahrattas ravaged Bengal, and by force of arms wrested from the Portuguese the strong-hold of Bassein and the island of Salsette.

Balâjee Bajerow died in 1761. As the office of Peshwâ was declared by him to be hereditary, he was succeeded by his descendants during many successive generations. The famous Ahmed Shah Abdâli, the sovereign of Kabool, gave the first check to the power of the Mahrattas, by defeating them in a desperate battle,* on the 17th of January, 1761; after which, for nearly fifteen years, their predatory incursions to the north of the Nerbudda were discontinued. There were many intestine conflicts carried on between the years 1772 and 1782, which ended disastrously for the Mahratta empire. But in 1784, the Mahratta chiefs made war against the petty independent States which bordered along their western frontier, and subdued each successively. In 1785-86, they were obliged to conclude a disadvantageous peace with Tippoo, with whom they had foolishly embroiled themselves; and thus they forfeited

* The Battle of Paniput.

many of their fairest possessions, till in 1790 they regained them once more, through their alliance with the British Government. In 1802, the Peshwâ (Bajerow II.) was obliged to take refuge in flight, when Jeswunt Râo Holkar's* army totally defeated the allied forces of the Peshwâ and Dowlet Râo Scindia.† The refugee proceeded to Bassein in December of that year, and there entered into a treaty with the East India Company. The federal empire was, by this treaty, virtually abolished, and in its place arose the independent States of Poonah, Scindia, Nâgpoor, Holkar and the Gwicowâr.‡ In the following year, General Wel-

* Mulhar Râo Holkar, of the *Doongur* or Shepherd tribe, was the founder of the Holkar dynasty in Malwâ. He was born in 1693, and rose to eminence under the first Peshwâ of the Mahrattas. He died in 1768 or 1769. Jeswunt Râo Holkar (mentioned in the text) was an illegitimate descendant.

† The founder of this race was Jyapa Scindia, the servant of the first Peshwâ, originally raised to power by his master. Dowlet Râo Scindia was a descendant, and succeeded to the territory of Oojein, which fell into the power of the first of the race, in 1794. The Scindia race were Mahrattas.

‡ A Mahratta chieftain, known by the family name of "Gwicowâr," (*Gaikwâd* in the Mahratta tongue.) Baroda was the capital of his dominions. The rise of the Gwicowâr's power was almost contemporaneous with that of the Peshwâ. The first of this race who attained to sovereignty, was a *Patél*, or managing proprietor of a village, by name Pillâjee Gwicowâr,

lesley (the Duke of Wellington) restored the capital of his dominions to the fugitive Peshwâ, and British forces kept his people in subjection for him. The final fall of the Peshwâ, and the entire dissolution of the Mahratta confederacy, were entirely owing to the insane hatred which the restored fugitive entertained towards the power which had reinstated him,—his intrigues at almost every court in India, proving him to be an incorrigible plotter against the British Government. His savage attempt to murder Mr. Elphinstone in 1817 was succeeded by hostilities, which ended in making him once more a ruined fugitive. A protracted war with all its attendant horrors, its enormous military expenditure and loss of revenue, appeared to be the unwelcome prospect before the British Government, as the wily fugitive frustrated every attempt at capture, even after he had been obliged to abandon the Râjah of Sattâra and his family, whom he had seized, and forced to accompany him in his erratic flights from one end of his former empire to the other. At last, in 1818, he voluntarily surrendered to Sir John Malcolm, who

who raised himself by stratagems and artifices to power, in much the same way as did his superior, the Peshwâ. The Gwicowâr dynasty was first politically noticed by the British Government in 1782.

at that time commanded in Malwâ, on condition of receiving a yearly pension of eight lacs of rupees (£8,000 sterling);—his dominions were then sequestrated, and his power annulled. He ended his life in a palace on the banks of the Ganges, near Cawnpoor, passing his last years in effeminate idleness and disgraceful debauchery.

Thus fell the Mahratta empire, and the Mahratta peasantry have still a pride in recounting the past glories of their ancestors, and still betray latent sparks of military fire and ambition. No territory in the whole length and breadth of Hindostan boasted of so many strong-holds as did the fallen empire of this belligerent people. Exclusive of the fortresses still held by the petty chiefs, or Jâghir-dârs, who, at the time of the entire dismemberment of the dominions of the Peshwâ, were permitted by the Company to retain their Jagheērs, there were nearly two hundred strong-holds scattered over the country under the Mahratta sway in 1817. For fear of these proving the lurking-places of banditti or rebels, the majority of them have been dismantled or entirely levelled.

I may now proceed with my journey, as I have digressed long enough *en route*.

The distance from Indore to Ajunta is one hundred and ninety-two miles. Unlike the high roads of the Bengal Presidency, this route is rocky and bad, and most ruinous to the springs of carriages, with the exception of the first seventy miles, which are in tolerably good repair. The entire country is covered with low hills; cultivation is more scanty, and the population apparently far less numerous than in the less hilly and jungly districts. The Simrole Ghât is passed at the thirteenth mile from Indore. This *Ghât* or Pass descends through the rocky hills to a level much below Malwâ, and is well worth seeing. The scenery is very wild, and the descent steep and wooded. The difference of temperature is quite perceptible by the time the foot of the Ghât is attained, and I found the heat most oppressive. I performed the first hundred and three miles by bullock-dâk, travelling day and night in my comfortable carriage. At Asseergurh I found my camp, and the plan I then adopted was to ride and drive alternately, according to my fancy, and the particular circumstances of time and road, travelling on an average from twenty to thirty miles per diem. My large Camp with the numerous retinue of servants kept up with me uncomplainingly, though the majority had to accomplish all the forced marches on foot. The bullocks were changed once or twice each day. I found the journey a most pleasurable affair altogether, in spite of my solitude and the great heat of the low hilly districts I had to traverse. Not long after passing Asseergurh, my camel-men walked off with their camels in the most cool and collected manner, decamping at the same time with all the advance pay they had received. I had no time to delay, and was forced to put all my baggage in hackeries, (bullock-carts,) changing them at every town or larger village, as the only way of carrying out my plan of "forced marches." I suffered greatly from constant fatigue and want of sleep, the intense heat preventing my travelling much by day, and the jolting consequent on the rocky nature of the route banishing sleep too often by night, even though I reclined in my carriage as comfortably as on the most luxurious couch. These districts must be fully ten degrees hotter than any part of Upper India. I remember at a place called Bodur, about forty miles beyond Asseergurh, in the Dâk-Bungalow there, feeling the heat absolutely prostrating. A hot blast blew from morning to night, and I lay on the couch exhausted by the feverishness induced by the very high temperature. A perfect Simoom raged out of doors, and as there were no *Tatties* to the house, the scorching wind seemed to wither every vital energy.

The only town of any interest after leaving Indore, is Boorhânpoor, whilom a famous city, the ancient capital of the Kandeish Province. It is situated on a fine plain on the north-west bank of the Tuptee River; latitude 21° 19′ N., longitude 76° 18′ E. About fifteen miles to the southeast is a range of hills that separate Kandeish from Berâr. Boorhânpoor is one of the best built cities in the Deccan. Most of the houses are constructed of brick, three stories high, with pretty *façades* framed in wood, and are invariably roofed with tiles. The Tuptee is a clear and beautiful stream of no great depth. On a high bank, close to the river, the Fort and Palace of its ancient sovereigns is still to be seen in extensive ruins. The Jumma Musjid is a fine pile of masonry constructed of grey stone, in a style peculiar to this part of India. Aqueducts amply supply the city with water.

There is a manufacture here of turbans and a sort of wrapper or shawl (the *Dō-puttah*) which is very handsome. It is a fabric almost transparent, with a fringe and border of gold; the colours of the stuff are principally purple and scarlet. The price of the turbans ("puggree") is from seven to fifteen rupees each, and of the *Dō-puttahs* from ten to forty rupees, according to the depth of the gold-border.

Boorhânpoor was taken, with the rest of the

Kandeish Province, by the Mahrattas about A.D. 1760, during the vice-royalty of Islam Khan. Since that period Kandeish has been progressively decaying. In 1803 the British army captured the Province, but afterwards surrendered it to Scindia. However, it subsequently again fell into the Company's hands, like almost all the native States of Hindostan.*

Very fine grapes are grown in the vicinity of Asseergurh, Boorhânpoor, and even as far down as Aurungabad. At or near Asseergurh, the direct road from Agra to Bombay follows a due southerly direction; I verged to the eastward, however, in order to visit the famous caves of Ajunta and Ellora.

I reached Ajunta on the night of the 25th February, after a long and difficult ride through the hilly country, which leads to the town. The proper name is "Ajayanti," which signifies

* The period of the British acquisition of Kandeish was in 1818. The sovereign power of the Peshwâ, to whom this Province belonged, was annihilated in the wars of 1817-18, which proved likewise so fatal to the Mahratta Empire. The whole of the Peshwâ's dominions were then incorporated with the British States, with the exception of Sattâra, which was given to the former Râjah. This State lies to the east of the great western Ghâts, and west of the Nizâm's dominions.

"the difficult or impregnable Pass." This quondam "town" is a mere village now, but there are some traces yet visible of greatness and importance long past. The immediate ascent to Ajunta is by a wide road, lately completed. The town stands on a table-land, at about two miles distance from the Ghât. At its northern entrance, there is an octagonal Seraï, of very striking appearance, and about six miles distant, are the caves I have alluded to, and of which I shall presently give a succinct account, though doubtless many an abler pen has already detailed their wonders. The Pass which has christened Ajunta, leads through the Berâr * mountains, fifty-three miles N. by E. from Aurungabad; latitude 20° 34′ N., longitude 75° 56′ E. The best way to reach the Caves would be to proceed there straight from Fardâr-

* Berâr is a large province of the Deccan, situated between the nineteenth and twentieth degrees of latitude. On the north, it is bounded by Kandeish, and Malwâ; on the south, by Aurungabad and Beeder; to the east lies the province of Gundwâna; and Kandeish and Aurungabad extend along the west. Berâr Proper is an elevated valley, ascended by a chain of Ghâts, or mountain Passes. It was once a separate Râj or kingdom, but its glory has departed long years ago. It formed (and perhaps forms still) a portion of the Nizâm's dominions, one of the few remaining *bond fide* Princes in the East.

pore,* a small village buried in the jungle. The caves are but three miles thence, (to the east of Ajunta,) and a very tolerable road has been marked out for the benefit of travellers. Wild beasts are said to infest the whole of this country, and in the neighbourhood of the Caves they used to be very numerous, only a few years ago. Even to this day, night-travelling is considered dangerous. There is a foot-path leading from Ajunta to the excavations, only three miles in length, shortening the distance by the road to one-half. This way is said to be particularly unsafe, as tigers inhabit the dense jungle, through which the lonely path has been cut. I was detained at Ajunta till near sunset, on the evening I had fixed upon for my visit to the caves, but in spite of the fading light, I resolved to proceed. I had not gone above a mile, when a gentleman rode up to me, and introduced himself as Captain R—, of the Bombay Infantry, who was surveying the district. Apologizing for the intrusion, he begged I would not think of risking my life by proceeding to the caves at so late an hour; —assuring me that two men had been recently killed on that very path by a tiger, and that similar accidents were of melancholy frequency. On

* Fardârpore is passed five miles before reaching Ajunta. It is situated at the foot of the steep ascent of the Ghât.

hearing this, I half promised to turn my steps towards Fardârpore, and to defer my projected visit to the caves until the following morning; my friendly monitor then rode away. When I reached the path, however, which diverges towards the Caves, I changed my mind, and resolved (perhaps somewhat recklessly) to pursue my original plan. I had a numerous escort of servants, Chuprassies and guides, and they implored me not to run so great a risk,—but I was exhausted with fatigue, and knowing my camp was awaiting me at the caves, I determined to follow my own counsel, and brave the tigers. We had no torches, and the night was pitchy dark. I confess that my heart sank, when I heard the trees in the thick jungle around us rustling, and the whisper of "Bâgh! bâgh!" (tigers) running through my trembling party, but I listlessly pursued my way, too weary and too indifferent to feel any serious alarm. One unhappy man, who was a straggler, never reached the Camp, and it is to be feared he fell a victim,— for what were supposed to be his mouldering bones were subsequently discovered on an adjacent wooded eminence. My presiding stars were however more propitious, and despite of my temerity, I reached the caves in safety, before ten o'clock, p.m.

There being no space in the vicinity to pitch large tents, such as are indispensable to travelling in the plains, I appropriated one of the subterranean dwellings as my domicile *pro tempore*. The ghost of departed deities did not haunt my slumbers, which were sound and dreamless, as those of wearied travellers generally are, when fortunate enough to find a bed to repose upon. " Tired nature's sweet restorer" visited my pillow, though the natives superstitiously shuddered when they saw me place my bed near a monstrous Idol, and fasten my mosquitoe-curtains with the aid of the various digits and noses in the neighbourhood!

Early next morning I made the round of the far-famed Caves, and had I not omitted to bring my sketch-book, I should have taken drawings of one or more. The latter part of the path to the excavations follows the bed of a river at present dry, but which becomes swollen and impassable in the rains. This river flows between nearly perpendicular hills, apparently parted for its especial convenience. The caves are found about midway up the ridge, on the right hand; and as the shape of this part of the hilly range is somewhat circular, so the caves—nearly thirty in number, separate and detached from each other—present a sort of crescent, and are all commanded by the eye in one view from any point near the centre. It is impossible to visit these subterranean wonders, and not marvel at their being—as they assuredly are—the work of man's hands. There are several compartments in each cave, divided by massive stone colonnades variously carved:—the walls are of stone, elaborately carved. Many of these caves are thirty and forty yards in length, and double that in breadth. They are all very irregular in shape and size; some consisting of one story, while others have double tiers, the outer façade of the upper being arched. The sculpture, both within and without these wondrous excavations, is very elaborate, and the whole series is a work of great magnitude. There are myriads of figures, many of colossal dimensions, representing gods, men, and animals. In one cave I observed a monstrous statue of a man, sculptured in a reclining position, supposed to be asleep on a couch. The length was upwards of twenty feet, and the rest of the figure in proportion. As I viewed these colossal statues, I thought that the native traditions must be true, and that these caves had been hewn out of the solid rock, and sculptured by men of different mould from the insignificant race of the present day,—in the olden time spoken of in Scripture itself—"There were giants on the earth in those days." There is some writing on the stone walls, in two separate places, one outside, and the other inside one of the caves at the further extremity of the range; but these are hieroglyphics of some unknown or forgotten tongue, for which no interpreter has been found. The characters seemed to me to have a remote affinity to the style of Persian caligraphy, but my cicerone scorned the suggestion. There are two caves entirely separate from the rest, and almost out of sight. I was assured that there is no possible approach to them. The footpath leading from cave to cave is narrow and rocky, flanked by the precipitous face of the scarp which terminates in the rocky bed of the river before mentioned; but this pathway comes to an abrupt termination at some distance from the two isolated caves. There was a little water just below, in a rocky basin in the bed of the river; but I am told this pool dries up as the hot weather advances, and even a temporary encampment in this vicinity becomes, in consequence, highly inconvenient.

In attaining the seventh excavation of the subterranean range, a narrow foot-path leads up a steep rocky ascent, and dismounting here, as the night was so dark, I walked up. There is shelter for cattle in the outer compartments of the seventh cave. Further on there is no possible way for a horse.

There is a good deal of painting in several of the subterranean chambers;—representations of flowers as well as of gods, men, deer, horses, and many other things. In several places, this painting is but little defaced; while in others, time has rudely destroyed every lingering trace of beauty. In one cave, I saw a large frame of canvas, on which Major Gill was drawing fac-similes of the decorated walls, by order of the East India Company. I was much struck with the artistic skill displayed in the difficult and laborious work. During so small a portion of the day do the sun's rays throw the requisite light on the walls, that Major Gill has but little time for pursuing his task, and each frame of painting takes him two or three months.

In the greater number of the caves, there is found a monstrous figure at the furthest extremity of the innermost compartment, facing the entrance. In this inner chamber, there are frequently several other statues of gods and idols, of the same inordinate size. The whole range of excavations is in wonderful preservation, considering how many centuries have elapsed since the forgotten architects called these wondrous chambers into existence. The pillars are for the most part in fragments, and the features or limbs of some of the figures are broken off or defaced, a digit or two being generally wanting; on the whole, however, the massive work has triumphed over time. There are some trees near the bed of the river, but the hills in the immediate vicinity are harsh in their outline, and nearly devoid of all vegetation, save the scorched up turf. Here and there a bush dots the yellow grass, but these spots of verdure are "few and far between."

"The mountain-grass by scorching skies imbrown'd,
The sunken glen, whose wither'd shrubs must weep."

Formerly Thugs* lurked in the dark recesses of

* The Thugs were a notorious class of public robbers, who were at one period the scourges of Hindostan. Their object was generally plunder, but also occasionally the gratification of private revenge. The peculiar mode they adopted of murdering their victims, has distinguished them by the name of "Phânsigârs," or stranglers. Their sly and adroit method of ensnaring hapless travellers was invariably attended with fatal success, while detection was impossible, or nearly so. Sometimes they placed a female accomplice in some secluded spot, if they heard of travellers journeying any particular route;—this syren would pour forth a harrowing tale of distress, which generally succeeded in moving the compassion of her auditors. If it were a single traveller, she would induce him to take her up behind him on his horse; then at an appointed spot, she would fling a noose round his neck, and dragging him to the ground, leave him to be quickly dispatched

these ancient caves, and it was consequently unsafe to travel through the surrounding country. Many murders and robberies were committed on hapless wayfarers, by those lawless and unscrupulous tribes. They are now, however, nearly exterminated throughout the length and breadth of the land. The wild beasts too, which so lately ranged these jungle hills in such alarming numbers, have been decimated by powder and shot. Only a year ago, my rash night-march through this deep jungle would probably have met with a far more tragic termination than a comfortable night's repose.

While this work was passing through the press, I saw an account of the Ajunta caves, in the 2nd Vol. of "The Trans. Asiatic Society," and as this account is the first ever published, (nearly thirty years ago,) of the wonderful excavations in question, I thought it might prove interesting to give a few

by her concealed associates. They often joined parties of travellers, apparently in the most innocent manner, without creating any suspicion, and thus followed their victims for weeks, perhaps, till having reached a secluded place, they chose a convenient time, (generally while they were cooking, or eating their food,) to strangle them all. They have been known to murder children for the sake of a rupee. All castes were found in these demoniacal gangs.

(This note may be unnecessary to the majority of readers, but I have subjoined it for the benefit of *ignoramusses !*)

extracts, as the work in which I found the Essay, is not easily procurable now. I therefore subjoin a few extracts, quoted *ipsissima verba*, from "Lieut. Alexander's Visit to the Cavern Temples of Ajunta."

"In passing a small party of the Nizâm's horse, the Duffadar (an inferior officer), saluted us with the customary compliment of "*Salam alicum,*" (Peace with you); and inquired where we were going. I told him we proposed visiting the caves: to which he replied, "*La illah illilah!* (There is but one God), you will never return: for *if* you escape the tigers, these stony-hearted robbers, the Bheels, will destroy you. *Khòdah hafiz,*" (may the Lord preserve you:) and taking leave of him, we rode out of the gate which led to the head of the pass, down which our road lay. After travelling some distance along a stony road, and passing several cairns, near which were many bushes covered with rags, pointing out the spot where unfortunate travellers had been destroyed by tigers, we suddenly found ourselves at the top of the precipitous *Ghât*, or Pass. The scene which now opened upon us was magnificent in the extreme. The vale of Kandeish was stretched beneath our feet, extending far into the blue distance, and enclosed by wooded mountains. Jungle, small lakes and streams scattered in every direction, diversified the face of the valley; and here and there amongst the trees, appeared the pointed top of a Hindoo Pagoda, or the white dome of a Moslem shrine. Near us, over the face of the hills,

> The bosom-folds of mist, the morning breeze
> Wreathed gracefully;

and bore with it the balmy incense of Oriental flowers. We now dismounted, and leading our horses down a precipitous pathway to the left of the Pass, found ourselves at the bottom, among sweet-smelling *kus-kus* grass. Directing our steps towards an opening between the deeply serrated hills, we arrived at the *bouche* of the glen, and fell in with a mountain stream, along whose banks lay the pathway to the caves, leading through low underwood, interspersed with trees and water-grass, fifteen feet in height; amongst which, not long before, three tigers had been killed. We had not far advanced up the glen, when a low whistling was heard above us to the left, and was quickly repeated from the opposite cliffs. This proved to be Bheels intimating to one another that strangers were approaching. The guide evinced some symptoms of fear; but on being remonstrated with, and encouraged with the hope of a handsome present, he proceeded onwards. Some of the Bheels showed themselves, peeping out from behind the rocks. They were a most savage-looking race, perfectly black, low in stature, and nearly naked. They seemed to be armed with bows and arrows. The principal haunts of these Bheels are in the Northern Deccan, along the course of the Nerbudda. They live entirely in the jungles, are in a state of great barbarism, and subsist by hunting, rapine, and plunder. Our fire-arms prevented their attacking us; and we were allowed to proceed unmolested. The glen, up which our road lay, almost to its termination, where the caves are situated, was remarkable for its picturesque beauty.

* * * * * *
* * * * *

The caves of which I am now treating, are excavated in horizontal strata of greywacke, with embedded portions of quartz, approaching chalcedony. Blood-stones, in which the portions of Jasper are larger than usual, may be picked up in a water-worn state, in the bed of the stream. Indurated felspar is also in abundance. * * * *

I conceive the age of the Caves of Ajunta, to be nearer three than two thousand years.   *   *   *   *

Though it was but a rapid glance that I had of these imperishable monuments of antiquity,

" *Quæ non imber edax non aquilo impotens,*
Possit diruere, aut innumerabilis
Annorum series,"

yet I was highly delighted with my excursion; and although many are the caverned Temples which I have explored, and many which I wish to revisit, yet to none would I sooner return than to those of Ajunta. Several of them I was unable to examine; but the *paintings* alone, in such as I had an opportunity of examining, would render them much more interesting to those who might desire to become acquainted with the appearance of the ancient inhabitants of Hindoostan, than the grotesque, though beautifully sculptured Deities of Ellora."*

I have purposely abstained from copying any account of the sculpture of the Caves, because Lieut. Alexander's description in no material point differs from mine. He says that the Buddhist religion is far more ancient than the Hindoo, and brings forward copious arguments, proving this interesting fact. In some other part of this volume, I have stated my own conviction to be the same, and there is ample proof found in the relics of antiquity, if the traveller will take the trouble to trace analogies with care and precision.

* "Lieut. Alexander's visit to the Cavern Temples of Ajunta. Vol. II. Trans. Asiat. Society."

CHAPTER II.

The distance from Ajunta to Roza, (or properly "Rowza,") where the caves of Ellora are found, is about sixty miles. The road is a mere cart-track the last sixteen miles, from the large walled-town of Phoolmurry, and very much cut up by ravines. I sent my carriage by the direct road to Aurungabad, which branches off at Phoolmurry, but as it arrived very much broken, I did not profit much by the arrangement. The cart-track from Ajunta to Phoolmurry is very tolerable, though here and there intersected by ravines and nullahs. Several rivers have also to be forded, but these in the hot season are very shallow, and prove no obstacle to the traveller. The country continues hilly in the distance, and the scenery is wild;—the greater part of the road was very pleasantly shaded with trees or bushes, while the warm air was impregnated with the delicious fragrance of the Babool,[*] and

[*] The Mimosa, or Acacia Arabica.

Jessamine blossoms. We passed several walled-towns, and a great many villages. As we approached Phoolmurry, the country became much intersected with ravines, but cultivation continued to flourish. Grapes were very plentiful at Phoolmurry, and they proved most refreshing in the oppressive heat of those sultry evenings. The whole of this district after leaving Ajunta, pertains to the Nizâm of Hyderabad, and the peasantry complain of the general grievance in almost all native states,—"Zōōlm,"—oppression and injustice.

The principal towns passed, besides Phoolmurry, are Sillode, Bunkinola, Ullun, Mahēlkinoola, and Puttree. There are very fine and extensive groves of trees near most of these villages, principally of mangoe, which impart a pleasing verdure to the hilly and otherwise barren landscape.

Rowza is situate on the narrow tabular summit of a ridge of hills, four hundred and fifty feet high, about six miles from the ancient fortress of Dowlutabad, of which a very picturesque view is commanded. The Nizâm government have built an excellent Bungalow for travellers, a little distance from the walled town on the road to the Caves of Ellora. A singular white-washed lofty gateway leads to the Bungalow, and to several mausoleums, both inside and outside the enclosure.

Though located in an excellent stone-built dwelling, I felt the heat most overpowering, even at Rowza, which formerly had the reputation of being a sanatarium,—so very pure was the air supposed to be.

On the 1st of March I went to visit the Caves, which take their name from the neighbouring village in the province of Aurungabad, called Ellora. The latitude of these famous Caves is 19° 58′ N., and longitude 75° 23′ E. Outside the village there is a very handsome temple, dedicated to Siva, beside other minor temples. About a mile to the east of the village is the mountain where these remarkable excavations of Hindoo temples occur. I feel somewhat at a loss how to describe these stupendous monuments of human skill, which have attracted so many travellers from afar. The principal excavations are at the foot of the Ghât, and extend for a mile or more. Most of them are very similar to those of Ajunta, but when it is considered that these chambers and sculptures are all hewn out of the solid rock, we may well marvel at the result. The whole is on a far grander scale than at Ajunta, and reckons among its attractions an unparalleled *chef-d'œuvre*. I allude to the "Kylâs," or representation of the heaven of Siva, which I shall presently describe *in extenso;* though without plates, it is almost impossible to convey any tangible idea of the wonders of the spot. There is no mistaking the fact of these excavations being *entirely* artificial, and not originally consisting of one or two isolated rocks, separated by nature from the main ridge, and by the hand of man, caved and sculptured merely. That stupendous sections of living rock have been hewn away, and completely severed from the hills of hard granite which intersect this part of the country, is manifest; because the summits of the different sections of the great Pagoda, in the centre of the insulated fane of Kylâs, exactly tally with the adjacent and corresponding points of the surrounding rocks in height and general appearance. Besides the great Pantheon of Kylâs, there are some fifteen other caves to the right and left of Kylâs, at the base of the same ridge, elevated a little above the plain-land. These are not excavated with the same *regularity* as those at Ajunta, but are scattered at irregular intervals.

The temple of Kylâs,* or the Paradise of the Gods, is well worthy of a few words of description, and though I can scarcely hope to give any adequate delineation of these beautiful monuments

* "Kylâs" is the especial Heaven of Siva and Pârbuttie.

of forgotten ages, I cannot entirely pass them by in silence. From the hill-side, Kylâs exhibits a magnificent front. Towering battlemented heights flank the splendid gateway on either side, and the whole is richly adorned with sculpture. There is a balcony over the portal, where tradition says musical strains used to be performed. The passage of the gateway is said to be 42 feet long, and on each side there are rooms 15 feet by 9, splendidly embellished with sculpture. The height of the gateway is 14 feet. This passage leads into a large area, in the centre of which is the principal Pagoda, which stands insulated, and thus the more conspicuous in its solitary and majestic beauty. Every part of this temple is minutely and elaborately carved with a profusion of ornamental and mythological figures and devices, while columns, friezes, pilasters, and pediments are lavishly scattered about. A distance of one hundred and fifty feet separates the galleries and colonnades from the central fane, which rears its proud crest to the height of a hundred feet. Beyond, and constituting the boundary of the court which surrounds them, are three noble galleries supported on pillars, containing sculptured representations of the mythology of the Hindoos, in compartments of granite scarping, in which I counted the figures of forty-two different deities. This unique piazza is eleven feet broad, and the elevation varies from seven to twenty feet. On the south side of the area there are chambers adorned with the figures of goddesses most exquisitely carved. In the court are the well-preserved remains of colossal elephants in stone, and an obelisk nearly perfect. To this obelisk, my attendant Brahmin-guides drew my attention,—remarking, that the men of those days were of so lofty a stature, that this pillar was their "chirâgh"*-stand, reaching only a little above the waist of these gigantic specimens of ancient humanity! The height of this pillar is about forty feet;—it is larger at the base than "Cleopatra's Needle," in Egypt, and like the rest of Kylâs, is hewn out of the living rock. The wondrous labour expended in excavating these stupendous works out of the solid mountain, must have been doubly great in the instance of Kylâs, since it is distinguished from the other excavations by not having the ponderous rocky canopy which overshadows the rest of the caves. There is a splendid fane, sacred to the bull Nundi,†

* Oil-lamp.
† The sacred Bull of Maha-Déo or Siva. It is his *Váhan* (or the vehicle allotted to each of the deities);—by some described as the emblem of justice.

which forms a part of the Pagoda, and fills up the central space. The rock, from which the Temples of Ellora are wrought, is of hard red granite, and it is difficult to account for these most stupendous monuments, without inclining to one of the two Brahminical beliefs regarding their origin, *i..e.*, either that they were called into existence by preternatural power, or that there were "giants in those days." The excess and wonderful variety of the objects presented to the eye as the traveller enters on this enchanted ground, are almost painful in the sensations of awe they inspire, while the impossibility of fathoming the real and primary origin of the wonders viewed, oppresses the mind. The more we gaze, the less can we comprehend, or *realize*, that all we see is the work of finite man.

The other most remarkable Caves at Ellora are known by the names of — Dus-Avâtar, Vishwa-Kârma, Râmeswar, and Dhēr-Wârra. I will give a short account of each in succession.

I. *Dus Avâtar.*—The Brahmins say that this cave, which is found in the centre of the range, has been so named from the ten* incarnations (*avátars*) of Vishnoo, which are sculptured in the several subterranean compartments. In my opinion there are as many *avátars* represented in the other caves, and this one has scarcely any legitimate claim to

* " Dus" means ten.

the distinctive appellation it has received from the priests. The best preserved piece of sculpture here is that which delineates the punishment, by Siva, of a demon who insulted his mountain-born consort, the fair Pârbuttie. There is a strange mixture of the Brahminical and Buddhist religions displayed in the idols and religious symbols found in this cave, but I will notice this point separately, after I have described the four caves I have particularly mentioned. The principal compartment of the Dus-Avâtar is ninety-eight feet in breadth, and a hundred feet in length. It has two stories; the roof of the upper is nearly twelve feet high, and is supported by forty-eight massive pillars, besides the twenty-two pilasters along the walls. The pillars separate the sculptured compartments, and the entire façade is open in front, admitting more than the usual allowance of light to illumine the singular subterranean treasures within.

II. *Vishwa-Kárma;* also called *Bisma-Kurm.* This cave forms a portion of the southern extremity of the hill, and with the aid of a little imagination, it would not be difficult to conceive it the appropriate and princely residence of gnomes of royal rank, as the very entrance seems to hold out rich promise of mysterious subterranean dwellings. This temple belongs exclusively to the Buddhist superstition, and a colossal image of Buddha stands at the extremity of the dark vista, of which a good perspective view is obtained from the threshold. The monstrous image is placed in a most imposing position;—the gigantic form partially revealed in the indistinct light of the gloomy cavern, and the majesty and perfect repose of the figure adding immeasurably to the solemn stillness of the dim and vaulted aisle. It conveys a feeling of terrible majesty and mysterious invisible power, which, since it affects even the followers of a more enlightened faith, can scarcely leave room for wonder at the potency of the charm exercised over the votaries of a dark and idolatrous religion, who, from their earliest infancy, are taught to reverence these senseless images as the presence of Divinity itself.

The Cave is eighty feet by forty-two, measured from the walls of the side-aisles; the height may be thirty-six feet. The extreme *depth* of the excavation into the hill is nearly two hundred feet. There are thirty pillars in all. The architrave which environs the cave, running along the top of the pillars, is adorned with sculptured figures. Above this architrave is the frieze, divided into compartments, in each of which is an effigy of Buddha, surrounded by four attendants. The roof of the cave is so excavated and sculptured as to appear to rest, along the cornices, on prostrate human figures,—the male and female being alternated.

The front of Vishwa-Kârma has been rendered quite perpendicular by the laborious hewing away of the *slope* of the hill whence the cave is excavated; the artificial scarp is very lofty, and as it recedes from the bluff promontory surrounding, the effect is unique,—the shade of dark trees adding to the picturesque beauty of the scene. In the rainy season, when all nature is so luxuriant in its verdure, and the adjacent waterfalls increase to a great volume, this spot is said to be singularly attractive to the lover of wild scenery.

III. *Râmeswar*.—This cave, according to the Brahmins, owes its cognomen to the fact of there being several sculptures in its dark recesses, commemorative of the nuptials of Râm* and Sēēta,† but I believe antiquaries incline to the belief, that Siva and his consort Pârbuttie have a more genuine claim to the temple in question.

Râmeswar is on a smaller scale than most of its gigantic neighbours. It boasts of a hall

* An Avâtar of Vishnoo, generally called Râma. Sir William Jones in his erudite work, places this incarnation 1810 years, B.C.

† The *Sacti* or Consort of Râm or Râma.

seventy feet long and about fifteen high; there is besides, an inner temple thirty feet square. Colonnades and pilasters adorn the large chamber, and they, as well as the walls and roof, are covered with carved figures, sporting and revelling in a very *un*-godlike style. There is one large group which forms a singular contrast to the frolicsome company around. This group consists of a horrible range of hideous skeletons. There are two ways of explaining the appearance of these figures, but the learned antiquarian inclines to the one which I shall first mention. In the adjoining compartment seven females are represented as engaged in the sacrifice of the "Now Râtree," (a celebrated festival in which *human* victims garnish the demoniacal altar,) and the group of skeletons is supposed to depict a starving family, (whence their leanness,) the father of whom is selling his wives and children for the sacrifice in question.

The other version is the one which the Brahmins prefer giving. They say that the skeletons commemorate a guilty family who pillaged the temples, and here garnered up their ill-gotten treasures; that the gods cursed them with famine and disease, in consequence of their sacrilegious robberies; and that they had the final judgment of seeing a thief run away with their gold and jewels in a bag, while their emaciated and miserable condition prevented them from offering any opposition. The alleged "thief with the bag" is carved in a corner of the compartment, and represented in the act of flight.

IV. *Dhēr-Wárra.*—This cave is supposed to have been for the "Dhērs," or low-castes. It is of wondrous and imposing size, but the sculptured effigies are much fewer and less elaborate. The name is modern, and the dedication to the lower castes quite supposititious;—not even founded on any genuine or credible tradition. The principal hall is a hundred feet long, and forty-five feet broad, exclusive of the recesses. There are stone platforms traversing the whole length of the cave, which are supposed to be intended for the accommodation of merchants and scribes, with their heterogeneous merchandize. As the Hindoos buy and sell in their temples like the Jews of old, the supposition is very plausible. At present the hall is littered and filthy from having been the asylum of cattle of all descriptions. This may perhaps account for the supposititious dedication to the "Dhērs,"—a race deemed only fit to be the scavengers of the earth.

Before leaving the magnificent caves of Ellora, I must say a few words on the religion to which they owe their origin, and wind up with a short account of some *items* regarding the excavations which I have omitted hitherto.

A mixture of Brahminical and Buddhist emblems is discoverable, even in the beautiful Kylâs, though this wondrous fane decidedly belongs to the former faith, which the prominent position occupied by the Sacred Bull of Siva, the mysterious Nundi, would of itself sufficiently attest. Those caves which occupy the immediate vicinity of Kylâs, in the centre range of the series, are likewise manifestly dedicated to Siva, as his *váhan*, the Bull, occupies the same prominent position in the interior of each. The four southern excavations are pronounced to be undoubtedly Buddhist by erudite antiquarians, while those on the northern side are of more doubtful character; some learned authors attribute them to the Jâins,* and others halt between two opinions, the emblems being typical of a mixed creed.

* The Jâins, by some supposed to be a branch of the sect of Buddha, hold some tenets in direct opposition to the religious faith of the genuine Buddhists. The founder of the Jâina sect was Rishabadeva, who was said to be incarnate thirteen different times. After him came in succession twenty-three sages and holy men, the Gōōroos of the sect, the last of whom was incarnate twenty-seven times. The Jâinas derive their name from "Jinoo," to conquer. The priests are called

The hill along which the caves are excavated slopes down gradually to the extensive plain on which the little wooded village of Ellora stands.

My guides drew my attention to a very singular fissure between the rocks, about five feet wide and nearly thirty deep, in the immediate vicinity of a very large cave. The sides of this fissure were scarped and perfectly perpendicular, but whether it be natural or artificial I am unable to decide. There was water lying at the bottom of the cavity, but it was in too small a quantity to admit of the supposition that the action of the water could have rent asunder the solid rock. If a natural phenomenon, it could have been by volcanic agency alone. I think I have elsewhere mentioned that the formation of the rock where these excavations occur is of hard red granite. The Brahmins gravely endeavoured to impress on my mind the astounding fact of the fissure above described being the "Chōōla"* of the mighty

Yatis, the laity, *Swárkas*. They all deny the supremacy of the gods, and the authority of the *Vedas*, and say that though there is a Supreme Being, he has no power to interfere in the regulation of the affairs of the universe. I have no doubt that the Hindoos, Buddhists, and Jâins were all *originally* of one faith, and that there occurred a great schism from which originated these three sects, so different, and yet so analogous.

* A *Chōōla* is the native stove used in cooking, or a fire-

architects of these wonderful temples! Their theory that those architects were men of giant mould, might be somewhat shaken by the observation of many of the galleries and compartments, which are of very moderate height and size. However, on my pointing out this little circumstance to the sacerdotal guides who attended me, I found they were by no means non-plussed by it, as I had hoped; for they quickly rejoined, that there were men of moderate stature, as well as a race of giants, engaged in the work.

The stone staircases are in several places yielding gradually to the relentless hand of Time, the great Destroyer; and in many parts, the stone walls—all massive though they be—have parted or sunk; several subterranean passages once open are now closed up for ever, while many a vaulted aisle can never more be penetrated by human curiosity. I observed many dark holes leading to unknown passages under-ground, but as the guides refused to descend with me into any which had not been entered, I could not gratify my love of adventure, though I most

place. Generally speaking, this primitive affair consists of two stones or bricks for the sides, and one for the back. The fire is placed in these bricks, and the cooking utensils at the top, resting on the stones over the fire.

earnestly longed to explore these hidden mysteries at any possible risk. The obscure holes I have alluded to, and many of the darker caves, both at Ellora and Ajunta, are full of monstrous bats. These horrid creatures flit wildly about in countless myriads, and infect the air with a most noisome smell.*

Before one of the largest of the excavations, there is a pool of water, and immediately above, on the perpendicular rock which frowns over the spot, are the water-worn marks of a magnificent cascade. The Brahmins informed me that there is a splendid fall of water here in the rains, and the sight must be beautiful. At this season of the year, the stream is dried up.

There is no writing of any kind in any of the Caves; conjecture must therefore run wild without some such guide amid the sea of doubts and difficulties regarding their origin, &c. I observed evidences of slabs of stone having been removed from the places where inscriptions might most probably have been found, and I have no doubt that all records have thus perished of the age and architects alike. My cicerone informed me, that on the conquest of this country, the remorseless victor ordered all these monuments of

* These bats are of the genus *Vespertilio Noctula*.

another religion to be burnt with fire. The uncompromising command having been partially obeyed, the ravages apparent may be considered the melancholy results of this tyrannical behest. The fact of the *mingling* of the two creeds—the Brahminical and the Buddhist—confirms the theory I advanced in a previous volume, as to these two religions having originally been one and the same.

I neglected to mention that in some of the caves, there are fine stone reservoirs, full of good water. In one of the excavations, there is a subterranean range of seven reservoirs, supplied by eternal springs, called the "Sât Sumoondur," or Seven Oceans, to which access is obtained by means of a dark, damp, vaulted chamber.

On my return from my visit to the caves, —to which, I may remark, *en passant*, there is a fine *puckha* road down the Ghât,—I went to see the village of Rowza. In spite of the promise given by its high stone walls of a large and flourishing town, all within the enclosure is *weehrán*, (in utter ruins,) and an air of melancholy desolation pervades the deserted spot. Scarcely half a dozen paltry habitations are now tenanted, and the once superior edifices are fast crumbling to decay. There is one building still kept up, which I went to see. It is the *Durgah* or Mausoleum of the great Delhi Conqueror, Alum-Ghir. The Mussulmans told me that this was the great Emperor who came from Delhi, and after making all these countries his own, departed this life at Rowza, where his bones now repose in peace and sanctity. His daughter died at Aurungabad, where a still more splendid Mausoleum is erected to her memory. There is a great deal of marble trellice-work in these tombs, the architecture of which resembles some of the more simple monuments at Delhi. I was followed out of the building by a score of religious beggars,—fat, sleek victims of pampered *poverty !* I ordered my servants to give them the "buckshish," (largesse,) which they clamorously demanded, in the shape of a good caning, and seeing my order about to be carried out by my obedient slaves, they took to flight, greatly to my relief.

I had the greatest difficulty in getting a single Coolie for the little baggage I had with me ;—the rest of my camp-equipage had fortunately been sent on direct to Aurungabad from Phoolmurry, on account of the indifferent cart-track between Phoolmurry and Rowza. I went myself to the hamlet especially inhabited by the Coolie-tribe, just outside the walls of the town. My servants having failed in securing any, I hoped to intimidate the people into compliance by my awful presence! But every attempt even to *find* a single specimen of the genus *homo* in the village above-mentioned, proved a miserable failure, though I rode through each wretched alley, and made my Chuprassie strictly search every native hut. I thought we had returned to the *women-villages* of Goolâb Singh's Illâka, where men were not to be seen. Weary at length of hunting, I enjoined my attendants to place the six loads on six of the strongest females they could find, who were accordingly impressed and carried off in triumph. I never saw an uglier race in my life; both old and young were inexpressibly hideous.

In a previous page I mentioned that there were some fine Mausoleums outside the city walls, and also within the enclosure containing the Travellers' Bungalow. During the period in which Aurungabad was the capital of Aurungzēb's dominions, Rowza was the royal burying-place; consequently its neighbourhood is thickly strewed with the tombs of saints and holy men of great repute. What struck me most forcibly was the insignificance of the Tomb erected over the last of the imperial and illustrious descendants of the celebrated Timur Lung, (or "Tamerlane,") who maintained the ancestral glories bequeathed by that renowned monarch. It was far eclipsed in splendour by the Mausoleum of a Moslem saint in its immediate vicinity—a man whose very name is almost forgotten.

CHAPTER III.

From Rowza to Poonah, *viâ* Dowlutabad, Aurungabad and Ahmednuggur, the distance is very nearly one hundred and seventy miles. The road from Dowlutabad is stony, and the latter mile is a rather steep descent down a Ghât. Before reaching this Ghât, I passed through the village of Kâghuziwâlli, where paper is manufactured in large quantities. The name of the hamlet expresses this,—" Kâghuz " being the literal Oordoo word for "paper."

No ingress is allowed to the fort of Dowlutabad without a pass, (a " Purwânnah," as it is called in the East,) from the Brigadier commanding the Nizâm's forces stationed at Aurungabad. I had therefore taken the precaution of writing from Ajunta to the Brigadier, so that the requisite Purwânnah might await my arrival at Dowlutabad. A Chuprassie met me at the foot of the Ghât with the pass, and the usual complimentary offering of fruit and flowers, (called a *Dâlly,*) sent by the Brigadier.

I was as much pleased with the Fort of Dowlutabad as with the famous Caves I had so lately visited, and explored the once impregnable fortifications with the greatest interest. This singular-looking old fortress is situated on an isolated hill of a conical form, while the ruins of the once important town, encompassed by lofty stone walls, extend along the base and front of the Fort-rock for a considerable distance. The space within the ramparts of the city is thickly wooded. Many a ruined and lofty Minaret rears its head amidst the crumbling habitations, and numerous tokens of departed greatness strike the eye while wandering through the grass-grown streets of the decayed city. But conspicuous above all is the fortified Rock; the bristling battlements rising proudly above the highest spires of the ancient town,—a melancholy witness of the lapse of ages, and the mutability of all things mundane.

High gateways, one within the other, and fastened by heavy iron chains, lead into the lower courtyard below the rock. All around is thick jungle, and I was told that tigers lurk in the wilderness there, but though often seen prowling about, they never injure any one. Occasionally one or two are destroyed by traps set in the covers for that purpose, in which they are easily caught.

A long flight of stone steps leads to the interior of the fortifications, and a draw-bridge spans the wide, deep moat, surrounding the inner section of the citadel. A little further on, a long ascending subterranean passage, pitch dark, winds through the heart of the Rock, and gradually emerges into daylight again about two-thirds of the way up the Fort-hill. This subterranean passage was so contrived that it could be almost *instantly* filled with deep water, by opening certain gates or bars:—thus strength and impregnability were ensured in times of war. This passage is now filled up beneath, and layers of wood and earth are placed as flooring, but the former contrivance could still be brought into play at will, by removing the obstructions.

There is a new Mosque near the crest of the conical hill, and above this temple the ruins of a former building have been converted into a modern Bâruh Durrie. Still higher, at the very apex of the cone, there is a small space built round, where on an elevated platform stands a monstrous gun. There are three very large pieces of ordnance measuring twenty feet in length, in different parts of the fortifications, besides several smaller ones.

In two or three spots, springs of water ooze out from under the rock, and the stone reservoirs which have been built there, are replenished from these concealed and inexhaustible sources. Thus the water is always at hand, fresh and pure; and from the fact of its being an inexhaustible spring, this Fort possessed great advantages in the olden time, in the event of a siege. One reservoir in particular was full of flowing water, clear and pellucid, sweet to the taste, and (despite the burning rock adjacent,) icy cold. I drank at this delicious spring when hot and thirsty from the long ascent, and thought I had never tasted aught so refreshing.

Near the top of the rock there is a square cavity, about three feet wide, into which steps descend, winding into the very heart of the hill. This narrow subterranean passage has never, in modern days, been thoroughly explored; but it is believed to have an outlet beyond the Fort, far below, and to have been formerly a means of communication with the city, with the secret of which the garrison alone were acquainted. There are all sorts of contrivances to ensure strength and resistance in the event of a siege, and with the boundless supply of water I have mentioned, the numerous defences of this old citadel must truly have rendered it quite impregnable in its palmy days. It commands the whole country round;—to the west is seen Rowza, with Ellora just below, and to the north-east, Aurungabad is plainly visible. The white houses of the cantonment lie to the right hand, while the wooded and ancient city stretches to the left,—distant half a mile or more. A line of hills extends to the right of Aurungabad, but beyond that, towards the eastward and southward, the country is level. Towards Rowza, the view is bounded by numerous hills and Ghâts in one or two unbroken ridges. Dowlutabad lies in latitude 19° 57′ N., longitude 75° 25′ E.;—as the crow flies, about seven miles north-west of Aurungabad. The height of the Rock has been estimated at upwards of six hundred feet above the town. It consists of an insulated mass of granite, the lower part of which presents a perpendicular cliff, being scarped all round. The scarp of the rock, down to the counter-scarp, may be two hundred feet in elevation; and the scarp below the glacis, about forty feet more, so the whole height of the scarped cliff may be two hundred and forty feet.

From the apex of the Fort-citadel, the old city

looked all jungle and ruins; the ramparts, constructed of massive stone, are, however, in comparatively good preservation, and are said by the natives to be three coss in circumference, though *what length* of "coss" appears uncertain.

There is a lofty Minaret on the plain-land, immediately below the Fort within the ramparts; but I did not venture to ascend it, as the guides declared it was not only unsafe, but that the bees which swarmed within, would alone render the undertaking utterly impracticable. Traces of rich enamel and paint still lingered here and there on the outer sides, and it was not difficult to see, that in days of yore, this must have been a very handsome building, glittering with bright colours. The town-gates are shut at sunset, and the clanking chains being locked, the keys are given to the Khiladâr, or warder, of the fortress, and on no pretext are they re-opened at night. The road from Rowza to Aurungabad runs along the outer side of the ruined city, and is very tolerable, with the exception of two or three rather bad nullahs:—the distance is about nine miles. There is no Bungalow, or any sort of habitation at all fit for a European traveller, either inside or outside the town-walls, and all the Mosques (usually very good substitutes in times of need) are open and exposed to the sun, with the exception of one large *Musjid*, a mile or more from the town. There is a very good encamping-ground, however, close to the ramparts, well shaded with fine trees, for those who have tent-equipage. I found the heat very overpowering; these latitudes are much more oppressive than the North-West Provinces.

Aurungabad is the principal cantonment of the Nizâm's army, and a brigade is stationed about a mile from the ancient city. There seem to be about a dozen houses in the cantonment. I saw nothing of the brigade, or its European Officers, as I was ill when the Commanding Officer and his wife called on me at the traveller's Bungalow. I should say, from certain circumstances, that the society is rather benighted in manners and *polish* at least. Having, however, received great kindness from Captain P—, the officer above adverted to, who, though a perfect stranger to me, was most obliging and considerate in his influential position as Commandant of the place,— for the sake of the " *one* righteous man," I will spare my "remarks reflective " on the rest!

Bullocks are much more frequently harnessed than horses; and as for the carriages, I am credibly informed, that they are modelled after the fashions prevalent before the flood, and which, even in Noah's time, were getting antediluvian, using that word in its modern sense.

At Aurungabad, I hired camels at an exorbitant rate, which were to reach Poonah (about 154 miles) in five days. The made road to Bombay commences at Aurungabad, and there are Dâk-Bungalows all the way, at distances of from ten to twenty miles,—a man being in charge at each, who is supposed to be able to cook for the traveller. I found grain and flour much dearer as soon as I reached the Bombay Presidency; the prices nearly amounting to double those of Bengal and the North-West Provinces.

Before leaving the ancient town,—so long the favoured residence of Aurungzēb, who changed its pristine name of "Goorka," into one more euphonious, and commemorative moreover of his royal self,—I must add a few words descriptive of the situation, &c. It is situated in latitude 19° 54′ N., and longitude, 75° 33′ E. It presents the usual symptoms of a deserted metropolis, *i. e.* extensive ruins, and a scanty population. It is situated in a hollow, and when approached from the north-east, its white domes and lofty Minarets are seen below, rising from amidst a grove of trees. Several stone conduits supply the city with excellent water from the neighbouring hills, and fountains spring up in the centre of the old town. The celebrated Mausoleum, erected by Aurungzēb over his favourite daughter, bears some slight resemblance to the Tâj, at Agra, though it is in every respect a less imposing edifice. Its domes are of white marble, and clustered like those of the beautiful Tâj Mâhul, but far inferior in size and splendour. In many places, *stucco* is substituted for marble, and the exquisite bas-reliefs are wanting.

Ahmednuggur is a small cantonment, where a Bombay Native Infantry corps is stationed. The Bungalows are much the same as those in the Bengal Presidency, and the Dâk-Bungalow is large, roomy and well-built, but the floors are uncarpeted, and there is no *khidmutgar* or *bawurchie* (cook) in attendance. As I had my own large camp, it was of no consequence to me, but to the majority of travellers journeying " post," the want in question is a serious *deficit*. There are a good many trees in the station, and hedges of prickly-pear seem the rage.

About fourteen or fifteen miles before reaching Ahmednuggur, the Kussoorie Ghât is ascended; it is easy for carts, and even carriages. After reaching the summit of the Ghât, a Plain dotted with trees is reached,—barren and uninhabited,—and there are higher ridges of hills all around, especially to the south-east. There is a Bungalow for travellers at this place, (called Emâmpore,) where a man who professes to be able to cook is in attendance. This rogue sells gram, grass, &c., in retail, at iniquitous rates, and a Bunniah must be sent for, from the nearest village, if travellers require flour, ghee, &c., which involves a delay of five or six hours, so that people ought not to go to Emâmpore without an extra day's provisions, unless their stock of patience be unusually large. There is also an "old" and a "new" road, and care ought to be taken in selecting the latter, as the other is long and rugged. The country is wild, and there is much beauty in some parts of the scenery. The nullahs are distressingly frequent; two or three rivers have also to be forded. The Godavery, a large and rapid stream in the rainy season, is fordable now, though with some difficulty. An iron rod extends across the river, supported on either bank by piers of hewn stones and wood. This supended rod is meant for the purpose of carrying the post at night, or when the river is swollen. It is also meant to aid and facilitate the passage-boats in the rains when the current is strong. They fasten the boat-ropes to the rod, and from the opposite bank by other ropes, (also fastened both to the rod and boat,) pull them swiftly across; the ropes ahead steadying the motion. The Godavery lower down in its course is perfectly navigable, and empties its waters into the Ocean. Toka, a good-sized village, stands on the right bank, while the small hamlet of Kygâon is on the left. There is a Dâk-Bungalow within a stone's throw of the river, close to Toka.

The ancient city and fortress of Ahmednuggur is not far from the British cantonment, and having been once a place of note, I will say a few words regarding it before I proceed to give an account of Poonah.

The Fort is constructed entirely of stone of a peculiar oval shape, and is perhaps a mile in circumference, with a great many round towers, and a glacis to protect such parts of the base of the wall as would otherwise remain exposed. The ditch is deep and broad, and the whole space within is commodiously vaulted for the reception of stores. The city is about three quarters of a mile distant from the Fort, and is also encompassed by a stone wall. The ancient Palace of the Sultan stands in the vicinity,—a massive structure surrounded by a deep moat. The whole of these buildings are decaying, and falling into irreparable ruin.

Ahmed Nizâm Shah established the independency of the State of Ahmednuggur, or the "City of Ahmed," about the year A.D. 1489. Four years subsequently, he laid the foundation of this town, and constituted it his capital city. He died in 1508. This dynasty lasted for more than a century altogether, and the *nominal* sovereigns of this family were still reigning at Dowlutabad in 1634, when that fortress being taken, all the Nizâm-Shâhi dominions became a province of the Mogul Empire. The *actual* dynasty of the Nizâm-Shâhi had in reality ended in the year 1600, when Bahâdur Shah, the infant sovereign, was taken prisoner by the Moguls, and confined for life in the fortress of Gwalior. Ahmednuggur shared the fortunes of the Delhi Emperor, until the death of Aurungzēb in A.D. 1707. It was then almost immediately seized by the Mahrattas, and formed part of the Peshwâ's dominions, until Dowlet Râo Scindia forced the Peshwâ to cede the Fort and district. In 1803 it was taken by the British forces under General Wellesley's[*] command, and secured to the British Government, by the treaty of peace concluded on the 30th of December, 1803.

Poonah is about seventy-two miles from Ahmed-

[*] The Duke of Wellington.

nnggur, *viâ* Gohrnuddy and Loonee:—the road is good for this benighted Presidency. The climate is said to be quite European in the rainy season, but when I was at Poonah it was oppressively hot; the Dâk-Bungalow was one of the worst I have anywhere seen.

The road from Ahmednuggur to Poonah is intended as an imitation of the "Grand Trunk Road" of Bengal, but though it is fully as ruinous to horses' legs,—being as hard as metal,—it is by no means as good; indeed the hilly nature of the country would not permit it, without very much more labour and expense than the authorities of this Presidency appear willing to lavish upon it. Hills are seen on every side, and the country is very pretty. There are a good many trees about the villages, and they look pleasantly green in the midst of barren hills. Supplies are procurable all throughout the district, but everything is expensive. Grass costs twelve annas (1s. 6d.) every hundred *pōōlas*, (small bundles,) and gram is from eighteen to twenty seers (36 lbs. to 42 lbs.) a rupee:—everything else in proportion. There are three or four Bungalows for travellers *en route*. I halted a few hours at Suroor (also called Gohrnuddy) and at Loonee.

Between Gohrnuddy and Loonee, a river,

called the Bēēmah, is crossed just before reaching the village of Korehgâon, once the famous scene of a protracted siege, when so many British officers lost their lives, in gallantly defending this post against the attack of the Peshwâ's whole army, estimated at twenty thousand horse, and several thousand infantry, mostly Arabs. This tremendous army, under the personal command of the Peshwâ, and viewed by him from an adjacent Height, were opposed by a mere handful of British troops, under the command of Captain Staunton. This little detachment consisted of a small portion of the Madras Artillery, the second battalion of the first regiment of Bombay Infantry, and some three hundred auxiliary horse. They were attacked by the whole of the Peshwâ's army, on the last day of December, 1817; and though all but three of the British officers were either killed or desperately wounded, the enemy were driven out of every position they attempted to occupy, and after ten hours of sanguinary conflict, desisted from the attack. The British troops had but just occupied the ground after a long and fatiguing march, and throughout the whole day, were forced to fight not only without food, but also without water. The following day was passed under arms, as the enemy were lurking about, but on the 2nd of January, the detachment retreated safely to Suroor, with all the guns as well as the wounded. It was indeed a gallant engagement, and a glorious triumph of British valour. A handsome obelisk commemorates the melancholy death of so many brave soldiers, and the names of the "killed and wounded," both men and officers, native and European, are inscribed on the opposite tablets. The two other sides are similarly inscribed in the language of the country. The obelisk is constructed of regularly shaped hewn stones;—its base corresponding. A railed enclosure, in which numerous Cypress trees mournfully wave in the breeze, surrounds the monument to the departed heroes. I rode inside the enclosure, and gazed on the spot with sad interest. How many a brave heart had on that memorable day suddenly ceased to pulsate;—how many a gallant soldier had been hurriedly called to his last account, while fighting for his country. Alas! how little could they who erected the obelisk, give balm and solace to the widowed and childless hearts, that mourned the loss of their beloved ones, thus rudely torn for ever from their sight. And *this* is *glory?*—the phantom for which a soldier dares so much, and gentle woman so enthusiastically worships and adores!

> "There's not a meteor of the polar sky,
>   Of such transcendent, and more fleeting light."

Well saith the preacher, "All is vanity; there is nothing new under the sun!" "'Tis true, 'tis pity,—pity 'tis 'tis true." And *where* are they gone, who fell on the very ground I trod a few hours ago?—

> "Gone—glimmering through the things that were:
>   First in the race that led to glory's goal,
>   They won, and passed away—is this the *whole?*"

Vain, however, are all such speculations, and "*all that we know is, nothing can be known!*" A satisfactory conclusion! But they fell, and nobly fell; and after all, has it not been said of death—

> "Why should we shrink from what we cannot shun?
>   Each hath his pang, but feeble sufferers groan
>   With brain-born dreams of evil all their own.
>   Peace waits us on the shores of Acheron,
>   How sweet 't will be in concert to adore
>   With those who made our mortal labours light!
>   To hear each voice we fear'd to hear no more!"

It saddens one to feel how small after all is the guerdon of valour—how many of the brave have fallen, and are forgotten as if they had never been; while fond hearts mourned their irreparable loss in distant solitude, and were but little consoled at the thought that they had fallen in the service of their country. How many precious lives have been sacrificed to this phantom, and too often sacrificed in unjust and unholy warfare. But I need not moralize,—young hearts will, to the end of time, glow at the relation of heroic deeds, and pant to be crowned with what they vainly hope will prove the *immortal* wreaths of fame and glory!

The famous besieged village is fast going to decay, but there are traces of many stone walls of great strength. The only water procurable in this hamlet has to be brought from the river, on the north-east side of which it is situated. The distance from Korehgâon to Poonah, is eighteen miles. The province of Beejapore was once an important section of the Deccan, extending from the 15th to the 18th degree of north latitude. Its length, twenty years ago, was estimated at three hundred and twenty miles, and the average breadth two hundred. The western districts are very mountainous, especially in the vicinity of the *Ghâts*, where hill-fortresses of great strength once abounded. The site almost invariably selected for these strong-holds, was on the summits of insulated eminences, with scarped sides. This rendered any outworks superfluous, as a single narrow path, easily rendered inaccessible at will, was the only means of reaching the fortress above. A strong wall crested the edge of the precipices; a much simpler and surer style of fortification than the one prevalent in the south of India, where numerous and intricate outworks are indispensable in connecting the rocks from the base to the summit of the citadel.

The sovereignty of Beejapore was founded in the middle of the fifteenth century, by Abou-ul-Moozuffir Adil Shah, from whom the dynasty obtained the name of the "Adil-Shâhi."* It terminated about two centuries subsequently (in A.D. 1689), when the city of Beejapore was besieged and taken by Aurungzēb, and the last Sovereign of the Adil-Shâhi dynasty, Sekunder Adil Shah, made prisoner. But though this empire has been regularly enumerated in the list of the *soubahs*,† subject to the throne of Delhi, it can scarcely be considered in the light of an acquisition pertaining to the Mogul empire. During Aurungzēb's reign, its possession was disputed in a most sanguinary manner, and his successors

* Shâh means King, and this is a derivation which stands for "pertaining to the King," or simply "Kingdom."

† A "Soubah" is a province. According to the Institutes of Akbâr, a soubah should consist of twenty-two "circars;" a circar of twenty-two "pergunnahs;" a pergunnah of twenty-two "tuppas;" and a tuppa of twenty-two villages; but this divisional strictness was never carried out. According to this rule, a soubah would be about three times the size of Ireland.

abandoned it to the Mahrattas. In 1818, the whole of this province became subject to the English. The capital of this once powerful province is Beejapore, the ruins of which are, to this day, most extensive. "City of glories now no more"—there exist few more striking instances of the instability of human grandeur. The fortifications were of immense extent, for between the wall of the fort and the outer wall of the old city, there was ample space for fifteen thousand cavalry to encamp. The natives assert that in its palmy days, it contained *nine hundred and eighty-four thousand inhabitants, and one thousand six hundred Mosques.* Of course this must be taken *cum grano*, as it is a preposterous exaggeration,—in my opinion at least. At present its extensive ruins prove that its former extent was of great magnitude certainly, but to credit the wild assertion I have retailed, would be illustrating the Scriptural simile of "swallowing a camel." Before leaving this,—once the most flourishing and powerful principality in the Deccan,—I will give the legendary history of the founder.

He was the younger son of the Emperor Bajazet, and the reigning monarch determined to put the boy to death, according to the cruel policy of the East, where no younger brother is tolerated near the throne. When the remorseless executioners went to demand the child from his mother, her passionate entreaties for mercy to her boy, the "apple of her eye," failed in moving her despotic sovereign, or his cruel myrmidons. *In extremis* she prayed for and obtained one day's respite, to prepare herself for the terrible trial ordained. During this inferim, she sent to the slave-market, and purchased a Circassian slave of the same age as her darling, who bore a fatal resemblance to him. One of the ministers who loved the mother, aided the child's escape, and favoured the deception which ensured it,—allowing the Circassian slave, who was dressed up to personate the young Prince, to be strangled in his stead. His body was shewn to the despot-sovereign as that of his youthful relative, who meantime was concealed till he was sixteen, when accident or treachery betraying his identity, he fled for safety to Persia. While residing at Shirâz, he had a supernatural vision which promised him sovereignty in India. He followed his evident *nuseéb* (fate), and left Persia without delay. The gods smiled on all his enterprises, and he rose in a few years to eminence in the state of Berâr. His historian, the romantic Ferishta, says that "the Hōōma of prosperity had spread the shadow of its wings over his head;" so upon the dissolution of the Bhâmanee* empire in the Deccan, he became the undisputed sovereign of a rich and noble territory. I must explain the expression "Hōōma of prosperity" before I proceed further. The "Hōōma" is a bird of good fortune, and whoever comes under the shadow of his wings—so the old legends relate—is sure to wear a crown. This fable has passed into an idiom.

The most beautiful ruins of the ancient city are the Palace (of seven stories), the Musjid in the centre of the capital, and the Asser-Mâhul, a glorious palace, which stands on the edge of the broad moat encircling the citadel, in what was, in

* The "Bhâmanee" dynasty began with the Deccan King, Sultan Alla O'Dien Hossein Kangoh Bhâmanee, (as many names as Queen Vic's last hope!) in the year of the Hejira 748, and Anno Domini 1347. The name "Bhâmanee," is derived from a Brahmin, who had been the benefactor of Alla O'Dien, the Long-Named, and was the first Hindoo who became the prime-minister of a Mussulman Prince. This dynasty scarcely lasted a century, when the kingdom was embroiled in civil dissensions, and finally split into five different monarchies, founded by the great officers of state, between the years A.D. 1489 and 1540, of which the Adil-Shâhi was the first:—established at Beejapore.

Aurungzēb subdued all these monarchies in the course of his mighty conquests.

olden time, the central quarter of the city. In this part, the ruin and decay apparent everywhere is still more noticeable, and all looks utterly desolate and deserted. The traditions and legends attached to the decayed metropolis of a bygone dynasty are legion, but I forbear retailing them, though I always heard them myself with never-failing interest. The sovereigns of Beejapore were said to be as princely in their pomp and power as the Mogul Emperors, and their studs of elephants were incredibly large, if Eastern historians do not romance. There is a small pool of water close to the handsome "Mosque of Mustapha Khân," which possesses an illimitable degree of sanctity in the eyes of Hindoos, as being fabled to have been originally brought all the way from the Ganges. Strange to say, it not only increased from a small jar-full to its present size,—a respectable pool,— but in order to assert its identity to the end of time, the hue of the water became *milky*. It really does possess this distinctive mark, and is perfectly wholesome I believe;—no similar tinted water is found anywhere in the vicinity.

This province displays a melancholy proof of the devastating effects of Mahratta despotism, misrule and anarchy. The once populous villages are deserted and in ruins,—the greater part of the country lies waste and uncultivated, overrun with jungle, and wild-beasts are the sovereigns of the present day. However, we must look for brighter days,—nor is the prospect entirely delusive, for the country, as far as population and cultivation are concerned, is improving gradually, and presents less desolate features than it did twenty years ago.

There is another river besides the Bēēmah, crossed between Ahmednuggur and Poonah. This is called the Gohrnuddy, and in most months of the year can be forded. It flows below Suroor, (a village also called Gohrnuddy,) where there is a Dâk-Bungalow. I observed two passage-boats lying near one bank, and two iron rods were suspended from pier to pier, as in the case of the Godavery before mentioned, to aid the passage-boats after heavy rain, when the river becomes deep, rapid, and totally unfordable, as well as to convey the post across on dark and stormy nights.

There was formerly a cantonment for British troops at Suroor,[*] but it has been given up. The

[*] Many years ago, Colonel Wallace, well known for eminent services in the Deccan, was buried at Suroor. His memory was so fondly cherished by the native soldiery, that all misfortunes, such as the dearth of grain, or any epidemic, were attributed to his ghost being disturbed, and they flocked to his tomb to do *poojah* (worship) to his manes; which holy act they imagined would quiet his perturbed spirit, and avert the impending calamity.

Cavalry Lines of the Poonah Auxiliary Horse are to the left of the Bazaar, and I observed four or five Bungalows, with trees and gardens environing them, still further to the left. Some are vacant, and one or two are tenanted by the European officers of the Auxiliary Horse I alluded to. The village is surrounded by trees, and the white Bungalows amidst the bright green foliage had a very pretty effect in the distance. There is a Hindoo Temple on the summit of a conical hill, a mile to the west of this place, which forms a conspicuous object in the landscape.

There is a river crossed before reaching the cantonment of Poonah, just below the city. This is the Moota-Moola, a compound of the Moota and the Moola, which form a junction close to Poonah, and subsequently flow into the Beēmah;—the latter river unites its waters with the Krishna,*

---

* The river Krishna rises in the Mahablèshwur hills, among the Western Ghâts, which are hereafter described. The source of the Krishna is not more than forty-two miles (in a straight direction) from the west coast of India. Thence it follows a south-westerly direction, until it receives the waters of the Warna river,—a medley of streamlets falling from the mountainous ridges. Turning then more to the east, the Krishna gradually receives the added waters of four other rivers—the Malpoorba, the Ghutpoorba, the Beēmah, and the Toomboodra —and, with a much augmented violence, empties itself into

not very far from Poonah, and the amalgamated streams fall into the Bay of Bengal. A fine stone-built bridge spans the Moota-Moola; and the view at this point is very striking. The broad deep river is fringed with verdant banks and fine trees, the green foliage of which is very pleasing to the eye, amidst the waste, hilly scenery around. The gardens adjoining each civilian's house were very pretty indeed, and the sweet scent of fragrant flowers attracted my notice as I rode past, on the evening I left Poonah for Panwell and Bombay. Though near its setting, the sun was very hot and oppressive; but as far as the Cavalry cantonment of Kirkee, (four or five miles from Poonah, on the Bombay route,) there are fine trees overshadowing the road. Kirkee is the station for Queen's troops, and at present the Tenth Hussars are there cantoned. The houses appear small, but all have pretty little gardens attached.

the Bay of Bengal, after a course of some seven hundred miles. As the Krishna flows through so mountainous a country, at a considerable level above the sea, its channel is consequently irregular, and much broken up by Rocks and Rapids, liable also to sudden and extreme fluctuations with regard to the amount of water. On this account, it is not adapted for inland navigation, though a great part of its course is navigated by light canoes,—a sort of bamboo wicker-basket, nearly round in shape, covered with half-tanned hides, and guided by paddles.

Poonah formed the capital of the Mahratta empire till the year 1818, when that kingdom was dismembered, and became subject to the British power. This ancient metropolis is situated in latitude 18° 30' North, and longitude 74° 2' East. It is about thirty miles to the east of the Ghâts, upwards of a hundred miles from Bombay, and seventy-five miles from the nearest sea-coast. Mahablèshwar, the only Hill-Sanatarium of the Bombay Presidency, is about fifty-five or sixty miles distant. A road has been made, and I believe it is adapted for carriages, but not having travelled on it myself, I do not vouch for its capabilities. The elevation of Poonah above the level of the sea is estimated at two thousand feet, and it is surrounded by hills a thousand feet higher, of trap formation, and of singularly scarped outline. In the days of native rule, these Heights were covered with fortresses, for which their position peculiarly adapted them in the eyes of Eastern engineers, but these have been destroyed or allowed to go to ruin, since 1818, as our Government found that they were useless.

The city of Poonah, which is at least a mile from the cantonment, is built somewhat in the style of Boorhânpore and Oojein.* The Hindoo

* Formerly the capital of the Scindia Mahrattas. Aboo

deities are painted on the old houses, and the streets are christened after them. But there are very few temples, and singularly few traces of its having been once the residence and capital city of a great dynasty. There is a temple on a hill, the "Pârbuttie Purbut;" and a fine view is commanded from this eminence. On a high mountain, south-west of Poonah, the once formidable fortress of Singhur is seen about twelve miles distant. This fastness is now in ruins, but it stands on the summit of a mountain, whither people resort, as a sort of sanatarium, for change of air. This Height terminates to the west of one of the ranges of hills between Poona and the Neera river.* The altitude is great, and the Fâzl, the ancient Eastern writer, so describes it:—"Oojein is a large city on the banks of the Sopra, and is held in high veneration by the Hindoos. It is astonishing that this river sometimes flows with milk." The city of Oojein is about one thousand seven hundred feet above the level of the sea, and is situated in latitude 23° 11′ North, and longitude 75° 35′ East. It boasts of a most remote antiquity, and a chapter in the Hindoo Mythological Poems, named the Purânas, is devoted to a description of it; also it is mentioned by Ptolemy, under the name of "Ozene;" and in Sanscrit it is called Ujjaegine and Avanti.

* This is a considerable river in the Deccan, which rises in the Western Ghâts to the south of Poonah, then passing eastward, divides the provinces of Beejapoor and Aurungabad, and near Nursinghur, in Malwâ, falls into the Beemah.

shape of the mountain irregular,—consisting chiefly of rugged eminences. There are other remarkable eminences in the district of Poonah, averaging four thousand feet above the level of the sea, viz., Loghur, Issapore, Kooâree, and Poorundur. Poonah is the only ancient "city" in the district of the same name, but there are many good-sized villages. The principal fabrics consist of coarse woollen and cotton cloths, and a few silken *sarhees* and other native garments. The manufacture of images, &c., is also extensively carried on in the city of Poonah, and they are unique and pretty, but very fragile. This manufacture consists of little figures (made of some composition), representative of the various classes of the natives,—parsees, servants, tradesmen and fakirs; also of different animals, idols, and other varieties. I do not know exactly what the "composition" used in the manufacture consists of, but when I suggested that it was very likely to be *clay*, the vendor became terribly irate, and went into a long explanation I could not fully comprehend, as he gabbled in the Mahratta tongue, instead of speaking the more refined Persian and Oordoo languages, with which I am acquainted. I advise all purchasers to beware how these itinerant merchants delude them into paying quadruple the value they will unconscionably ask. My head-servant purchased about thirty figures of every description for me (representations of the various classes of servants, gaily attired), for about sixteen rupees. The man first asked *me* fifty-two rupees for the same lot, and but for my servant, I should certainly have paid him five-and-twenty or thirty at least, and then have fancied that I had made a good bargain.

The other manufacture of the city of Poonah, that I have seen, consists of baskets, boxes, fans, &c., made of *kus-kus*, (the sweet-scented grass used for tatties, before described,) ornamented with pieces of velvet and beetle-wings. I also observed some beautiful fans of peacocks' tails, covered with devices of various sorts in beetle-wings. One man brought several pairs of sandal-wood bracelets, very handsomely carved, and coloured black; but these may or may not be the peculiar handiwork of this city.

The Dâk-Bungalow at Poonah is one of the hottest and dirtiest I ever entered. The room I was condemned to occupy (being the only vacant one in the establishment,) was about seven feet by four, guiltless of bed, table, or chairs; filthy, unswept and uncarpeted. In the evening I retired to my more luxurious carriage, the interior of which I arranged as a couch, and pulling the heavy curtains down, fell asleep, much exhausted by heat and feverishness. But my sleep was not destined to last long, and I was to get a sample of the polite manners prevalent in the Bombay Presidency. The only servants attached to the Bungalow were a *Peon** and a dirty "Mess-man," as they call the Portuguese table-attendants at the staging Bungalows of Bombay. All my own baggage had gone on ahead;—so, in taking possession of my carriage at night, I had no option, there being no bed in the miserable room allotted to me. The delightful "Mess-man" pretended to believe that I meant to go away surreptitiously, to avoid paying the immense fee † of the Dâk-Bungalow hire! When he asked me for it, I simply answered that I was not going away till the following evening, and fell asleep without giving the subject another thought.

About half-past ten o'clock at night two gentlemen (or men *calling* themselves by that title?) cantered up to my carriage, and most insolently demanded why I had withheld the rent! I awoke considerably bewildered and alarmed, and

* A man generally employed in the revenue or the police; a Government servant corresponding to the "Chuprassie," in the Bengal Presidency.

† In the Bombay Dâk-Bungalows, this fee is eight annas (one shilling) per diem, or half the Bengal rates.

merely replied that I had no intention of going away for another day. On this, these *gentlemanly* visitors replied,—" Oh yes, you did intend to go, and you must be the Mrs. Handyside complained against, for non-payment at the Kondepoorie Bungalow." "Kondepoorie?" I rejoined, frightened, and still scarcely awake,—" I never was at the Kondepoorie Bungalow!"—I could not for some time remember the names of the halts I had made from Ahmednuggur, so really *scared* was I at this sudden and untimely attack, but on reference to my Journal, I found that I had passed the disputed stage in the dead of the night, when I was in my carriage, between Gohrnuddy and Loonee. I immediately ordered my Sirdar to pay the day's fee, and still much alarmed, I lay down silently, pulling down the heavy blinds of the carriage windows.

Such an unprovoked and wanton attack, without any explanation asked, thus insultingly to tax a lady with cheating, and to charge her with falsehood, are "gentlemanly" manners I had never before experienced in all my long travels. Can this be the tolerated custom of the Bombay Presidency? I ought to illustrate them in a page or two devoted to themselves alone! I was also much obliged for being mistaken for any "Mrs. Handyside, who had been complained against at Kondepoorie,"—that name not being mine, all sweetly euphonious though it be; and as for the Kondepoorie Bungalow, I passed it in a deep sleep! The "*gentlemen*" above alluded to, I will spare the disgrace of seeing their names in print, for I have managed to-day to trace them out, and have given them a *gentle* reprimand, which I hope may have the desired effect. I consider it the very height of Christian charity to forbear from inserting their names (and rank in the gallant Bombay army) here, for the admiration of all who may chance to read.

CHAPTER IV.

From Poonah to Panwell is a distance of about seventy miles, good made road, but very hilly. From Ahmednuggur to Bombay by this route, and from Panwell *viâ* Tannah, (avoiding, of course, the direct sea-route,) a public phaeton runs, which is built to carry two passengers and a servant, besides luggage. Having my own carriage and camp, I did not try the conveyance, so cannot pass any opinion as to its merits or demerits. The mails from Agra are carried in carts drawn by one horse, very light in order to ensure celerity over the worst ground, and much the same as in the neighbouring and more enlightened Presidency. I reached Panwell,—where my land-journey came to a conclusion,—on the 13th of March, annihilating the distance between Poonah and that place in three forced marches, which completely knocked up my Camp, and gave me several days' fever after my arrival at Bombay. I shall never forget the terrible heat of Panwell,—so utterly exhausting in its enervating effects, damp and heat being mingled in the most sickly manner. The Dâk-Bungalow was the worst in this heathen Presidency, and totally unfit to exclude the burning rays of the sun, which beat fiercely through the imperfectly-tiled roof. Half distracted with fever, I passed a miserable day there, and yet I could not even indulge in the *dolce far niente*, which would have been my only chance of relief. To escape from this Pandemonium, I was forced to exert myself all day, engaging boats for my large Camp, and making every preparation to enable me to leave for Bombay by the evening tide, and thus escape the cruel purgatory of a further residence in this Tartarean abode of discomfort. But before proceeding to Bombay, let me describe the country, &c., which is traversed *en route* to Panwell, for the elevated and healthy districts of the Deccan are exchanged for the malarious low-lands of the horrid Concan, about three-and-thirty miles from Poonah.

From the latter city to Kundâlla, the country is very barren and hilly, though, where wooded with trees, extremely pretty. Kundâlla is a paltry village on the verge of the Bhore Ghât, the boundary between the Deccan and Concan, and the Illâkas of Poonah and Bombay Proper. There are several Bungalows at Kundâlla, as this spot, from its beauty and picturesque situation, is resorted to by Europeans, especially during the Rains, and the climate is reputed particularly salubrious. These European visitors are principally the miserable inhabitants of Bombay, who fly here for healthful breezes, during their dismal monsoon, when the "rains" wildly imitate the ancient deluge in volume and perseverance, in order to avoid becoming the victims of melancholia and liver-complaint—the inevitable consequence of long exposure to such a climate. *Quant à moi*, I found Kundâlla very hot, the wind quite a simoom in its scorching power, so I cannot say if the delicious climate reported to prevail during the rainy months be fact or fiction. The scenery is beautiful, I allow, but even that may apparently not be enjoyed in uninterrupted tranquillity, as the following instance will illustrate. One evening I took a ride as far as the Bhore Ghât:—the descent commences about half a mile from the village, and when I reached this spot I observed a couple of tents pitched by the roadside on the left hand, from which two or three natives rushed out, and in English demanded peremptorily my name, rank, and destination:—at the same time extending a paper for me to read. In this eccentric document was verily written in Queen's English, that travellers were expected to answer the above home-questions. Oh, Bombay Presidency, land of Kafirs! thy "manners and customs" are, verily, most unprecedented and peculiar!

I returned the paper, and as I trotted down the hill, laughingly replied, that my name and destination were an awful mystery, and one I could not think of revealing! I had not gone far before I halted to view the extensive prospect, which opened out from the summit of the descent, and while so employed, a Sowar* came from the tents inquisitorial, and halted close to me. He had evidently my mysterious self in his eye.

I kept him a good half-hour waiting, and then I turned back. I asked him, just as I was galloping off, if he had found out who the stranger was; he looked surprised, but said nothing, and I observed him watching me till I was out of sight. (I wonder if this be a branch of the detective police?)

The Bazaar of Kundâlla is in a sort of street: the main road runs between the two rows of Bunniahs' shops. There are some ten or twelve Bungalows on the various points and hills surrounding, scattered over a space of half a mile or so. Paths run in various directions, and the

* A Trooper, or mounted Soldier.

houses are many of them quite out of sight of the main road. One path leads to a high hill, from the summit of which a beautiful and extensive prospect is commanded. Not only Panwell but Bombay, and the blue sea beyond, are distinctly visible to the naked eye.

As I rode along the *inner* range of the Ghât, I could almost have imagined myself in the far distant Himalayas once more,—no plain met my gaze, only wild hills and khuds on every side. But the warm evening air, so different from the bracing winds of the well-remembered hills of the north, quite destroyed the illusion.

From the commencement of the descent of Bhore Ghât, the view is extensive and pleasing:— a confused succession of wooded hills to the right and left, and in front the wide plain stretching out, dotted with villages and trees, while the broad ocean lies beyond in infinite expanse. There is a great deal of jungle about Bhore Ghât, and a man with whom I was conversing yesterday evening, during my half hour's halt at the spot, told me that tigers abounded in the woods, and one in particular roamed at large night and day, and by my informant's account, was a regular man-eater. He had the credit of having lately devoured ten or twelve people! I shall take care to pass the jungle before the "shades of evening close around us," as I have no ambition to form the unlucky "thirteenth," and I feel sure that if my bones were to lie on Bombay ground, my spirit would know no peace.

I remained three days at Kundâlla, wishing to recruit my worn-out people by a good rest, previous to the long march of thirty miles into Panwell. My object in not halting at either of the Bungalows *en route*, built expressly for travellers, was the reported unhealthiness and suffocating heat of the Concan. The first Bungalow after Kundâlla is Kūppowlie, about six miles distant, at the foot of the Ghât,—very hot and very dirty. The next is Chowk, twelve miles further, also very objectionable.

While I was at Kundâlla my servants reported to me the illness of one of my stud, poor "Begum." The Syce appropriated to the animal begged I would give her a *gallop* to bring her round. I was amused at the course of medicine proposed, though in the absence of better advice, I adopted the suggestion. It was past sunrise, but I did not hesitate to give my sick favourite a long and rapid canter for nearly an hour, up hill and down dale, in the more secluded vicinities of the village, where I could gallop without impediment. The main road is disagreeable to ride or drive along after sunrise, or indeed, I may well say, daylight, on account of the immense traffic which throngs the thoroughfares from morning to night with carts, bullocks, and buffaloes, very heavily laden. Cotton seems at this season of the year to be the principal article of commerce.

I left Kundâlla on the 12th, at near sunset. The same inquisitorial people rushed out, but this time I took no notice of them, galloping past the tents, nor did any one attempt to follow me. A mile and a half further brought me to the Custom Houses, where toll is levied on every one; *viz.*, eight annas for every laden cart, and one rupee for every four-wheeled vehicle; one anna per horse; one pice per goat; one pice per man's load. Such were the tolls levied on my people and Camp, and they thus appropriated some five rupees of my specie. This was before I passed,—and when I rode by, a Chuprassie came up and demanded one anna for toll, to pay for the passage of my steed. I stopped to read the placard, and not being in the habit of carrying "coppers," I civilly told the man to send some one to my Sirdar, who was not far on ahead; but two men ran after me, insolently demanding the base metal there and then. After taking the trouble to repeat, that not being aware of the toll, I had omitted taking money from my Sirdar for the purpose, I rode on. My importunate creditors, on this, absolutely caught hold of my bridle;—one touch of the whip, and my gallant steed bounded impetuously on, prostrating the youth who had been so valorous! I stopped at fifty paces distance, and turning round, enjoyed a good laugh at the toll-keeper's expense; but I kindly told him his anna would be given by my servants on demand, notwithstanding his impudent importunity.

I do not know what this toll is instituted for. Probably to defray the expenses of making and repairing the road, which is constantly necessary, so thronged with carts as it is. I believe some Parsee has taken the contract of this Ghât from Government, and pays half a lac yearly. I should opine that he makes a dozen times that amount, as in the course of two days I did not see less than five thousand carts, laden bullocks, and other excisable items. Cotton is exported in enormous quantities, and all traffic passes this way.

The road is very broad and metalled, the inclination by no means great. My carriage got down very well, with the drag on, nor did my baggage carts meet with any accident. The descent is wooded, and all the surrounding hills are covered with bushes and jungle. The Ghât is five miles long, and the village of Kūppoolie, where there is a Dâk-Bungalow, is at the foot. The Bazaar lines both sides of the road, and all supplies are procurable. There is a puckha Tank a little above the village, to the right of the road in descending the Ghât. It is fortunate that the road is so broad, because perpendicular precipices frequently flank the made route, and carts or carriages *meeting* would in a narrower path inevitably come to grief. I cantered and trotted the whole way down, without any other impediment than the numerous carts and bullocks, many lying wheelless or useless. Kūppoolie is a hot, dirty place, and no traveller ought to waste a day there, if he can possibly avoid it. And, (as I think I have mentioned before,) the next village where there is a Dâk-Bungalow, is Chowk, twelve miles from Kūppoolie, and the same distance from Panwell. The village of Kâlapore is half-way between Kūppoolie and Chowk. Shops here likewise line the two sides of the road, and supplies are procurable, but no water fit to drink. The village of Chuchoole is between Chowk and Panwell; no Bungalow, but supplies procurable. All other villages are off the road. Chowk is a very large Bazaar. It was eight o'clock, p.m., when I arrived at the Dâk-Bungalow there, and so oppressively hot, that I was constrained to dine outside. I observed a great difference after passing into the low lands below Bhore Ghât, where even at night the air felt quite oppressive; and during the Tartarean days, the heat was absolutely prostrating;—and yet not a sign in any room of a Punkah. (Oh! this barbarous region of Salamanders.) I observed a small tent, like our Hill *Pawls*, pitched near Kâlapore. It was the "Camp" of some Bombay officer, "marching" on duty!* And there sat the Salamander contentedly at the tent door! The road is metalled the whole way, and from the foot of the Ghât to Panwell runs at a slight inclination, besides a few short ascents here and there. The Ghâts rise like a wall all along the country, but even in the Concan there are hills, mostly separate and disjointed, some conical, others of markedly pointed and angular shapes. To the very shores of the sea, hills are found. There are a good many trees in this district:—I observed some very fine Mangoe trees, and several Palms stud the landscape. Though but a gunshot from the sea, not a glimpse of its blue waters is visible from this Bungalow. A

* Such a tent we would not allot for a stable in hot-weather marches in Bengal.

hotter and a dirtier place my eyes never ached to see before!

I went this morning to the place where the boats are kept. There are three kinds for hire,—the "bunder-boat," the "cotton-boat," and the "dingee." The former resembles the Budgerow of Bengal; the second is for baggage, or bales of cotton, whence it derives its name; and the "dingee" is for those who cannot afford the bunder-boats, and are forced to voyage, *in formâ pauperis.**

---

* See next page for the Rates of Fare.

RATES OF FARE.

BUNDER-BOATS.	For Fair Season, from 15th Sept. to 31st of May.									For Monsoon, from 1st June to 14th September.					
	For a Boat comprising a crew of 13 men.		For a Boat comprising a crew of 11 men.		For a Boat comprising a crew of 9 men.		For a Boat comprising a crew of 7 men.		For a Boat comprising a crew of 13 men.		For a Boat comprising a crew of 11 men.		For a Boat comprising a crew of 9 men.	
	Rs.	As.	Rs.	As.	Rs.	As.	Rs.	As.	Rs.	As.	Rs.	As.	Rs.	As.
From Panwell to Tannah	10	0	9	0	8	0	7	0	15	0	13	8	12	0
,, Bombay to Colset Bunder	12	0	11	0	10	0	9	0	18	0	16	0	15	0
,, ,, Bhewndy	13	0	12	0	11	0	10	0	20	0	18	0	16	0
,, ,, Bassein	13	0	12	0	11	0	10	0	20	0	18	0	16	0
,, ,, Nagootnah	13	0	12	0	11	0	10	0	20	0	18	0	16	8
,, ,, Elephanta and Butchers' Islands	5	8	5	0	4	8	4	0	8	4	7	8	6	12
Per day	5	8	5	0	4	8	4	0	8	0	7	0	6	0
On board Ship at Middle Ground	5	0	4	8	4	0	3	0	9	0	8	0	7	0

RATES OF FARE.—*Continued.*

| | Fair Season. || Monsoon. ||
Cotton-Boats.	Rs.	As.	Rs.	As.
In Harbour, per day	2	0	2	12
,, half a day	1	0	1	12
To Panwell or Tannah	5	0	7	0
To ditto ditto and back	7	0	10	0
To Nagootna	7	0	10	0
To ditto, and back to Bombay	10	0	12	0
To Elephanta	3	0	4	0
To ditto and back	4	0	6	0

| | Fair Season. || Monsoon. ||
Dingees.	Rs.	As.	Rs.	As.
For trip of two hours	0	8	1	0
For every additional hour	0	2	0	3
For a whole day	1	8	2	0

I engaged a bunder-boat for myself, and two cotton-boats for my horses, baggage, and the half of the servants I could not accommodate in my barge. I will give the land route by Tannah, in the appendix to this volume, in case any one might prefer it to the sea voyage.

Panwell is situated on the River Pan, to which the tide flows up, several miles from the harbour, and in consequence the water is as salt as the sea. The situation,—in the midst of a salt morass,— must necessarily be very damp and insalubrious, but its proximity to the sea and Bombay makes it a very busy spot, where commerce on a considerable scale is carried on, which justifies the selection of the locality for a prosperous mart. The latitude of Panwell is 18° 59′ North, and the longitude 73° 15′ East. This is the grand ferry to Bombay, which is about twenty-two miles distant; the passage may be performed in seven or eight hours if the tide favours. On our voyage we passed the island of Elephanta, where the famous cave is found, and I went to see it. After Ajunta and Ellora I thought comparatively little of it, though it has appeared wonderful to those who have never seen the superior marvels of the former. The caves at Elephanta were in the same style as those near Ajunta, as far as size and sculptured figures went, but instead of the crescent range of numerous caves, those at Elephanta are single,—only one large and one small, half-way up a hill, the latter above the former. The figures of gods and animals I need not describe, as they are much the same as those previously detailed, only in a more dilapidated condition. There is a reservoir of water in the large cave, supplied by a fresh spring. The hill is wooded, and commands a fine view of Bombay and Salsette. There are a few huts at the foot, but I could not obtain the milk I wanted for my morning meal at any price. I saw a couple of tents pitched very near the caves, but I do not know who were the inmates. They were, however, very Samaritans to me in my need after the hot walk up the hill; they most kindly sent me a cup of tea, as I was exploring the cave, and supplied my Khidmutgar with milk, after he had failed in every effort to obtain it elsewhere.

I observed some men extracting toddy from the Palm trees. This liquor when fresh is merely a little sour, and is largely drank by the natives:—after sunrise it ferments, and forms an intoxicating beverage, and then I imagine it is still more largely partaken of. The method which the natives employ in mounting the lofty spiral trees is very singular, and merits recording. Having tied their ankles loosely together, they pass a band round their waist, which at the same time is made to encircle the tree likewise, and placing their feet to the root of the tree, they lean upon the band, and with hands and feet nimbly climb up the stem without branches, sometimes fifty feet high. The ligaments I have alluded to, used for the waists and ankles, are frequently manufactured of long strips of palm-leaves torn off just as they are about to mount. I have seen little children clamber up to the top like monkeys, when the cocoa-nuts were wanted for thirsty travellers, who refresh themselves by drinking the cold delicious milk contained in the shell. When the toddy-gatherer ascends, he carries in his hand or *cummerbund*, (waist-cloth,) a hatchet to make fresh incisions, or to renew the old ones, and besides this he must burthen himself with an earthen jar, to bring down the toddy, which is received in pots of burnt earthenware tied to the tree and emptied every twelve hours.

My boat was an hour and a half in performing the passage from Elephanta to Bombay, and we moored in the harbour of the city, off the Bunder* or Ghât of Mazagon. This Bunder is of stone, and similar Ghâts stretch along the whole coast included in the harbour. Mazagon is three miles distant from the Fort, and consequently very inconveniently situated for people who have business to transact, as all the public offices are, without exception, within the ramparts of the Fort.

There is a great desideratum in Bombay, in the total want of good hotels. Those in the Fort are said to be not at all respectable, at least for ladies, and the only way of managing a temporary residence in this Presidency, is to pitch

* A *Bunder* simply means a port or harbour, but I never heard it used in any part of Bengal in that sense. Its only signification there is a monkey or baboon.

a tent on the Esplanade. Except during the stormy months of the Monsoon, this wide piece of level is covered with the tents of travellers, and the scene presented to the eye is very enlivening. The large "single-poled," and "double-poled" tents, each with its stable and kitchen canvass spread quite close, are ranged in *lines*, from the sea backwards to the road which constitutes the Mall, or morning and evening drive. The row next the sea is solely and exclusively reserved for invalids, by order of Government, and a certificate is requisite from a medical man, before the Executive Engineer can permit any traveller to pitch his tent there. Owing to my being in very indifferent health on my arrival in Bombay, I obtained the medical certificate at once, and the day after my arrival in the Presidency, I had my tents pitched in this favoured line. I arrived in my carriage, ill with an attack of low fever, and as I observed the clouds of sand flying over that "line" in particular, I wished I was *not* entitled to its honourable place. What I suffered there I should find words too faint to describe. The heat was appalling, and the perfect hurricanes of dust which blew night and day were distracting. The fierce rays of the tropical sun pierced with intense and killing power, through the thin canvass roofs and walls, and the minute particles of sand searched their way through every impediment, besides covering the beds, couches, tables,—everything—with a deep coating of sand. It was no use rubbing it off, because the next minute a sandy blast swept through the camp again. Dinner was principally composed of sand in various forms, and I must confess I did not approve of the novel condiment. Though my tent was within ten yards of the rippling waves at high tide, I used to awake in the morning weary and unrefreshed; exercise fatigued me to depression, and during the hotter hours of the day, a wandering sensation of the brain came over me, and in half unconsciousness I used to lie on the couch for many consecutive hours daily, almost in a stupor, if undisturbed. There was not actual pain in the head;—merely a dull pressure on the brain, and a visionary, dreamy state of the intellectual faculties. I have at times fearfully thought "Is this the preliminary stage of *mania?*" If I wished to transact any business, mental or corporeal, I was forced to do it in the early morning; for after nine or ten o'clock these painful sensations gradually clouded the brain, and any attempt to read or write only made the *cervicular* compression more distressing, and the wandering of the mind more perceptible. In spite of the sand, the "sea-breeze," (so called *par excellence*,) which usually sets in about ten or eleven o'clock a.m., was an invaluable boon in this torrid zone; and when, through the kind hospitality of friends, I moved to a good house in Colaba, (the furthest extremity of the Island of Bombay,) where its accompaniment of sand could not intrude, I used to pine and languish each day for its advent. The extremity of Colaba, where my friends lived, was near the Lighthouse, and the beach in that vicinity is rocky and not sandy, so the breeze was doubly welcome. The house, too, was built at an elevation above the sea-level, and the welcome airs of the expansive ocean had full and unfettered play. But soon after sunset, an oppressive lull supervened, and almost invariably the nights were close and suffocatingly hot, not a breath of air stirring.

I went for a week in search of lost health to Mahablèshwur, the Bombay Sanatarium, of which I will give an account in a subsequent chapter. The sufferings I have endeavoured to describe, both preceded and succeeded my Hill excursion. I had the misfortune to lose the steamer on the 17th of March. Only arriving in Bombay about a couple of days previously, I had formidable arrears of work to get through, before I could attempt to move. I found all my heavy baggage lying in a most neglected state in the Godowns of Messrs. Thacker and Co. in the Fort, when I had been vainly imagining that they were half-way home, as they left Julundhur three months before I did. Again I lost my passage per steamer "Achilles," of the 1st of April, having returned from Mahablèshwur only two days before with a dreadful cough and cold, and entire disappearance of voice. I did endeavour to start, however, and on the day of sailing, made superhuman efforts to get my baggage packed and to arrive on board in time, but though the bunder-boat I was in, reached within a steamer's length of the "Achilles," the Captain either did not, or *would not* see the signals made by my boat's-crew to wait our coming, and under our very eyes, (quite within hailing distance, but for the boisterous wind that was blowing,) sailed away! Three of my Bombay friends were in the boat with me, and our chase was exciting. We followed for a considerable distance, the high and favourable wind giving us a chance, till the Pilot was dispensed with, and the steamer sailed away in earnest. However, all things considered, it was just as well I could not go, in the state of my health at the time, for the vessel was crowded to excess, and I was too ill to *rough* it in any way. The lady who had one half of my cabin, Mrs. M——, had a lucky escape, as my cough would have probably kept her awake all night, so incessant and violent were the paroxysms which momentarily convulsed my worn-out frame.

In mentioning the Hotels at Bombay, I have avoided all allusion to the Hope-Hall Hotel at Mazagon. In the first place it is out of the way, and in the second, the landlady is not a very civil or very honest person, if I am to judge from the day I spent under her auspices. I could only get a *tent*, and I was but twenty-seven hours in the place, for which she brought me a bill of nearly thirty shillings for my sole self! And when I remonstrated mildly at the imposition, being a palpable overcharge on the advertised rates, to say she was *rude* would be too mild a term, because she used language which surprised me into speechlessness. My reasons for leaving the place, were the heat, bad food, myriads of mosquitoes, *et hoc genus omne*, from whose combined attacks, I was forced all day to retreat within the small enclosure of my mosquitoe-curtains, as the sole hope of preserving my sanity intact. This obese, self-satisfied dame sat all day in the verandah of her house, and I could not but observe that, however ungracious and extortionate she was to me, she was very different towards her gentleman-lodgers, with whom she seemed on the best of terms. To argue the matter with this virago was out of the question; so paying her ten rupees, eight annas, I left the precincts, only too glad to get away.

My journey to Mahablèshwur, I will give in its original Journal-form, but I must first devote a short chapter to an account of the Island of Bombay, and its most prominent class of inhabitants —the Parsees, or poetical Fire-worshippers.

CHAPTER V.

BOMBAY.

THE Island of Bombay is situated in latitude 18° 56′ North, and longitude 72° 57′ East. Originally Bombay was merely a succession of small islands, with numerous back waters; the greater part of the soil producing rank vegetation, at one time dry, and at another overflowed by the sea. In consequence of this, to inhale the air engendered by this vegetation was considered so fearfully unwholesome, that the old writers on India allot *three years* for the average duration of life passed in this Presidency! A river, called the "Goper," which rises in the hills of Salsette,*

* Salsette is an island formerly pertaining to the Mogul Empire, and is separated from Bombay by a narrow and shallow strait. A causeway now connects it with the main island. The surface of Salsette is an alternation of hill and dale, and the valleys, especially in the southern quarter, are well cultivated. This island is remarkably rich in mythological antiquities. There are some very extraordinary excavations found here, called "Kennery," resembling those of Ellora, though far less extensive.

and disembogues itself into the channel which formerly severed that island from Bombay, when swollen by floods, used to rush in at the breaches situated towards the northern extremity, and after traversing a very large extent of ground, finally discharged itself into the sea. The various petty islets and larger islands which, before Bombay belonged to Great Britain, were quite separate and distinct, are now intimately connected together by the numerous buildings, houses, &c., which have sprung up under British rule, and where once divided by arms of the sea, bridges or vellards now connect the banks and shores together. The once distinct islands are still known by separate appellations, and Colaba, Salsette, Bandora, Girgâon, Caranjah, Byculla, &c., &c., have boundaries of their own, all being comprised under the *generic* name of " Bombay." The vellards are very massive works of stone, and have proved a great convenience to all ranks and classes; for in former days boats were requisite where now the causeways form the thoroughfares. The vellard which connects Colaba with the part of Bombay where the Fort and Town are found, is of recent construction; and in this vicinity a very considerable tract of land has been redeemed from the sea. Where some years ago the ocean rolled at high tide, fine buildings and extensive warehouses have sprung up. During my residence of four months in the island, I watched the progress of redeeming a large level piece of ground, at present useless from the fact of the sea washing it twice a day. This "level" is close to the vellard near Colaba, and in a year or two, what is now a salt marsh, will have been raised sufficiently to allow cotton to be stored there in bales during the dry season. The process of "redeeming" is, in the particular instance in question, most offensive to the olfactory organs; for rubbish of all kinds is brought in carts, and heaped up there hourly. But Bombay is famous for its non-Arabian perfumes, which exhale from various parts of the island;—for instance, at or near all the Bunders without exception; and worse than all is a particular spot on the only riding-ground near Colaba, along the level sands between Colaba and Malabar Hill, which I christened "*Araby Felix*." I used to dread riding past this fragrant spot, and my gallant Arabs soon learnt to break into a violent gallop at the first breath they scented, notifying our approach to " Araby." This part of Bombay is called the Backwater Bay, and but for a long ridge of rocks which extend from Malabar Point to Colaba, and which, though concealed even at low-water, are still not far below the surface, this bay would form an excellent harbour. As it is, only very small craft can enter, and these are merely fishing-boats and small barges carrying timber, which is all stored in Girgaum, close to Backwater Bay. The ridge of rocks above alluded to excludes *sharks* from this bay, and, in consequence, it is the only safe place for sea-bathing. Every morning and evening, numbers of natives, principally Parsees, are seen performing their ablutions in the briny waves, and many gallant horses are daily led far out into the tide for the same purpose. Not that I approved of the latter custom;—my stud were never so victimized.

The harbour which is situated on the eastern side of the island, is a very fine one. During the Monsoon, particularly, a large concourse of ships of all nations may be seen riding at anchor in this port. The Fort looks out on the harbour, and the sea washes the greater part of the walls on three sides, while the esplanade stretches across the fourth. The town, which is built within the walls of the Fort, was constructed partly by the ancient masters of the island, the Portuguese, and partly by the British subsequently. As I have elsewhere mentioned, all the public-offices are within the ramparts, and all business is transacted there. The "Colaba Company" have Godowns, &c., at Colaba, and a very fine range of houses, three-stories high, (inclusive of the "Godown floor)," called the "Grant Buildings," are let out on hire, unfurnished. During the Monsoon, I found these apartments cooler than any other part of Bombay, and in consequence of this, I left the house of my kind friends at Colaba, and spent the month of June and beginning of July in an elevated apartment which commanded every breath of wind, and after the Monsoon set in, was always cool when the wind blew as it almost invariably did; at nights, the temperature became actually cold. I used to leave the opposite windows wide open, regardless of the rain which drifted several feet into the room, or the thorough draft which is thought so dangerous in England. I used to ride every morning at daybreak, whether ill or well, and take an inspiriting gallop on the sands, even if torrents of rain fell, and hurricanes of wind blew. To this rigorous discipline, I contend that I owe my life! otherwise, verily should I have fallen a victim to melancholia and disease of the brain,—so terribly did the climate of Bombay affect my health from first to last. While I am on the subject of the effects of the climate, I may as well say a word about the climate itself. The

Bombay-ites vow, that hot and humid though the Presidency is allowed on all hands to be, it still is *healthy!* It is true I only saw the island during very unfavourable seasons,—first, the hot weather, then a month of the Monsoon,—but in my humble opinion, the sickly, blanched faces of very young children, as well as adults and those of maturer years, sadly contradict the foolish boast. There can be no manner of doubt, that the climate is debilitating to the last degree, and promotes low spirits very rapidly. The very sea-breezes bear moisture in every breath, and far from conveying the bracing effects of similar breezes in Europe, one feels as languid and depressed as if the burning Simoon blew from the ocean, or as if every breeze were heavily surcharged with deadly malaria. There is another wind prevalent in Bombay, especially during the night, which blows when the sea-breezes are still, and this is called the "land-wind." By all accounts it is most dangerous to be exposed to it, especially during sleep. People who are not sufficiently guarded, often have their features distorted, or their limbs crippled for life, by a sort of fatal paralysis. One night while driving in my Equirotal on a march through the Concan, I slept in my carriage, leaving the doors open on account of the excessive closeness of the temperature. I could scarcely observe any perceptible wind, but the natives told me it was the destructive land "hāwa"* which was prevailing. In spite of their warnings, fatigue and heat overpowered me, and with open doors I fell fast asleep. In the morning I awoke with rheumatic pains in all my limbs, and instead of feeling refreshed by the long night's slumbers, experienced a most distressing lassitude, and a *worn-out* sensation. I probably escaped still worse results by the wind being very light. Poor Ghaussie, who had for several weeks past been suffering severely from rheumatic fever, became very ill at Bombay, but he found relief when I made arrangements for his sleeping where the land-wind could by no possibility reach him.† There is no "cold weather" in Bombay, such as the more favoured residents of Upper India enjoy, and the rains are most trying to the constitution. The Monsoon bursts in the end of May, or early in June, and is ordinarily ushered in with a violent storm, or succession of storms, accompanied by tremendous thunder and lightning.

* "Hāwa" means wind, air.

† To all who know anything of India, it may be almost superfluous to observe that the native servants very rarely sleep in beds, and are generally accustomed to roll themselves up in a sheet or blanket, lying on the hard stone verandahs outside, or the inner vestibules, if there be any.

The burst of the Monsoon which I saw, had nothing so terrific as the *avant-courier* of the heavy rains which fell during the last month of my residence, —perhaps in pity to my nervous fear of " Indra's instruments of wrath ! " The hurricanes of wind and rain which devastate the island throughout the months of the Monsoon, I can testify to, however. Often in my morning rides have I experienced the greatest difficulty in stemming the force of the gale, and very frequently finding it impossible to ride home *against* the wind, I have been forced to canter on, away from my residence, in the most pitiless down-pour of rain, till the blast moderated sufficiently to allow me a chance of keeping my saddle, instead of being perforce blown off. The quantity of rain which falls during the Monsoon is very great, more than quadrupling the fall in the neighbouring districts of the Deccan—Poonah, for instance. The average exhibited by the rain-guages in Bombay is upwards of a hundred inches from the beginning of June to the end of September, and the damp is so great, that mildew gathers in one day on the tables, floors, &c., ruining books, clothes, furniture,—in short, every thing that can be ruined,—with hopeless celerity. During this dismal season, few people boldly run the risk of open doors and windows as I did, during my séjour in the Grant Buildings, revelling in the cold blasts, and heedless of the accompanying rains. The miserable inhabitants who *can* get away, hurry to Poonah,—and those who are unable to leave their avocations in the Presidency, keep every door and window hermetically sealed, (instead of open, as is practicable during the same season in Bengal,)—a matting constructed of grass and leaves encloses the greater part of the houses, thereby producing a suffocating temperature, hot, damp and air-less, which is indescribably trying. I said above that the unhappy residents of Bombay migrated to Poonah, and not to the hills, as is the case in the other Presidency. Alas! miserable Bombay! thy beautiful highlands form no sanataria during this unpropitious season. The Mahablèshwur hills, however delightful during seven or eight months of the year, are not habitable during the rains, and are deserted by white and black bipeds alike. I am told that nearly *four hundred inches* of rain fall in four months. If this be true, and my informant was a gentleman of reputation,[*] I suppose it rains night and day incessantly. Unhappy Presidency! no wonder thy denizens rail at Bengal and its dependencies! All " envy, hatred, and malice;"

[*] The learned Professor P——n.

but those who are so much more highly favoured, ought not to trouble themselves with wrath, but rather smile in derision at all jealous attacks. Poor Major Jacob, the reputed author of the abusive pamphlet which created so much stir in India! He must have indited it on finding all his full-dress uniform spoilt by mildew, or when prevented from meeting the ladye of his love, by ten inches of rain incontinently falling at the trysting time. *Le Malheureux!*

There are numerous Bunders in the harbour of Bombay—the Apollo, the Colaba, the Boree, the Mazagon, &c., &c., all paved and substantially built up. The light and graceful vessels of the Yacht Club glide swiftly along, and their speed is very great. The model upon which almost all the craft belonging to this club are fashioned, is the simple fishing-boat of the island, and those which are constructed with the strictest fidelity to this model, are the swiftest.

The extreme difference of climate between this presidency and the Punjâb is illustrated by the fact that in no month of the year, (not even in the hills, I believe,) can ice be made. All the ice used, comes from America; whereas, in the Punjâb, in *one* station alone, *ten thousand maunds* (or about 820,000 lbs. English weight) of ice were made in less than two months, last cold weather, all of which was stored in ice-pits for summer consumption.*

The hard metalled roads which intersect the island in every direction are ruinous to horses' feet, and riding is with difficulty *properly* enjoyed in the presidency. A gallop "across country," as in the far north-west, was a bliss I no longer could command, and I pined for it more than I can express! The only "rides" are the eternal and monotonous fashionable haunts of the Esplanade, the sands between Colaba and Malabar hill, the race-course, and the "flats." The latter are about ten miles from Colaba, and as the macadamized roads intervene, this riding-ground is as much lost to the Colaba people as the sands are to all residents in the neighbourhood of the "flats." Moreover the "flats" are a mere marsh in the rainy

* To the majority of my readers it may scarcely be necessary to explain the simple process of making ice in India, but it may be as well to describe it for the benefit of the uninitiated. Water is placed in numerous shallow earthen vessels, and exposed all night. The ice thus made is put into the pits every morning, and grass is spread thickly below, every care being taken to preserve the ice. Even at Julundhur, where the ice-club was not composed of many members, and the quantity made not so very great as in larger stations, upwards of *fifty* men were daily employed in the above work. (Julundhur is the station alluded to in the text.)

months. All the "made" roads are kept up by heavy taxes levied on the permanent inhabitants, such as the wheel-tax, horse-tax, house-tax, &c.

There is a very pretty kind of manufacture here in ivory and sandal-wood, inlaid; of which desks, work-boxes, and every possible description of articles are made, and sold at very moderate prices. Boxes of camphor-wood, brought from China, and warranted to exclude insects, are also sold, of various sizes and prices.

The "manners and customs" of the Bombayites are quite different from those of the sister-presidency. The servants are not half so respectful in their manner or language;—they are more highly paid, but are fewer in number. Many of them are Portuguese, who wear European clothes, but rarely speak any language save an incomprehensible medley which it is difficult to define. There are Parsee servants too, but these are all very expensive, and will never engage in any menial capacity. What are called Khansâmahs * and Khidmutgârs † in Bengal, are here termed

* Correctly *Khânsamân*; *i. e.* "lord of the paraphernalia,"—from "Khân," lord; and "samân, paraphernalia. The ordinary word "Khansâmah," is a corruption.

† "Khidmut" simply means, if literally translated, personal service. "Khidmutgâr," however, is used amongst the Anglo-Indians to denote a table-servant only.

Bootlèrs, (the native corruption of the English word "butler"!) They are all far less particular about *zât*, (caste,) than in the sister-presidency, because the serving classes are much lower in Bombay and Madras, and they rarely have any "zât" to lose. I think all dispassionate people will allow that Bengal servants are by far the best. There was great competition for my large retinue, when I was dismissing them, and they were bribed by high wages to remain in the presidency after I had given them their *rōōkhsut* (leave). All labour is dearer, and the system in force is very bad, where native workmen are concerned; it is very difficult at times to get a smith or carpenter.

The fruit in Bombay is very good. The mangoes have long been famed, and grafts are taken to Malwâ, and the north-west provinces. I have tasted very good pine-apples and plaintains, and melons and oranges are plentiful. I am told grapes also grow, but are not so fine as those in the Deccan. The greater part of the grain consumed in the island is imported, and *dōōb* grass,—the rich green grass so fattening for horses in Bengal,—is almost unknown all throughout the length and breadth of the presidency, and utterly so in Bombay itself. All the grass consumed is brought from neighbouring islands and districts, and after being stored in great ricks, it is sold by retail at exorbitant prices, so a "grass-cutter" is useless, for his "occupation is gone."

There is a cathedral in the Fort, and there are also numerous churches of the different persuasions of Christians scattered over the island. There are several public buildings—the Elphinstone College, the Town-hall, &c., &c., all of which have been described so often, that I will not linger over the detail. The beneficent works of Sir Jamsetjee Jeejeeboy, the well-known Parsee knight, are beyond all praise, and many a destitute invalid has had cause to bless his munificent liberality, when carefully tended, with good medical aid at hand, in the splendid hospital he has so nobly erected. Before leaving the public buildings of Bombay, I must say a few words on the Lunatic Asylum, and its talented and indefatigable Superintendent, Dr. William Campbell, whom I am proud to reckon in the number of my most esteemed friends. This establishment for the insane has long existed in Bombay, but it owes its present efficient state to the labours of the Medical Superintendent, who has devoted all his energies to the task he has undertaken. I have repeatedly been over the Asylum; and the feelings of deep sadness and uncontrollable depression induced by the melancholy sight of creatures like ourselves, fallen to a par with the beasts of the field,—with reason dethroned, and intellect extinguished,— were agreeably soothed by the manifestation everywhere apparent of a tender care for their welfare, and a gentle leading back to sense and decorum. The unfortunate lunatics owe much to their kind-hearted, talented master, who has (I believe entirely at his own risk,) introduced *occupation* into the establishment, as a means of cure. It is most interesting to see the elaborate works that these creatures bereft of reason can be taught, and when in God's good time their minds are restored, they will be able to make a profitable use of the trades thus acquired. I saw weaving, rope-making, cotton-cleaning,* and spinning; mat-manufacture, straw-hat and bonnet ditto; and cane-work chair, stool and basket-making of very pretty and intricate patterns. All this gives occupation to the poor maniacs and idiots, and as no one is in any way coerced to work, only gently *coaxed* thereto by offers of some trifling reward, or extra indulgence, the benefit derived is most wonderful in detail. It was quite touching to see how Dr. Campbell was beloved by one and all

* There are very fine machines for this department, in an out-office built for the purpose.

of his unfortunate patients, European and native, and his gentle voice spoke kind and cheering words to all, evincing the interest he took in their little plans and occupations. If the sight of faces un-illumined by the light of reason always saddened me deeply, I never viewed this receptacle for the insane without feeling impressed with the magnitude of the charge committed to the Medical Superintendent, and charmed with his admirable method of fulfilling it. Should these lines ever meet his eye, I hope he will understand the friendly feeling which prompts this humble tribute to his merits, though he needs no one to point them out, so well known must they be in the land where he toils.

This short account of Bombay would be incomplete without a few words on the people who overrun the island, possessing nearly all the houses and lands. I need hardly say, I allude to the Parsees or fire-worshippers, famed in song. On the Esplanade they are seen driving about in very different style from most natives. They are more numerous by far than the European population of the better class in Bombay; and on the Mall, I used to observe them in the proportion of at least five to one of our countrymen, driving better carriages and more costly horses. They are much fairer than the natives of India, from whom they differ considerably in costume, and there are many good-looking men amongst them. I have seen none of the higher class of the Parsee ladies, but I am informed by credible eye-witnesses that there are several really beautiful women of that race in Bombay. Sir Jamsetjee Jeejeeboy (knighted by our Queen,) is a fine-looking old man, and his wife, who is a fat old woman, is always called "*Lady* Jeejeeboy"! His son has a beautiful wife, whose charms by far eclipse, saith Report, those of the greatest English belles ever seen in Bombay.

The following extract, descriptive of the Parsees, I copied out of some book, two or three years ago, but as I made no note of the author, I am sorry I cannot mention his name.

"Besides the native hordes and castes, Bombay and Gujerat contain nearly all the Parsees or fire-worshippers to be found on the continent of India, the feeble remains of the once predominant religion of the Magi. According to their own traditions, after the Mohammedan religion was promulgated in Asia, and began to pervade Persia, the ancestors of the Indo-Parsees retired to the mountains, where they remained until the overthrow of the Persian monarchy, and the death of Yezdijird, the last sovereign. Finding the religion of their native country wholly overthrown, and themselves outlaws, they wandered towards the port of Ormus, then governed by a branch of the old royal family, where they resided fifteen years, during which they acquired the art of ship-building, for which they are still celebrated. At the expiration of the above period, they quitted Ormus, and proceeded to the island of Diu, where they sojourned nineteen years, but finding it too small, embarked for Gujerat, where they first lighted the Atish Baharam, or sacred fire, and spread themselves over the country. At present, they are dispersed among the towns and villages along the north-western coast of India, and in 1815, were estimated at 150,000 families.

"The Zendavesta, or Sacred Book of the Parsees, is the only work known to have been written in the Zend language, and is believed by them to have been the composition of Zoroaster, in the reign of Gushtasp, (supposed to have been Darius Hystaspes,) or about his era. Although the writings of Zoroaster are alluded to by the ancients, the name of Zendavesta does not occur for 1500 years after the period when they are supposed to have been published. The original work of Zoroaster is said to have contained 21 *nosks*, (or books,) of which only one entire nosk, conjectured to have been the twentieth, is now extant, and a very few fragments of the others. The greater portion of the Zendavest is a series of liturgic services and prayers for various occasions, and is totally destitute of any literary merit.

"No existing religion, the Jewish excepted, has continued from such remote ages, with so little apparent change in the doctrine or ritual. Different opinions, however, are held regarding the nature of the world. All the laity consider Ormuzd the author of good, and Ahriman the author of evil but many of the priests assert that all things originated in Zerwan or Time, and that Ormuzd was only the first of created beings. They admit, however, that Zerwan has ceased to operate, and that good and evil flow directly from Ormuzd and Ahriman. Ormuzd is all light, purity and excellence, and inhabits the primeval light; Ahriman, all darkness, impurity, and wickedness, and inhabits the primeval darkness. Cayumers, the father of the human race, was created by Ormuzd; but Ahriman attempted to destroy him, and attacked the revolving sphere, but was repulsed and precipitated into hell. The modern Parsees, even the sacerdotal class, know little or nothing about the theory of their own cosmogony, the whole of which, however, is evidently Chaldean, and often forcibly reminds us of Milton's "Paradise Lost." Sin and misery found their way into the world, and continued to increase until Zoroaster promulgated the law, and instructed man in the will of Heaven. The whole Parsee system is founded on the supposition of a continued warfare between good and evil spirits, which pervade all nature, and religion teaches us how to gain the assistance of the first, and to escape from the snares of the last.

"The grand visible objects of Parsee veneration, are the elements, and more especially fire,—light being considered as the best and noblest symbol of the Supreme Being. The sun, moon, planets, stars, and even the firmament, are consequently objects of profound veneration; but they have no temples considered as the residence of the Deity, or of any superior angel; their fire-mansions being merely to preserve the holy element pure and unextinguished. Of the latter, there are two species in Gujerat, the Behram and Aderan; the first composed of 1001 kinds of fire, the last of at least 15 or 16 kinds. These varieties of combustion are procured from different materials, such as the fire from the friction of wood, from a funeral pile, from a kitchen fire, &c. The Behram fire, that most reverenced, is only to be found in their temples, viz., at Udipoor, (a town near Damaun,) at Nausaree, and at Bombay. In their original country, the greatest number of Guebres, or fire-worshippers, are collected in the city of Yezd, situated about 230 miles south-east of Ispahan, where they are said still to occupy about 4,000 houses. They are very industrious, but greatly oppressed by the modern Persian Government, being taxed at 20 piastres a head, besides suffering endless extortions.

"The Parsees have various classes of priests, of whom the chief are the *Destoors,* or expounders of the law; and the next the Molids, who are the officiating priests, and superintend all religious ceremonies; but the last rarely understand the prayers they recite, or the books from which they read. They are, like the Levites, a peculiar tribe, the priesthood being hereditary in their families; but they have no salary or fixed allowances, and no chief-priests, or supreme ecclesiastical head, while many follow secular employments. Neither is the Parsee an exclusive religion; converts, generally children, being admitted; but no Parsee can drink out of the same vessel with a person of another religion, for fear of sharing in his sins and trespasses. The Parsee is one of the few religions that has no fasts, and as to food, all birds and beasts of prey are forbidden, as also the hare and dog. By their own law they may eat beef, but in India they generally abstain. The Parsee females have long maintained an unspotted character for chastity, which may be accounted for, from their being placed by their religious tenets on a level with the men.

" Planting trees is a meritorious work, and they cut down fruit-trees with great reluctance. In Bombay, they never practise as professional gardeners, but Parsee merchants and shop-keepers abound. Others act as servants; many as ship-carpenters and liquor-sellers. They are certainly a most active portion of the population, and retain within a tropical latitude, the fair complexion, hardy constitution, and activity of more northern climates. As the life of a Parsee is a constant warfare with evil demons, in the conducting of which vigilance is indispensable, the watchful animals, such as the cock and the dog, are highly respected.

"Their reverence for the elements prevents their throwing any impurities into fire or water, and to their respect for the latter may be ascribed, in all ages, their aversion to sea-voyages. In like manner, their reverence for fire restrains them from following the trade of a smith; neither do they enlist as Sepoys, pretending that they dare not defile the sacred element by the use of fire-arms. Hence also they never bury their dead, for fear of defiling the earth; but leave the bodies to moulder away, or to be consumed by birds of prey on the towers where they are exposed, guarded by a dog, who is expected to bark when he sees the demons approach to seize the soul, which is supposed to hover round the body for three days and nights, in the vain hope of being reunited. The corpse is also watched by sentinels, to see which eye the vultures pick out first; if the right, it is a good sign, and if in addition the dog takes a piece of bread out of the mouth of the corpse, no doubt remains respecting the beatitude of the deceased. Should any one survive after having been taken to the place of skulls, he is shunned by all as having had intercourse with impure demons, until purified by a priest; but such an event very rarely happens.

"The Parsee being a religion of ceremonies and prayers in an unknown tongue, has scarcely any effect on the morals of its professors, and indeed, little influence of any kind, except as connected with the prejudices of caste. The priests are in general not only disliked, but despised, and little attended to except by the females. Like the Hindoos, the Parsees show some desire to be esteemed by the individuals composing their own peculiar tribe, but have little regard for any extraneous opinions, and appear totally insensible to any remote check of religion. They are bold, active, and persevering in the thirst for gold, and many of their merchants by superior enterprise and address, have accumulated large fortunes. On the other hand, like all Asiatics, they are tyrannical when in power, regardless of truth, and not the less esteemed by their own sect for the want of it. They are luxurious and voluptuous, and frequently generous. Their great expenditure takes place on the marriages of their children, on which occasions, (like the Hindoos,) they waste immense sums in childish show and folly. Their houses of recreation on the island of Bombay, are generally a little distance in the country, and sometimes handsomely furnished after the European fashion, in which mode the disposal of their table-equipage is arranged. Like them also, they indulge freely in luxurious food, and rather exceed them in their potations of wine. But notwithstanding all their faults, the Parsees are certainly the most improveable caste in India; being free from Hindoo and Mohammedan bigotry, and in every respect more resembling genuine Europeans, than any other class of natives at present existing in southern Asia."

It is an error to say that the Parsees have any religious abhorrence to a sea-life; for though they never were a really maritime people, they constantly embark as traders on the most distant and perilous voyages, and are extensively engaged in ship-building and other mercantile transactions connected with the sea.

When their dead are exposed, and sentinels watch to see which eye will be first plucked out, it has been mentioned above what augury is drawn from the attack on the right. Should the luckless sinister orb, however, be the first *bonne bouche* chosen, then the relations mourn the defunct as one eternally damned. The place where corpses are exposed is generally a cylindrical building, placed on a mound, somewhat apart from the town or village. This structure is open at the top, and about fifty-five feet in diameter and twenty-five feet in height, filled up to within five feet of the top, with the exception of a well in the centre, fifteen feet in diameter; the part so filled being terraced with a slight declivity towards the well. Two circular grooves, three inches deep, are raised round the well—at the respective distances of four and ten feet. Grooves of a similar height and depth, and at the outer part of the circle, four feet distant from each other, are carried straight from the wall to the well, communicating with the circular ones, to carry off the water. The tomb by this means is divided into three circles or partitions—the outer for the men, the middle for the women, and the inner for the children. There the bodies are respectively placed, wrapped loosely in a piece of cloth, and left to be devoured by vultures and beasts of prey. This is why the Parsees are forbidden in their ritual all food made from "birds or beasts of prey." Myriads of these disgusting harpies are seen hovering about the charnel-houses of this sect. The tomb-keeper, or the friends of the defunct, in process of time throw the bones into the well in the centre,—the receptacle built for this purpose. From the bottom of the well, subterranean passages lead in different directions, and prevent the cavity from being filled up. Some wealthy men build a charnel-house for themselves, constructed on the above model. I saw one of these gloomy places at Mhow, in Malwâ, and unimpeded, I went all over the place. The corpses were put on iron railings, over a pit, to allow of the bones dropping down when the vultures had finished their revolting carnival. In a room adjoining was the sentinel who watched the eyes of the dead, and in his little chamber, the holy fire eternally burned, and was never extinguished. The whole building was on a mound, surrounded by a wall.

The Parsees possess the chief wealth of Bombay, and own numberless houses, which they let out to rent. Many of the heads of firms and flourishing mercantile houses are wealthy Guebres, and their incomes are very large.

The Parsees were driven from their country by the Mussulmans at the conquest of the kingdom of Persia in the seventh century, when

Yezdegird, the last king of the dynasty of Sassan, was overcome by the Kalif Omar, and forced to take refuge in the mountains of Khorassan,—where, after maintaining himself for some time, he died, A.D. 652, (or year of the Hejira 32,) and in the 21st year of the Yezdegirdian era. His granddaughter became the wife of the Mussulman ruler of Persia, who thus claimed the right of inheritance, as well as that of conquest, over the kingdom of "Irân."

Fire is the chief object of external worship among the Parsees; in each *átsh-khána*, or firehouse,* there are two fires, only one of which the vulgar eye may behold; the other, called "Atsh-Baharam," is kept in the most secret and holy part of the temple, and is only approached by the chief-priest. As it must not be visited by the light of the sun, the chimneys are so constructed as to exclude its rays while carrying off the smoke. Though I regard as an exaggeration the assertion that "one thousand and one fires," of different kinds, are required to compose the Atsh-Baharam, this fire, if once extinguished, can only be replenished by bringing sacred fire from the altar, at Yezd, in a golden censer, by land.

* The native servants call the hearth and mantel-piece, both indifferently, the "âtsh-khâna."

The sun and the sea divide, with fire, the adoration of the Guebres, and I have seen them every morning and evening, muttering their prayers, in a low, murmuring tone, with their faces turned towards the rising or the setting sun,—making profound obeisances to the sea every minute. They are very regular at their devotions, and sometimes the women go in a body to worship at the sea-shore.

The Parsee very seldom marries more than one wife, unless she has no children, and then she invariably gives her consent to his taking unto himself a second spouse. They marry their children when very young, (at five or six years of age,) and the little wife is at once introduced into her juvenile husband's family, and brought up with him. The women are not shut up, like the natives of India; but though I know several gentlemen who have been admitted to interviews with the Parsee ladies of high rank, it is a well-known fact that the Guebres have insensibly imbibed a little of the native prejudice, and prefer keeping their females excluded from all masculine gaze out of their own family.

The superstition of the *dog* introduced into the charnel-house, as related above,—also that of the dying Parsee being required to fix his eyes on a dog, which I have frequently heard mentioned,—have a two-fold source. Some say that the fire-worshippers hold the belief that the dog guards the soul at the moment of its separation from the body; and others assert that the superstitions connected with this animal arise solely from the Parsees having been saved from shipwreck on their emigration to India, by the barking of the dogs announcing their approach to the land on a dark night.

Bombay owes its primary importance to the Portuguese, to whom it was ceded in A.D. 1530. They erected a Fort, on account of the noble harbour, but as the capital of the Portuguese in India was Goa, Bombay was for some time comparatively neglected. There have been two derivations assigned to the name:—one from the Portuguese, *Bom Bahia*, a good bay; and the other from the Hindoo goddess, Bomba Davi.

This island was first ceded to Charles II. in June, 1661, as part of Queen Catherine's portion. In March, 1662, a fleet of five men-of-war, commanded by the Earl of Marlborough, was despatched with five hundred troops, under Sir Abraham Shipman, and arrived in Bombay in September, 1662, to take possession; but as the English Admiral demanded "Bombay and its dependencies,"

(Salsette and Tanna,) the Portuguese evaded the cession, on the plea that only Bombay could be claimed. Two years afterwards the British were glad to accept Bombay on any terms, as the island (Anjediva) to which the troops had been removed, was so deadly in climate that four-fifths of them had been swept away. Mr. Cooke, who may be considered the first Governor of Bombay, was the only surviving commander when that town was thus inauspiciously taken possession of, and though so gloomy a beginning offered but little promise of future prosperity, the "desert" soon rose into a thriving and populous settlement, in the hands of the British. In March, 1668, by letters patent, the king of England transferred the island of Bombay from the crown to the East India Company, on the guaranteed payment of £10 in gold (as annual rent) on the 30th of September, each year! So unprofitable at the time was deemed the royal acquisition!

Shortly after this cession, the revenue of the island was estimated at £2,823 sterling—a much more considerable sum in those days than in our own time. However, the whole island continued very insalubrious, and in 1691-2, it was ravaged by the plague. In 1708, such was the continued weakness of the settlement, that the Bombay Government considered it politically requisite to decline receiving an envoy from the King of Persia, for fear he should observe this weakness both by sea and land. In this year the rival East India Companies united, and Bombay gradually rose in importance and power. In 1813, the annual revenue of the Presidency amounted to 6,420,569 rupees; in 1824, to 16,206,900 rupees. I mention this to exhibit the gradual increase; but as the statistics of after years are so well known, I will not add any further remarks on the subject.

Salt is an extensive article of commerce at Bombay, and I saw the mode of collecting it by evaporation, all throughout the island, especially near Sion.* The sea was let in through sluices into vast fields, whence its egress was prevented by low embankments. As the briny waters evaporated, the salt lay thickly at the bottom, and was taken up and stored in great

* Sion is a small town and fort on the island of Bombay, about ten miles from the Presidency, at the opposite extremity of the island. It stands on the top of a small conical hill, where it commands the passage from Bombay to Salsette, and was of importance when the Mahrattas possessed the latter. At the foot of the little hill of Sion is the vellard built across a small arm of the sea, which separated the two islands. This arm of the sea was first bridged over in 1805, at an expense of 50,575 rupees.

pyramids, bricked over to preserve them from the chances of climate. I observed the same process at the island of Santa Maura, (one of the Ionian group,) where I saw on the sea-shore at least a dozen salt-heaps, each perhaps one hundred feet in circumference. There the salt forms a most profitable article of revenue, and I have no doubt the Bombay Government find it equally lucrative.

I will now resume my journal, which I have so long deserted, and it will conduct the reader to the Bombay sanatarium of Mahablèshwur, and the mountains of Malabar in the Madras Presidency. On my return from the latter, I visited Bassein and Tannah; and a cursory account of each will be found in the sequel.

MAHABLESHWUR. (Hills.)

(Elevation above the Level of the Sea, about 4,500 Feet.)

Distance by Marh, about a hundred miles by water, and thirty miles by land.

23rd March, 1852. *Tuesday.*—I arrived here this morning after a very trying transit both by sea and by land. I only took a small quantity of luggage and my horse "Goolâb." Six servants accompanied me. We all went on board at sunset on Sunday, but the tide having gone out, and the wind being completely lulled, we did not leave the harbour till midnight. I left my tents standing on the Esplanade and three servants in charge: the rest of my large Camp I paid up and discharged previous to leaving Bombay. All my horses I also disposed of, merely retaining Goolâb till my passage should be secured by one of the "Overland" steamers.

I begin to think it a beautiful and effective *ruse* to have got out of that hot Bombay, and thus to have escaped from all my overpowering business, which appeared daily to increase instead of diminish. Some kind friends have promised to clear off all arrears of work for me, and to take my passage, &c., during my projected absence of a week, so I have avoided no end of trouble. The "kind friends," in question, are to be pitied, however.

But to return to my journey.

I commenced by saying, we left the harbour at midnight on Sunday, in a Bunder-boat,—my little nag also on board. We all embarked from the Boree-Bunder, the only ghât practicable for horses. The tide was so low that when I arrived at the water's edge, I found my boat was anchored at some distance, and I had to go out to her in a dinghie.

When the morning of Monday broke, I found we were off Colaba, a fort about an eighth of the distance (by water).

We reached Bancoot, which is a port at the entrance of the Marh river, at two o'clock, p.m., having accomplished the long voyage between Colaba and Bancoot in eight hours. A very high wind blew in our favour the whole day, and every soul on board (excepting the boatmen, of course,) suffered much from sea-sickness. I could not stand the effects of the violent motion in the cabin, so I remained on the upper deck both night and day. The dews at night were heavy, and I felt very ill, in spite of the curtains I erected by means of poles to save myself from sun by day and dew by night. The coast was perhaps pretty, perhaps ugly,—I was far too miserable to take note of aught.

The sea ran so high when we were turning into the direction of the Marh river, that the waves nearly swamped our boat, and I was obliged to go below at last. The foam wet me through even in the cabin, and I must allow I felt rather anxious about our safety.

The river once gained, there was no more sea-sickness on board, but our progress was slow in proportion to the loss of the propelling wind. After going some four miles, the men were obliged to take the sails down, and ply their oars. We did not reach Marh, the terminus of the voyage, till two o'clock, a.m., on Tuesday (yesterday). The distance from Bancoot to Marh, by water, is eighteen coss, or thirty-six miles.

The breadth of this river seldom averages more than a hundred yards, (after fairly leaving the sea,) and the hilly, wooded banks are very picturesque. The distance from Bancoot to Marh, as the crow flies, is not ten miles, but the river winds in a most tantalizing manner. At Marh there is a staging Bungalow; and ponies, bullocks, and carts;

also Coolies and *humáls*, (*kuhárs* or bearers,) are ready at a moment's notice. The fixed rates of hire are as follows :—

From Marh to Mahablèshwur.

	Rupees.	Annas.	
Ponies for lading	1	4	each.
Bullocks, ditto.	1	0	,,
Carts, as far as Kunéisur, the foot of the Ghât	2	0	,,
Coolies, to Mahablèshwur, from the foot of the Ghât,	0	5	,,
Humâls, ditto,	0	6	,,
Coolies, from Marh to Mahablèshwur, the whole way	0	10	,,
Humâls, ditto.	0	12	,,

A phaeton, drawn by two horses, can be hired from Marh to Kunéisur, where palanquins and riding ponies are kept by the same Parsee who runs the phaetons, that convey the traveller to Mahablèshwur from Kunéisur;—a palanquin, for seven or eight rupees; a pony, two rupees, for the twelve miles. The phaeton costs the same for one or two passengers, from Marh to Kunéisur. There is a land-route from Marh to Bombay, *viâ* Nagotna; but as I mean to return that way, I shall defer all notice of it at present, beyond remarking that the phaetons run on to Nagotna from Marh, and that the cost of one or two seats for the entire distance from Nagotna to Kunéisur, is alike forty-two rupees. I preferred riding my own horse the whole way to this mode of travelling, so I cannot pass any opinion on it.

The first (staging) Bungalow on the road, is Polâdpoor, also called Kolâkpore, twelve miles from Mhar or Marh. The next is Kunéisur, six miles further. At this Bungalow I passed the whole of yesterday, as my baggage had not come up. My stupid servants had sent it on bullocks, and those animals are slow beyond conception. I exchanged them for ponies at Kunéisur, and sending these on about sunset, waited myself till eight o'clock, p.m., in order to dine before starting, as it was already so late. The road is a made one, and very good all the way. There are many short ascents and descents even during the first eighteen miles; but I rode it on one horse, very easily in two hours or less. The last twelve miles consist principally of two steep ascents, divided by a similar descent.

I was told that I should find it too steep to ride! I not only rode the whole way, but the greater part of the distance by night, when heavy clouds made the thick darkness visible. The road is not half so steep as the last three miles from Syree to Simla,—far better made, and broader by four or five feet, at the lowest average.

The hills rose higher and bolder as we ascended the Ghât, and the air became very cold. As I was alone, I kept near my servants, and we went so slowly, that repeatedly I fell asleep, and nearly dropped off my horse. At last, about one o'clock in the morning, I halted on the road,—stopped the pony carrying my bed, and entering an empty hut, made myself comfortable for the few remaining hours of the night, sending on nearly all the servants and baggage. I rode up this morning, and can testify to the beauty of the hills and of the richly wooded landscape. Having seen, however, scenery so much more grand and magnificent, I was not struck by the extreme beauty of the Mahablèshwur Hills as powerfully as others have been who have never beheld the more wondrous loveliness and grandeur of the lofty Himalaya and its peerless Snowy Heights.

Through the kindness of Mr. S——, of Bombay, I am fortunate enough to have a very good house here, during my short stay. The compound surrounding it is so large, and so well wooded, that I feel delightfully sequestered. The air is deliciously cold, the morning mists have all cleared away, and the sun shines brightly now. The station is four miles at least from Mahableshwur (Proper), the village whence it derives its name, where there are Hindoo temples, and a famed spot for pilgrims of that religion. The elevation of Mahableshwur is 4,500 feet above the level of the sea, being lower than Simla by nearly 3,000 feet. On a clear day, the ocean and the river of Marh can be seen with the naked eye from certain points in and near the station, and vessels may be distinguished sailing to and fro. There is a spot, called "Elphinstone Point," which commands a very extensive view of the sea, river, and surrounding hills. There is a church here, and the houses are numerous, covering a large extent of hill. Good made-roads intersect the station and its vicinity.

26th March, 1852. *Friday.*—I leave the Hills to-morrow;—but before I go, I must add a few words descriptive of Mahableshwur, as I shall not have another spare moment for days, most probably. I applied for the phaeton to Nagotna, for the whole or even part of the way, as poor "Goolâb" will never carry me seventy-two miles on end at my favourite pace;—but Lord Falkland and others have pre-engaged all the vehicles, so that I cannot procure one for the next three or four days. As I cannot delay, I must manage the best way I can without it.

I went to see Mahablèshwur, which is a small village, about four miles from the European station. A good made road leads to it,—and two miles further on, to "Elphinstone Point," where there is a Bungalow built for the convenience of visitors. There are two temples at Mahablèshwur, —one called Krishna, and the other has the honour of christening the village. The former contains the spring, reputed as the birth-place of the river Krishna, which flows through a narrow valley, flanked by perpendicular hills, a thousand feet below. The water is made to issue out of the mouth of a stone deity, (the spring being invisible,) and falls into a reservoir beneath. It must have an underground passage, for it issues forth some distance below, from a third temple, out of the mouth of another deity, and falls into a basin similar to the first. It re-issues, after a further subterranean passage, at the side of the hill,—the abrupt precipice forming this side, being close to the third temple. At present there is not much water in it.

I visited Elphinstone Point yesterday evening, so poor "Goolâb," what with the morning and evening work, had to carry me some thirty miles. The "Point" commands a truly magnificent view: —the ocean is quite visible, and the river of Marh is seen meandering through the valley. The little port-town of Marh appears absurdly close, and yet to reach it from this spot, thirty-six miles must be traversed. It does not seem above six or seven as the crow flies.

This Point is on the brink of a very abrupt precipice, with nothing to break the dizzy height;—I felt quite giddy when I looked down. The ground below is all rock and precipice, and the perpendicular khuds, together with the generally impracticable nature of the ground, make all idea of a direct road to Marh mythical, and most hopeless. I was fortunate in getting a clear view, as during the greater part of the day, thick mists obscured the atmosphere, and rendered it impossible to see ten yards' distance. I observed a tiger-trap laid between Mahablèshwur village and "Elphinstone Point." A pleasant reminder, truly, as evening came on! Almost immediately afterwards, I saw an animal moving through a thicket within twenty yards of me, but the dense foliage prevented my distinguishing its species. I drew up my horse on his haunches in the midst of a sharp canter, and hesitated for a moment, as I made sure it must be a tiger. But *only* for a moment. The next instant I cantered on; for, tiger or no tiger, if I wished to see the "view" I had heard so much of, this was my only chance. As I really believed I had seen a tiger—the trap proving that they haunted the neighbourhood—I think I showed some courage in going on, all alone as I was. So this quality must be inherent, or acquired, even in the gentler sex!

Yesterday morning I visited a tank below the Station hill, which the natives told me was called "Yenna," or some such name; and I went a little distance down a road in that direction, called the Bâee road. There is also a very good route to Sattâra, which station is fifteen coss distant. It is possible to reach the Neilgherries by a land-route from Sattâra, but the sea-route from Bankoot to Calicut, and thence by land to the Neilgherries, is by far the best and shortest. If I cannot secure a cabin next month as far as Suez, I shall take a trip to those hills before the May steamer starts, as I believe they are very well worth visiting.

The soil of the Mahablèshwur hills—stone, rocks, and earth—is all red; and the made roads look very pretty, resembling our English parks, where the paths are purposely covered with red gravel. The very *metalling* of these hills is all of red stone, pounded and powdered.

There has been a great deal of rain since yesterday evening. The mists became so dense long before I could get home, that I was very nearly lost in them. I could not see an inch before me, though it was not long after sunset, and in turning a corner I was within an ace of falling over a precipice. It began shortly after to rain heavily, and did not clear up till nine o'clock this morning. It is deliciously cold and fresh now, and the sun is shining joyously. The air feels so soft and balmy, though cold, that I think regretfully of my sojourn in this place being so near an end, and look forward to the humid heat below with absolute horror. All the people drive about here in carriages, which are brought up by Coolies from Kunéisir.

No wonder that the roads are so numerous and good all throughout these hills. The red rocks and soil are very easily managed;—whereas in the Himalaya, the impracticable rocks prove a formidable impediment, as they would have to be laboriously and expensively blasted for miles together. Were Elphinstone Point in the Simla district, I do not doubt that a road would long ere this have been made far more direct to Marh. If the Bombay-ites had only visited Kanâwr, they would see *what* can be done in the way of road-making through *real* " mountains:"—the solid rock blasted for miles, and the road built up frequently with an elaborate labour quite incredible to those who have not had ocular demonstration of the fact.

There is a made road hence to Poonah, which is some sixty miles distant. A great difference exists between the British Himalayas and these hills, with regard to the mode of agriculture. In the former, the luxuriant fields of cultivation are disposed in terraces regularly cut along the slopes of the mountains, with beautiful regularity and care. But here, the little cultivation visible is desultory and irregular, and the verdant terraces of the north are completely unknown.

I remember, some two years ago, meeting an officer in the Queen's 15th Regiment of Foot, who had come up to see his brother at Simla. This gentleman entirely upset my gravity, by showing me some sapient remarks recorded in his diary, regarding the phenomena presented in the mountains he was visiting, of myriads of "*natural terraces!*" I asked him, gravely and inquiringly, if he had also made a note regarding the cultivation being as spontaneous as the terraces were "natural," and assured him that the fields of wheat and barley he saw, were all the wild produce of beneficent Mother Nature. (He believed me implicitly, and doubtless, subsequently made use of my valuable suggestion!)

BOMBAY.

Distance from Nagotna, by land seventy-two miles, and by water about thirty-six.

12th April, 1852. *Monday.*—I left Mahablèshwur on Saturday afternoon, the 27th ult., at two o'clock, p.m. Illness has prevented my attempting to chronicle my journey before, as I have been an unwilling and helpless prisoner for days to a sick bed. I have lost my passage Home too, and my thoughts are now fixed upon my cherished visit to the Blue Mountains of Malabar,—deferred but not forgotten. To return to my trip from Mahablèshwur to Bombay, of which I have not as yet said anything.

Having failed in obtaining a seat in the phaeton which runs to Nagotna, owing to the concourse of visitors rushing up at the time of my departure, I mounted my own gallant steed Goolâb,* and cantered down the Ghât as fast as I could. In the steepest parts, of course, I was obliged to slacken my

* Which I should have before informed my readers is a Kashmir pony, thirteen hands high.

speed, but I reached Polâdpore in two hours' time. The rapid pace and the great heat combined, had exhausted both steed and rider, so I went up to the Dâk-Bungalow to rest in the shade for half an hour. I was feverishly thirsty, but all I could get in this Goth-ish place, was a very tepid questionable-looking fluid the Khidmutgar persisted in calling "water," and which I was forced to imbibe in inordinate quantities to quench my raging thirst.

After leaving the Bungalow, I cantered to within two miles of Marh, when "Goolâb" most unconditionally gave in, and my utmost persuasion could not coax him out of a walk. A thirty miles' ride in the sun is not very pleasant at any season of the year on *one* pony, but at the end of March in this killing climate, it was most annihilating work, and on my arrival at Marh, I threw myself on the bed in the only unoccupied apartment of the Dâk Bungalow, utterly worn out. My cough became so distressing, and my pulse beat so feverishly, that I felt I could ride no more that night. No phaeton was to be procured, and as I wished to reach Bombay in time to sail per "Achilles," I was forced to hire a wretched conveyance from the Messman, in which I could travel in a recumbent position. This conveyance had *no* springs, and Heaven forefend that I should be condemned again to endure the purgatory of that miserable night! Sleep was quite a myth, and before the day broke, I became so very desperate, that I called for my horse, determined to ride till I dropped, rather than remain in this conveyance worthy of the days of Noah. But my pony was nowhere in sight, so I lay down once more in despair. About eight o'clock (on the morning of the 28th,) we reached Indapore, a Dâk Bungalow twenty-four miles from Marh, and eighteen from Nagotna. It is situated on an eminence a hundred paces to the left of the road. Here I remained till two o'clock, p.m., in the vain hopes of some better conveyance arriving. But my evil stars continuing adverse, I mounted Goolâb at last, and rode to Nagotna, in a desperate frame of mind, cross and ill. Goolâb went at a moderate trot the whole way, but if I attempted to urge him faster, he drew resolutely up, and mutely declined to go. So I took the hint, remembering the adage, "Quand on n'a pas ce qu'on aime, il faut aimer ce qu'on a !"

I reached Nagotna at five o'clock, p.m., and found my baggage and servants had arrived. A gentleman in the Bungalow sent me two bottles of iced soda-water, like the prince of Samaritans, seeing me arrive wearied and hot. I shall remember him in my prayers, for his timely aid, though I do not even know his name.

We embarked at sunset in a Bunder-boat, which had been sent for me from Bombay, and I hoped my troubles were now at an end. The place of embarkation at Nagotna is a mere Nullah, which by the ebbing of the tide, is left for miles too shallow to be navigated. We had only gone some six miles, when the same cause detained us for hours in the said arm of the sea. At seven o'clock, a.m., we were off "Kurza Bunder,"—Bombay in sight—and I began to look forward to a breakfast on shore. Vain hope! We knocked about the mouth of the harbour till *midnight*. The boat's crew were intoxicated, (apparently,) and behaved in so singular a manner, that I became seriously alarmed, and requested to be put on shore at Kurza Bunder. I might have addressed myself with equal chance of success to the unruly winds of heaven! The crew preferred the stormy passage from Kurza to the sandy, desolate shore opposite— backwards and forwards through the livelong hours of day and night, and with all sails set, this same tempestuous passage was made over and over again. They could not, or they would not, enter the harbour. The terrible sea sickness, which overpowered me, forced me to remain on the poop, and more dead than alive, I braved the sun and dew alike, terrified and ill. One of the boatmen, who was evidently under the potent influence of *B'hang*, or some such intoxicating drug, became more and more frantic in his gestures and language as the evening came on, and about 9 o'clock I and many others in the boat very nearly met with a watery grave. The wind was raging more tempestuously than ever—the wild waves threatened each moment to engulph our helpless bark, and still we tossed about the stormy mouth of the harbour, from point to point, as if our boat were possessed by the Foul Fiend himself, or the unquiet wraith of the Flying Dutchman. Each moment I thought would be our last, and distracted by seasickness, wet to the skin by the breakers, which scattered their briny foam on my unsheltered cot, I gave way at length to the feelings of despair and misery which overpowered me, and with passionate tears, frantically entreated the boatmen to land me *anywhere*—rather than pretend to be reaching Bombay, when for seventeen hours we had continued to perform the same stormy passage, inability or unwillingness rendering our entrance into the harbour an apparent impossibility. I addressed the Tindal, or head of the boatmen; but the intoxicated individual I have alluded to above, rushing across the deck, and jumping up the ladder leading to the tiny poop, (which was more than half occupied by the bed on which I was at the moment seated,) harangued and gesticulated with insane vehemence, shaking his great black fists in my face, and madly endeavouring to precipitate me into the surging waters of the angry sea,—only restrained by the combined efforts of my terrified servants, who prevented his getting on the poop. In the small space, so confined and circumscribed, in which the wrestling took place between this wretch and my servants, there was momentary danger of one or other being upset. My slight couch reeled with the stormy wind, and one of my people was obliged to sit by it, for fear of its being tilted over by the combatants, even if the tempest spared the fragile structure. I shall never forget that dreadful night:—a crew of intoxicated and infuriated natives, one of whom appeared ready to proceed to all extremities—a desperate storm raging round us, the black and foaming waters of the "Great Deep" looking doubly terrible in the uncertain and flickering light of a shadowed moon—her radiance dimmed and darkened by heavy, portentous clouds, which only foretold further miseries for our hapless boat, if it remained exposed to the gathering blasts much longer. How we at last reached Bombay, I hardly know, for the rest of my "durance vile" was passed in a fortunate state of insensibility to all things mundane. Overcome with terror and illness, I looked as one "who sleeps the sleep that knows no waking," and perhaps, this awed my bacchanalian crew into sobriety and comparative decency;—at all events, my servants informed me, that after coming up to my couch and gazing with alarm on my pallid and senseless features, so ghastly in the dim moonlight, they made every exertion at last to reach the Bunder, which was easily attained after four hours' proper navigation.

The following day I took care to report the whole matter to the proper authorities, having first, on arrival at the Boree Bunder, taken the timely precaution of handing over to the European in charge of the Ghât, all my refractory crew. I am happy to be able to add, for the credit of justice administered, that the wretched men received the utmost limit of chastisement permitted by law.

The route to Marh I described in my former journey:—from Marh to Nagotna was new ground. There is an excellent *made* road, though not quite level, which passes inland, losing sight of the sea almost at once.

The Bungalow I mentioned at Indagurh is the only staging-house *en chemin*. Between Mahablèshwur and the first Bungalow at Parrgâon, six miles, I observed, as I rode down, a Fort, on a rock to the right hand, which escaped my notice during my nocturnal ascent. I was riding alone, and saw no one who could enlighten my ignorance as to its origin or present use.

17th April, 1852. *Saturday*.—The climate of Bombay has so seriously affected my health, that I feel it is absolutely necessary to try change of air, before I attempt the hot discomforts of the Overland Journey to England in this trying weather. I have resolved therefore to leave Bombay to-morrow, in the English ship "Ursula," as the Captain thereof has promised to land me at Calicut, on the Malabar coast, that I may take a run up to the Neilgherries, and be back at Calicut in time for the last "coasting steamer" of the season, on its return to Bombay, as no vessels ply on the coast of Malabar after the monsoon has once burst. The journey by *land* from Malabar to Bombay would be too trying for an invalid at this season of the year. My cough continues most harassing, and is wearing me to a shadow. I have also a return of the former anomalous and distressing sensations in the brain, and I languish to return to a more genial climate. *Pour comble de malheur*, I learn by letters from the Punjâb, that the weather in that part of the world is even *un*-seasonably cool and pleasant, so that I might have been enjoying it all this time, instead of grilling here, since my voyage to England has been thus unavoidably postponed beyond my original calculations.

CALICUT. (On the Malabar Coast.)

Distance, about six hundred miles from Bombay.

24th April, 1852. *Saturday.*—Arrived here this morning, after a passage of five days and ten hours, per "Ursula," from Bombay. We had adverse or light winds a great part of the time, otherwise we should have been here two days ago. The "Ursula" is a fast-sailing ship, and distanced one or two others which left the harbour of Bombay several hours before we did. I found the heat very great on board—the thermometer steadily rising as we approached this latitude, which is easily accounted for, as we are considerably nearer the equator here than at Bombay.*

Calicut consists of a small station, and a large native town, entirely in the Madras style—all heat and cocoa-nut trees. The natives are a fine-looking race, as far as size and stalwart make are concerned, but *beauty* is wofully at a premium in either sex. The men wear a most eccentric head-gear, in the shape of a straight hat fitting close to the head, and rising from the forehead to a couple of inches higher than the crown, surmounted by a regular umbrella—the whole concern made of a sort of leaf-matting, in one piece, secured by strings tied under the chin. The Coolies, shop-keepers, bearers, all adorn themselves with this funny hat,—and on consideration, I cannot help admiring the sense which prompted so useful an appendage—useful alike when the sun shines or the rain falls—a " march of intellect" rarely to be equalled in this land of heathens.

The harbour of Calicut is an open road-stead, with a slight surf near the beach, on account of which the boats are all small and flat-bottomed. As soon as I reached the shore, a *tonjon* and eight bearers met me, and brought me to this Dâk-Bungalow. The

* The town of Calicut is in latitude 11° 15′ North, and longitude 75° 50′ East.

thermometer stands now (noon) at 98°!—I need make no further comment on the heat. The province of Calicut is a sub-division of the Malabar province, extending along the sea-coast between the parallels of 10° and 12° N. lat. It is one of the principal countries of that extraordinary Hindoo race, the Nairs. The former Calicut Râjahs were of this tribe, and the distinctive and honourable appellation of the "Tamoori Râjah" was bestowed on the sovereign by the natives. The ladies of this tribe were called Tambooretties, the male sex having a prescriptive right to the appellation of Tamboorans. The fair sex of the most exalted, as well as the lower ranks, had most extraordinary customs regarding marriage—unprecedented indeed! They married, but it was deemed scandalously improper if they lived with their *soi-disant* husbands, whom indeed they were never permitted to see alone. They always resided in their brothers' houses, and the fathers of their children were studiously selected from the Brahmins (or Nambouries, as they are there called). The Râjah was chosen according to seniority in the *female* line, and was regularly crowned. He aspired to higher rank than any of his progenitors, the sacred Brahmins, and was held inferior only to the invisible gods themselves.

These pretensions, though fully admitted by his subjects, were repudiated, however, by the Brahmins. The pride of this race of royal scions was very great; the Râjah was always called "the Zamorin" by the British. In 1767, when Hyder Ali invaded Malabar, the Cochin Râjah quietly submitted to pay the required tribute; the Zamorin, however, did not follow the servile example of the neighbouring prince, but proudly and unconditionally declined all submission, and, after an unavailing resistance, he was made prisoner. Even in this extremity his spirit did not succumb. Determined to die rather than submit, he set fire to the house in which he was confined, and perished in the conflagration. Several of his personal suite, who had been accidentally excluded when he shut the door, subsequently threw themselves into the flames, and perished with their proud and honoured master.

The province of Malabar extends along the western coast of India. Its former limits were from Cape Comorin to the river Chandraghiri, in latitude 12° 30' North. When the term "Malabar" is applied to the whole tract of country from Bombay to the southern extremity, it is erroneous though very common: the other modern subdivisions are Cochin and Travancore. Malabar lies immediately below the Western Ghâts, and the sea is almost everywhere in sight. The country is low, but broken, and much intersected with extensive ravines, rivers and back-waters; the whole extent is densely shaded with forest and jungle. The uplands are comparatively barren, and the greatest part of the population resides on the margins of the streams and in the deep ravines. The low country is excessively hot, and the vapours and exhalations are very dense. A prodigious quantity of this ærial moisture accumulates, and remains night and day in a floating state, sometimes ascending to the mountains—but being checked by the cold in those high lands—descending again immediately. This continues till the setting in of the monsoon, when the whole is condensed into rain, of which some falls on the low country, some on the mountains, and what remains is blown across Mysore, over the Seringapatam valley.

Rice is widely cultivated throughout Malabar, and valuable timber is obtained, especially in the uplands of the province. In the low country, bamboo and cocoa-nut trees overrun the district, and are very profitable. Pepper and the fruit of the jack-tree form the remaining staple produce of the province.

The dress of the women is remarkably scanty, even for Orientals, and their beautiful figures are displayed more than in any other part of Hindostan. They simply wear a petticoat, very scant and thin, or a *dhotie*,* such as the Hindoos use in the sister-presidency. The upper part of the figure is generally quite unadorned—perhaps like the fair "Lavinia"—their beauty is, "when unadorned, adorned the most!"

Occasionally a transparent muslin scarf of spotless purity is thrown over the back of the head, but in no way concealing the perfectly symmetrical form. And I must say it *is* symmetry itself, for more grace and beauty I never before beheld;—the nymphs seemed so modest withal, so unconscious of the unusual nudity of their persons, that I called one or two to my room and had a long conversation with them through an interpreter. Very few of the Malabar peasants can speak the Hindee or Oordoo I am accustomed to—the Malabar tongue is totally different.

The Mohammedan inhabitants of the province are called Moplahs, and among them is a set of

* A long piece of muslin, about a yard and a quarter broad, so ingeniously wound round the lower part of the figure as to form flowing trousers, leaving the legs bare from the knee downwards.

fierce, bloody-thirsty, bigoted ruffians, who have rebelled repeatedly against the British power, and have given considerable trouble to the government.

Wild elephants are very numerous in the jungles of Malabar. Not long ago, a lady and gentleman were travelling in palanquins, carried by sixteen men each, along the very route I am taking, when the conveyances were suddenly put down on the road, and the two-and-thirty brave carriers took to instant flight, uttering wild cries of "The elephants! the elephants!" The lady was asleep and never heard anything, but the gallant escort jumping out of his palky, hurried to the fair sleeper and dragged her out of the conveyance, before she understood the meaning of his frantic and unceremonious haste. They had just time to rush wildly down a slight declivity and hide themselves in the underwood, when the gigantic monster came up to the deserted vehicles, and imagining them to be still tenanted, first trampled them to atoms and then contemptuously scattered the *débris*, leaving the luckless travellers to reach Ootacamund the best way they could. An awful and mysterious silence has been preserved regarding the *names* of this pair, and under frightful penalties has my silence been purchased! so as I am dying to reveal the secret, I had better go on to some other subject.

But first let me mention the predicted horrors in store for me in the Arricode wilderness. This very elephant is said to be prowling *yet* along the road, being an outcast from his brethren—outlawed for his horrid ferocity even among the ferocious. Report saith that this fiend is ready to waylay any passengers, and only awaiteth his opportunity. He was tracked two days ago by a keen sportsman, (one Mr. Rowland Hunt,) up a water-course to the foot of a rugged Height, far beyond the usual range of the "elephant-jungle," and his track was distinctly marked for miles on miles along the very road I am to ride. But I am resolved to brave all this; though verily I have no reason to be partial to any of the elephant tribe, even tame ones. It is a well known fact that very frequently elephants become *must'h** even in a tame state, and they then become most unmanageable. Occasionally they get loose and range the jungles, carrying death and destruction everywhere, destroying men and animals with equal ferocity, tearing up huge ancestral trees in the vast forests—their own comrades of the jungle fearing and repelling their approach. There was a very famous elephant of this sort last year (or the year before) in the Dehra Dhoon,

* Mad, ungovernable.

known by a heavy iron chain being still fastened to his great ankles.

But even before they become as bad as this, they have very frequently wild and unmanageable fits even in their tamest state. I have already observed that I had no reason to feel fearless with regard to these animals in any way;—the fact is, one of this genus very nearly terminated my sublunary career about three years ago. I was mounted on an elephant, sent by the Râjah of Nâhun,* as a particular mark of respect. [The sequel would almost suggest that he had been bribed to attempt my life, which he slyly effected under the cloak of especial honour paid.] This *Hât'hie*† was an incarnation of Satan, and after various

* Nâhun was formerly the capital of the principality of Sirmoor. It is a fine open town, situated in a level spot of table-land, on the summit of a lofty hill, which forms part of the north-western boundary of the Kyârdar Dhoon. The elevation of Nâhun is 3,207 feet above the level of the sea, and in winter, snow lies there two and three inches deep. A magnificent view is commanded from the top of a neighbouring peak of the extensive plains beyond Sirhind and Sehârunpore;—the latter is between forty and fifty miles, N. by W., distant from Nâhun. The view to the north is bounded by the Snowy Mountains—the icy peaks of the lofty and distant Range of eternal snows so white and glittering in the far horizon.

† Hât'hie means a male-elephant; the feminine is *Hât'hnie*.

playful pranks at the very outset of the march, incontinently left the road at the second mile, and careered away in the direction of the Kyârda Dhoon, a wilderness of forest-trees. The Mahoūt had no power over the unwieldy brute, and vainly dug deep into his head the sharp-pointed iron instrument, the only weapon used to guide these monstrous animals. Faster and faster we went, while terror tied my lips,—which was more than could be said of my native Abigail, who was seated beside me, or of the driver perched on the neck of the runaway demon. *Belle Diâne!* how they wept and screamed, as if tears or yells could avail; and if death *must* come, how much better to meet it with a calm and undaunted front! However, in the emergency, I spared my lectures, and contented myself with despising the timidity displayed. Faster and faster we went! I was forced to hold on, "like grim Death," or the rapid motion would have swept me from the padded cushion* on which I was perched. We came at length to a Nullah, or dry ravine, with abrupt and precipitous sides. Methought, "this *must* stop our mad career." But no; not a bit of it; my sable Abigail rolled off, like a bundle of clothes, just as we reached the bottom of the Nullah, in a

* Called a "Guddee."

most cozy manner; and her forced exit was followed by that of all my effects, such as pillows, parcels, &c. I had hardly time to remark her release before we were up the other side of the ravine, and " away, away to the Kyârda Dhoon."*
Now, I will allow that the said valley is most rich in wooded beauty, greatly to be admired by all lovers of the picturesque:—but place the most devoted of the genus in my helpless position, and, believe me, he would not have had much leisure to gaze on the " wooded beauty," except to utter rapid anathemas on the said beautiful trees, the pride of the forest. As we approached, I figured to myself death in all its horrors;—my limbs

* A valley not far from Nâhun; it takes its name from an old *ghurry*, or fortified post, fifteen or twenty miles south-east of Nâhun, in lat. 30° 28′ N.; and lon. 77° 30′ E. The valley lies between the town of Nâhun and the river Jumna. The jungle is so dense, that in the rainy season, in order to escape the pestilential exhalations and miasma, the inhabitants of the valley used to make annual migrations; and the marshy soil was so luxuriant that, during their absence, long rank grass and thick underwood had sprung up, and obliterated all traces of their labours. This valley was formerly in possession of the Ghōōrkhas, who were expelled by the British forces. In former times this Dhoon was well-peopled and well-cultivated, according to ancient accounts; and its subsequent insalubrity may be attributed to the rapid over-growth of jungle from neglect.

torn asunder by the spreading trees, or hanging, like Absalom, by my long hair, the cherished pride of my youth! The Mahoūt meantime was equally alive to the perils of his position, and to my horror, I observed him preparing (in the midst of his baby-tears,) to slip off the trunk of the elephant, and leave me to my fate. For the first time since the commencement of our dangerous elephantine-gallop, I opened my lips in remonstrance and wrath, eloquently representing my helpless position:—even in the event of the elephant coming to his senses, how could I guide him back to the road? The gallant Oriental youth was ready with a philosophical reply to my earnest remonstrances, far from satisfactory to me at the time. "Ap ke jân ghéa," said he, "owr méra jân keōōnh nōōkhsân kurrengé?"* and he was gone, and I was left alone in my helplessness! My favourite dog was with me, and I resolved to save the life of my pet, if mine were really to be so sacrificed; so I looked out deliberately for a favourable spot, and threw my faithful little companion as softly down as our rapid motion allowed. I felt a pang when I saw the poor creature remain motionless as long as I could see it, but the ex-

* Or Anglicé; "Your honour's life *is gone,* and why should I sacrifice mine?"

treme danger of my own position soon recalled my thoughts to more selfish considerations, and I shuddered to contemplate my own certain doom, if I remained on the elephant much longer. A few minutes, and we should have entered that dense jungle, now so terribly near, where I knew a fearful death awaited me—to be, perchance, torn limb from limb, and trampled to death at last by the infuriate beast, so wildly careering on to my destruction.

> "We near'd the wild wood—'twas so wide,
> I saw no bounds on either side;
> 'Twas studded close with sturdy trees,
> That bent not to the roughest breeze."

A few seconds, and it would be too late to choose my fate! With desperate resolution, but unwavering presence of mind, I jumped from my elevated seat to the ground, just before we reached the fatal forest. How I managed it, I cannot well explain, but fortunately I never lost my presence of mind; for, I remember, that just as I was about to take the terrible leap, on observing that my foot had caught in a loop of the rope-gear, I very calmly disentangled it with one hand, while I held on with the other. Had I been flurried, and jumped when my foot was thus held captive, most dreadful would have been my end, as I must have been dragged along the ground *head-foremost*, my foot being imprisoned above, and thus have met a cruel and agonizing death. As it was, I reached the ground in safety, and though the shock of the fall from so great a height, stunned me for two or three hours, a merciful Providence spared me from any fracture of limbs, or dangerous contusions. I suffered a week's fever;—but the recreant Mahoūt was, by order of the Rájah, imprisoned for *a year* in the Nâhun jail, and he was, moreover, mulcted of a year's arrears of wages, and received five-and-twenty lashes before going into the dungeon. The elephant was not found for several days, and then he was in a very wild and unapproachable state;—so the natives informed me.

Four o'clock, p.m. Same day.—I have been in despair about my projected trip to the Neilgherries, finding it very hopeless getting a dâk laid by *any* route under four or five days' time. Every person who comes to Calicut in the wild expectation of escaping at once to a more genial climate, labours under a delusion from which he will only too soon awake, when actually here. There are two roads to Ootacamund from Calicut; one *viâ* Pâlghât and Coimbatoor,* the other, by Arricode

* The route from Calicut to Ootacamund, by the above, is as follows:—

    1. Baypoor, B . . . . . 6 miles

and the Koondah Pass. The latter is the more direct, and I mean to pursue it. As my arrangements can only be made half way, (I cannot afford even one day's delay,) I shall be obliged to "rough" it; but I have purchased a pony to carry me when my dâk fails, and I have made up my mind to start this evening, whatever the inconveniences *en route* may be. I have received every aid and assistance from Mr. Conolly, the collector of Calicut, to whom my best thanks are due for enabling me to get away at all. I have copied out the instructions he gave me, and subjoin them

2. Tanoor, B	13	miles.
3. Batulpoodyanguddy, B	9	,,
4. Tirtallah, B	16	,,
5. Patamby, B	4	,,
6. Wunyomkollum, B	11	,,
7. Lackadycottah, B	8½	,,
8. Palghâtcherry, * B	16	,,
9. Wulliam River	15½	,,
10. Coimbatoor, * B	15½	,,
11. Goodaloor, B	11	,,
12. Matypollium, B	9	,,
13. Summit of Coonoor Pass, B	12	,,
14. Ootacamund, * H	9	,,

Total distance . . 153 miles.

N.B.—In the above route, "B" stands for Dâk-Bungalow; and when "*" is added, it is to intimate that there is a military or civil Station there likewise. "H" stands for hotel.

for the guidance of travellers.* The Kotwâl of this place, when he came to receive my orders

*(*Verbatim copy.*)

"A boat can ascend the river from Calicut to Ariacode in about eight hours. There is a small public Bungalow at the latter place. The road from Ariacode to Wundoor is hilly. Wundoor is a fine and open country, four or five miles from the Jungle, and is perfectly healthy at all seasons. The public Bungalow is a good tiled one. The Sisaparah, or Koondah Bungalow, is situated about two hundred yards to the left of the top of the Ghaut; this and the Avalanche Bungalow are wooden buildings; in both of them there are fire-places. The Bombay travellers, who bring horses with them, will find the Koondah route the shortest and best. On landing at Calicut they should immediately write to the Collector of Malabar, or, in his absence, to the Calicut Cotwal, to secure a well-manned boat and a Munchal, and their horses should be posted at Ariacode, Wundoor, Cholakul, Walaghaut, Sisaparah and Avalanche, so as to enable them to be ready at these different stages on the morning of the third or fourth day. The road from Wundoor having been only lately opened, natives have a great dislike to proceed along it, stating their fear of elephants as the cause; but there are only seven miles of jungle at the bottom of the Pass to be traversed, and in reality there is no fear during day-light. Any number of bearers can be got from Calicut to the foot of the Ghaut, but they will not ascend the Hills, so bearers must be ordered in advance from the Postmaster, at Ootacamund, to meet the traveller at Cholakul.

"With horses baited, and the other requisite arrangements made beforehand, it is quite possible, starting from Calicut in the afternoon, to reach Ootacamund by the following evening."

regarding my journey, strenuously endeavoured to dissuade me from pursuing the Arricode route, as the road is so very jungly, and infested not only with wild elephants, but also with tigers and wolves. He told me pathetic tales of people being trampled down by the former, and torn to pieces by the latter, and conjured me not to risk my life thus rashly. Having fully resolved, however, on the particular route in question, *coûte qui coûte*, I paid but little heed to his remonstrances.

ARRICODE.

Distance from Calicut by the Baypore river, about twenty-seven miles.

25*th April*, 1852. *Sunday*.—I arrived here at eight o'clock, a.m., accomplishing the voyage in nine hours. The Baypoor river is about a mile from the Dâk-Bungalow at Calicut, and I was carried to the boat in the same conveyance in which I am now to proceed dâk. This conveyance requires a few descriptive words. It is called a "muncheel," also "munzil," and is an excellent imitation of the hill *Dandy* of the Himalayas, with a moveable top; the sole difference being that four men carry the Muncheel, and two only are required at a time for the Dandy.

The boats on the Baypore river are all small. The largest resemble the Bengal "Budgerow" in miniature, but there is no cooking cabin of any description—a serious inconvenience indeed. When I called for tea this morning, we were obliged to moor the boat, and the water was boiled on shore. The bearers of my dâk, called the "Boees," row the boat, which no Bengal bearers would ever condescend to do. The river is narrow and shallow; the banks densely wooded, and the scenery of wild beauty. The Neilgherry hills are distinctly visible at almost every bend of the winding stream. A wooden bridge spans the "Baypore," close to the spot where we embarked, but it was so dark last night, I could make no particular note of the vicinity.

There is a Bungalow here, but no servant beyond a Sepoy in charge. The heat is very overpowering, the thermometer standing at 98° in the house now, at one o'clock, p.m. This Bungalow is a mile from the place where we left the boat, and part of the road is along the shore, and part through the village;—wooded, hilly scenery on every side. Plaintains and cocoa-nuts seem the staple commodities of the place. All I have taken to-day has been the "milk" of a fresh cocoa-nut, which is as refreshing as it is unwholesome. My pony has just arrived, *by land*, and though the heat is intense, I shall now proceed on my journey. I do not understand the Malabar tongue, and my refined Oordoo is quite at a discount here. Ghaussie, who is with me, is equally at a loss. The "Muncheel" is ready, so now for the Blue Mountains of Malabar, and the wild elephants *en route*.

WUNDOOR.

Distance, fourteen miles.

26th April, 1852. *Monday.*—Six o'clock, a.m. —Before leaving, I must chronicle my arrival here, though a slight attack of fever almost incapacitates me from the slightest exertion. We did not arrive till long after dark. I was chilled and feverish then, and went to bed without breaking my fast. A storm of thunder, lightning, and rain, came on before we had accomplished two-thirds of our journey, the road was wooded and jungly—so my illness is not quite unaccountable. Half-way there is a small Bungalow, but knowing I had no time to spare,

I did not halt, though the storm was at its height at the time. The river Baypore re-appears just below this half-way Bungalow, and we crossed it in a boat. The road is a little hilly, very wooded and pretty, but by no means good, or adapted to any wheeled conveyances. I now proceed in the "Muncheel" to Chola, (or "Cholakul,") through the jungle of wild elephants, while Ghaussie rides my pony.

CHOLA, OR CHOLAKUL. (FOOT OF KOONDAH PASS.)

Distance, eleven miles.

Same day, eleven o'clock, a.m.—I feel so ill, my pulse beating 120°, that I fear I have got an attack of jungle-fever, and unluckily here my "dâk" stops, so I *must* ride. It would not be safe to halt in this jungle under any circumstances.* There is only a miserable hut here, with a Sepoy in charge—no supplies of any description procurable.

* A lady and her daughter, a Mrs. and Miss M——, travelled this route the day after I arrived at Ootacamund. Yielding to the feverish feelings which so frequently come on, (especially after any exposure to cold or wet,) in these jungles, they passed the night at Chola-kul. They fell the victims to their impru-

The road from Wundoor to Chola is a good pathway, generally level, but the country is of a hilly nature, wild and jungly, the wood consisting principally of bamboo trees. The rank vegetation and the redundant underwood strongly remind me of the Sikhim Hills, or rather the jungle near the foot of those hills. I saw one wild elephant with huge tusks, *close* to the road, but it did not molest us. The heat is very great, and I am too feverish to write more. In three or four hours' time, *Deo volente*, I shall be in a colder region.

SISPARA. (CALLED COMMONLY BY THE NATIVES "CHEE-CHEEPARA.")

Distance, eleven miles.

27th April, 1852. *Tuesday.*—Arrived here yesterday evening at sunset. The road is a very good bridle-path, but no carts could, in the very wildest imagination, be taken an inch of this

dence, for within a week both mother and daughter died of the jungle-fever. I saw the announcement in the newspapers before I left Malabar. The malaria in these jungles is indeed fatal in its effects on the constitution, and during sleep especially, the deadly miasma too certainly operates.

route. From Cholakul, the ascent up the Koondah Pass commences. The jungle continues, but the trees change from bamboo, &c., to the different varieties of rhododendron, oak, and other hill-growing species. At half-way from Chola to Sispâra, is Wâla-Ghât, where there is a hut,—a rude construction, but sufficient protection in a storm. There are coffee plantations, about a couple of miles distant, (off the road,) and the jungle is being rapidly cleared away for them.

There is a magnificent view from the top of this Ghât, when the clouds and mists obligingly make themselves scarce. The sea is seen beyond the wooded plains stretching over the range of the Koondah mountains, and the little river of Baypore meanders through the wilderness. It is quite possible to discern ships sailing on the ocean with the naked eye; and as the crow flies, I do not believe the Koondah's highest summit can be thirty miles from the sea.

The Bungalow at Sispâra is a wretched place, principally built of wood. Rain fell heavily here, not only all last night, but for several hours this morning. I am passing away the moments of my imprisonment the best way I can. I got wet through yesterday evening on the ascent of the Ghât, and I believe rain is constantly deluging this section of the hills. A beautiful creeper grows here in wild luxuriance, of velvety purple tints. It has four petals, of three different shades of purple. This plant is called the "Sispâra creeper," but I have noticed it equally at Wâla-Ghât, and indeed all over the Koondah mountains.

There are numerous wild-flowers between Wundoor and Chola, but I will only particularize two or three kinds which struck me most. One is of a bulbous species, the upper flowers of a beautiful pink, while lower down the stem grow smaller and *different coloured* flowers, the outer petals yellow in hue, and the centre nearly black. The other flower which attracted my notice, as I passed through the elephant-jungle, was of the lily species, but very much larger than the English varieties. A third plant I may also mention, as it is not found on the Himalayas. The flower is exactly like a small English geranium, of a bright scarlet tint, but scentless. The leaf is not at all like the geranium leaf, however, being much longer in shape, and far from fragrant. The flora of this country is so well known, that it is useless my adding my crude ideas and observations on the subject. Indeed, as my visit to the Blue Mountains of Malabar will be so very hurried and partial, I shall only be able to give a slight sketch of them.

AVALANCHE. (Called by the Natives "Ablanjee.")

Distance, eighteen miles.

Same day.—Just arrived. I have performed this march on a Mahratta pony, accomplishing the distance in three hours;—had I been mounted on my beautiful "Phœnix," one third of that time would have been nearly enough. The pathway averages some four feet in breadth, and the numerous ascents and descents are very slight and gradual, in comparison even with the more civilized Himalayan roads. The scenery (after losing sight of the Koondah Pass) appeared to my palled eyes tame and uninteresting. The green undulating hills, with clumps of wood, had nothing to strike the eye—no bold peaks, no awful precipices, no wondrous chasms, and I was proportionately disappointed.

There is a hut half way from Sispâra, where it is possible to take shelter, or halt for breakfast, if a traveller be not *too* particular as to his quarters. Close by this said hut I observed the marks of elephants' feet, along the very path I was pursuing, and I looked forward with some dread to a *rencontre* with one of the gigantic tribe before I reached Avalanche, but I did not halt or delay in consequence. It is raining again, thunder and lightning being the pleasing accompaniments. I find I am far less timid now than formerly in these awful storms—a very satisfactory discovery, by the way! This place is called "Avalanche," on account of a land-slip, which very imaginative people think bears a resemblance to the mighty snow avalanches of the Alpine regions. A very great license such people must give to their fertile imaginations, for in my humble opinion there is not the ghost of a likeness between the two.

Fowls, eggs, rice, &c., are to be procured here, —also milk; and for horses, "Coolty." This Coolty is the Madras substitute for gram, and is a species of pulse. It is always boiled previous to use, and is said to be fattening. At Sispâra *nothing* is to be had, not even milk, as there is no village near. Coolty at eight seers the rupee, can be purchased from the man in charge of the Bungalow, but no supplies are procurable for Christian bipeds; so let all travellers be warned, or they will be starved as I was, from want of some such friendly caution, pre-administered. I have fortunately brought a goat with me, so I can always ensure a cup of tea, and that is at all times consolatory (to me). There are plenty of jungle-fowl in these mountains, and "shikâr" of all sorts is tolerably abundant. I will hereafter enter into further detail.

The thermometer exhibited in the shade to-day at Sispâra, 63°; at Avalanche, 66° at noon, and 63° at sunset. A difference, it will be observed, of 35° between this and Calicut.

A Peon or Chokeydâr is the only servant entertained by government for these staging-Bungalows, except at Wundoor, where the attendant functionary professes to be a cook; however, from my knowledge of these Bungalow domestics, I should not feel much disposed to trust to his culinary skill. The Bungalow is prettily situated here, and there is a striking and beautiful repose in the still landscape, which must be very refreshing to the blasé denizens of the heartless "world," flocking hither as they do from the large stations in the plains, or even from the mountain-sanataria, where all is brilliant turmoil, and hollow frivolous gaiety, palling and wearying at last even to satiety.

OOTACAMUND. (Elevation 7,361 feet above the level of the Sea.)

Distance, fourteen and a half miles.

30*th April*, 1852. *Friday.*—I arrived here early on Wednesday, and I have spent two days with E— P—, whom I found here, much to my delight. I have also met with an old friend of my childish days, Nina S—, now Mrs. G—. I reminded both herself and her *caro sposo* of their days of courtship, and told her I remembered well how *entêtée* she used to be once upon a time! Such reminiscences are sometimes troublesome, but the happy Benedicts in question enjoyed the "light wit" as much as I did.

Yesterday morning mounting my new purchase, the Malabar pony, I climbed the summit of Dodabèt Peak, the highest point south of the great Himalayan range. Its elevation is 8,760 feet above the level of the sea, and a very fine view is commanded on every side. To the north stretch out the burning plains of Mysore, and on a clear day the distant city of Seringapatam is distinctly visible. To the right of Mysore are seen the stations of Coonoor, Coimbatore, and Pâlghâtcherry. Ootacamund is entirely exposed to view, the houses being scattered over slightly undulating hills, the rich green sward bespangled with countless myriads of lovely wild-flowers. The little lake relieves the monotony of the scenery, which, pretty as it indubitably is, has too little variety, too few bold or striking points, and no stupendous Heights white with everlasting ice and snow,—is too *tame*, in short, to satisfy eyes now palled with the long contemplation of the majestic features of the Himalayan mountains, and the remote and glorious wastes of the regions of perpetual snow. With the people of the Madras presidency, I fear this confession will rank me as a stupid and heterodox character, and in imagination I hear the denunciations poured forth on my affectation and want of taste.

There are four stations in the Neilgherry Hills—Ootacamund, 7,361 feet in elevation; Coonoor, 5,886 ditto ditto; Kotagherry, 6,571 ditto; and Dimhutty, 6,330 ditto. The first is the principal one of the four.

An excellent hotel flourishes at Ootacamund, and a second is in embryo. The only public buildings of any size that I saw were a church and the club-house, but my very circumscribed visit scarcely permitted any extensive observations, and as I before remarked, I can only offer a very slight and imperfect sketch of the Blue Mountains.* The lake is a narrow strip of water, between three and four miles long, and as a carriage road encircles the basin, a good drive of seven miles may be had all round. There are a few carriages here, but riding is far more adapted to the hills. The roads are very tolerable, and throughout Ootacamund, pretty level, but not so good as on the Mahablèshwur Hills.

There has been a good deal of rain since my arrival here; the "oldest inhabitants" say, however, that the monsoon has *not* set in. Ootacamund is entirely exposed to the full force of the south-west monsoon, but a range of mountains protects Coonoor during those stormy months. However, in October, November and December, the north-east or Madras monsoon prevails there. During the prevalence of the south-west monsoon, numbers of people flock to Coonoor, from the neighbouring sanatarium, and a very good hotel has been built to accommodate this influx of visitors, besides several private Bungalows.

The climate of Ootacamund is said to be more equable than that of most of the other sanataria.

* *Neil*, blue, and *Ghiery* or *Gherry*, mountain.

During my short residence, the thermometer has exhibited the following heights:—

		Sunrise.	Noon.	Sunset.
April	28th	63°*	62°†	62°
,,	29th	61°	64°	63°
,,	30th	61°	63°	61°

N.B. The thermometer stood in a room the whole time, on the same spot.

Before leaving the subject of the Blue Mountains of Malabar, I will give a slight topographical account of them. These hills are situated between the parallels of 11° 10′ and 11° 32′ North latitude, and 76° 59′ and 77° 31′ East longitude, from Greenwich. Their greatest extent, in an oblique direction, from S.W. to N.E., is about forty miles, and their extreme breadth perhaps fifteen. This estimated breadth is tolerably constant throughout, and if the fact of the great undulation of the surface be taken into consideration, the superficial extent may be computed at nearly seven hundred square geographical miles. These mountains form the abuttal of the immense table-land of central India, beginning with upper Hindostan and the Deccan, and continued through Mysore, limited on the east by the faintly-marked line of the Eastern Ghâts, and on the west by the bold range

---

* At Avalanche.   † In heavy rain.

of the Western Ghâts. From the table-land of Mysore,* the Neilgherries rise to the elevation of 3,500 feet, and a deep fissure divides them from the Eastern and Western Ghâts.† On all the

* Mysore is a large province lying between the parallels of 11° and 15° North latitude, enclosed on two sides by the Western and Eastern Ghâts. It consists of an elevated plateau, from which rise many lofty hills and clusters of hills, containing the sources of numerous rivers that fertilize the neighbouring low country. Barometrical observations give the altitude of Mysore from nearly 2,000 to 4,600 feet above the level of the sea, according to the points measured. The latter elevation constitutes the highest mountain in Mysore. The formation of the rock which forms the basis of the whole country, is sienite, being quartz, felspar, hornblende, and mica, mingled.

† The Eastern Ghâts are a chain of hills, commencing in the south about latitude 11° 20′ North, extending to the banks of the Krishna, in latitude 16° North, separating the "Carnatic Balaghât" and the "Carnatic Payeenghât," (which extends along the coast of Coromandel.) The average elevation is less than that of the Western Ghâts, the highest altitude being 3,000 feet. The "Western Ghâts" are better defined than the former, and extend from Cape Comorin to the Tuptee, or river of Surat, where they bend eastward in a wavy line parallel to the river, and are afterwards lost in the hills in the vicinity of Boorhânpoor. Their distance from the sea-coast varies from forty to seventy miles, and at one point the chain approaches the sea as near as six miles. The whole extent includes 13° of latitude, with one break in the ridge, sixteen miles wide, through which the river Paniany flows

other sides they rise abruptly from the low-lands of Malabar and Coimbatore, in a precipitous mass between five and seven thousand feet in altitude. There are three distinct ranges, of much the same elevation, but presenting very varying features in the grouping as well as the general aspect. The table-land on the summits is much undulated, and swamps, free from miasma, are found in the valleys. Dodabēt Peak forms the line of separation between the north-east and south-west monsoons, all the mountains to the west of the peak being subject to the influence of the latter. A belt of dense jungle completely environs the base of the hills, rising from 2,000 to 3,000 feet along their declivities. This belt is of varying breadth—nowhere less than six miles in extent, and nowhere exceeding twenty. After the belt of jungle is surmounted, there occurs ordinarily a line of demarcation (an open space nearly destitute of trees) above which the Alpine character of the vegetation and forest begins to be distinctly observable, and the jungly underwood almost entirely disappears, rich grass taking its place. The boldest and most picturesque scenery

---

into the Western Ocean. The elevation of this chain of mountains varies from two to six thousand feet above the level of the sea.

is presented on the side of the Koondah Range, which rises in vast rocky precipices, five and six thousand feet in elevation, quite inaccessible from the low-lands beneath. From these Heights, most magnificent views are obtained; and, apparently quite close, lies the boundless expanse of the dark blue ocean,—the surface so calm and placid in fine weather, so awful in its wrath when storms sweep over the fathomless deep, and the mountain waves lash the foaming waters into white and stupendous breakers.

The table-land, diversified by long undulating ridges, with deep valleys interposing, is sometimes beautifully wooded, sometimes carpeted with luxuriant grass and countless flowers. The abundant supply of moisture preserves the surface of the ground in a constant state of verdure. The western face of Dodabēt descends with a slope of considerable abruptness—wooded hollows and swampy valleys forming the varieties presented to the eye. Kotagherry is situated on a table-land, after one or two of the above valleys are traversed, and the range has become broken into numerous small conical rocky hills. The country is less wooded here, and is intersected by deep valleys debouching into the low-lands below. One of these dales is called the "Orange Valley," from the number of orange and lime trees found in it. The elevation of this valley is between 4,000 and 5,000 feet above the sea-level, and as it is confined by steep hills, the temperature is proportionately high. Dimhutty is lower than Kotagherry, and is situated on a plateau between that station and the Orange Valley.

The mean temperature of Ootacamund is 52° 28';—a long course of meteorological observations places the maximum at 77°, and the minimum at 38°. The extraordinary effect of radiation, evaporation, and the forced* descent of the colder columns of air, is to reduce the temperature of the valleys below freezing point, and even in the spring, thick ice is found. If a person were to test the effect of the radiation at the bottom of the valley, by descending on a dark, clear night, he would feel a sudden and powerful chill, proving thereby his entrance into a colder column of air. When the stratum of air above is transparently clear, the valleys below are wrapped very frequently in dense fogs, from the cause above stated.

The geological formation of these mountains is primitive—almost wholly composed of sienite

* "Forced" by their superior weight, and unobstructed by any disturbing wind in their passage.

of a very hard description. Quartz has been found near the Koondah Ghât, and beds of decomposed felspar elsewhere. Crystals of garnet, and veins of ore, both iron and gold, have also been detected; but only in places where the prevalence of dense and malarious jungle renders all extensive research impossible. The water found on the hills is of two kinds— one hard and containing iron, the other delightfully soft. The soil of the hills is very rich, and cultivation abundant, considering the amount of the population. Barley, *bháttoo*,* poppies, garlic, onions, wheat, &c., are cultivated extensively. A few fruits and numerous vegetables are also produced. Potatoes, cauliflowers, cabbages, beet-root, celery, and peas, are to be had in plenty in the bazaars. Beautiful flowers can be horticulturally cultivated, besides the numerous and fragrant wild varieties, with which the hedgerows and jungles abound,—the wild rose, so divinely sweet, the eglantine, the honeysuckle, the geranium, and the jessamine. The butter-cups and daisies recall our native land, and the merry days of childhood,—

"The days when we went gipsying, a long time ago."

* This grain resembles "Love-lies-bleeding," and is of the same blood-red colour when ripe. It is called in the Neilgherries, "Keereemow."

The rhododendron is here a fine forest-tree, as in the Himalayan mountains, and glows with thousands of rich scarlet flowers, from the end of October to the beginning of April. The horticultural plants are—the dahlia, (of many kinds,) the geranium, the verbena, the rose, the heliotrope, and all the English varieties of garden plants. The fruits are—apples, pears, peaches, plums and strawberries;—the latter, and also gooseberries and cherries, grow wild, but are only fit for tarts.

Woodcock and the ordinary jungle-fowl abound in these mountains. Elephants, bison, tigers, bears, wild-hogs, cheetahs, hares and jackals form the favourite "shikâr" of sportsmen. Porcupine, elks,* jungle-sheep,† and ibex, are also occasionally found, and hunted.

The last topic I shall descant upon, before closing this hasty sketch, is one of peculiar interest, as it relates to a very singular race, whose origin is yet enigmatical. These are the "Todars," who claim to be the original tribes of these hills—the veritable aborigines. I went yesterday evening to one of the *Todar-munds*, (or their apo-

---

* The "Sambah."

† So called up here, but they are more correctly a *bonâ fide* species of deer.

logies for villages,) and was much entertained by my visit to this curious people. I believe a very able account of the race emanated from the pen of Captain Harkness, some twenty years ago; and though I have not met with the work in question, I have no doubt it gives all particulars, so that any further description is almost an act of supererogation. I will content myself therefore with a very few words on the subject.

The appearance of the Todars is decidedly prepossessing; the men are fine, tall, stalwart figures, with handsome faces, and soft curly black hair— the features prominent, and classically chiselled. The women are fairer than the men, and have very long and beautiful hair, flowing round them in redundant natural curls. They are good-looking, and have a good-tempered, laughter-loving expression. Their features are regular and classical, but as their figures are enveloped in a sort of dingy mummy-like wrapper, it is not easy to say what they are like. The whole race, male and female, are above the average height of even European countries; and in their appearance and habits, they are so completely isolated and singular, that it is impossible not to regard them with curiosity and interest commingled. They do not congregate in towns or villages, but lead a strictly pastoral life, the principal branches of every family living quite separate. The number of the whole race does not exceed five hundred, and it is said they are gradually diminishing. Perchance the next century will find them vanished from the face of the earth. Their "munds" are simply a collection of wigwams. These huts have been likened to the canopy of a waggon. They are formed of thatch, supported on wooden posts, and the only entrance is a very tiny door about two feet high, and one foot and a half wide. I endeavoured to creep in, but the smoke of the fires which were lit inside for cooking purposes, nearly stifled me at the very entrance, and the filthy habits of the people still more effectually frightened me away.

Their language appears to be quite different from any of the Asiatic tongues, and apparently impossible of acquirement, as no one has been known to master its simplest rudiments. Moreover, they have no written language whatever, nor any outward symbols of their ideas.

The only notion they have of religion is rough and indistinct. They make obeisance to the rising sun, and believe that the soul goes somewhere—*c'est tout!* This unknown locality they term "Hoomanorr." The women are famed for anything but virtue, and their domestic institutions are too bad to describe, so I will not advert to them further. On the occasion of my visit to the Todar-munds, I was accompanied by Mrs. G— and her brother, Mr. S—. The Todars crowded round us, full of mirth and curiosity; jabbered away very fast in their pectoral language, and freely examined our clothes, &c., with no appearance of shyness. They had learnt at least *one* word of Hindostanee, and importunately clamoured for "buckshish," which Mr. S— gave them very good-naturedly, but failed in satisfying their rapacity. Yet they were so merry and good-looking, that it was impossible to be aught but amused at their freedom. I noticed that they had all uncovered heads—men and women—and the luxuriance of their hair was quite remarkable.

The literal meaning of *Toda* is "man," by which term they *rather* proudly (and coolly) designate themselves, *par excellence!*

CALICUT.

Distance, by the Koondah Pass and the Baypoor River altogether, ninety-six miles.

5*th May*, 1852. *Wednesday.*—I need not describe my trip, as it was very much ditto repeated of the one *en route* upwards. I accompanied Captain and Mrs. C——, very delightful people, from Sispâra to Calicut, and my solitude was thus pleasantly broken. I had also the pleasure of finding here an old and esteemed friend; so, as we all go back to Bombay together, in the " Steam Navigation Company's" steamer, I expect quite a pleasure trip, instead of a sick and solitary passage—the wind being fair and light, and there being as yet no decided appearance of the Monsoon, notwithstanding the heavy rain we have had during the last week.

Between Ootacamund and Sispâra, before I joined Captain and Mrs. C——, I had a second *rencontre* with one of the elephant tribe, but escaped unhurt, as in the Cholakul jungle. I had distanced my servants, and was riding alone. My weary pony (who was not worth his salt,) was flagging wofully in his speed, when I came upon the unmistakeable elephant-tracks, so freshly imprinted on the earth that I felt they must be recent. I looked around for assistance, but no human being was near. I tried to urge my pony into a gallop—and he obstinately declined to move at all. In this extremity, at no great distance from the road, I observed the tracks verging off in the direction of a spring of water, and a few seconds afterwards, to my horror, I spied the monstrous animal behind a tree, not fifty yards off. I observed he had but one tusk. Had he attacked me, I must have fallen a victim, for no persuasion or coercion could hasten my recreant steed. But though, at one time, I thought the enemy approached defyingly, he let me pass on. It soon after rained heavily, and I came up to some huts, the remains of a Bungalow once built on the spot, where I took shelter. Here I found Mr. Hunt—the great English sportsman before alluded to—who informed me that this elephant was the "one-tusker," well known in these parts, said to be an outcast from his fraternity, and extra-ferocious. How grateful was I for my providential escape, when I learned the full extent of the danger I had incurred. The late rain has diminished the temperature here, nearly ten degrees since my last visit to the place. The thermometer to-day exhibited, at sunrise, 75°; noon, 81°; sunset, 79°.

BOMBAY.

5th July, 1852. *Monday.*—Long continued illness has prevented my resuming my diary, and the debilitating effects of this deadly climate have totally incapacitated me, of late, from all exertion, bodily or mental, after six, a.m. Complete exhaustion prostrated every energy by sunset, and I could then do nothing but lie down in a state of physical debility closely approximating to stupor—from which I only succeeded in rousing myself for my delicious cold plunge-bath, or my short morning gallop before sun-rise, each day. I have had, however, nothing to chronicle, except a visit to Bassein and Tannah, of which I will presently give a short account, and the "bursting" of the south-west Monsoon a month ago. As for the said "bursting," I have been spared all storms of thunder and lightning, and a deluge of rain seems to constitute this "Monsoon"—ceaseless rain accompanied by hurricanes of wind.

Shortly after my return from Calicut, I visited Bassein, starting with a party from Apollo-Bunder in a Bunder-boat one fine, hot evening. By day-break we found we had made comparatively little progress; so, about ten o'clock, we moored our boat at a wharf, the name of which has entirely escaped my recollection. In some ruins situated on a hill, our breakfast was prepared. At three o'clock, p.m., we returned to our boat, and in spite of the remonstrances of the boatmen, who declared that both tide and wind were adverse, we resolved to attempt the passage to Bassein, which was actually in sight. However, after a tempestuous knocking about for five hours, during which interval we did not progress a mile, we were forced to return for dinner. That important business being consummated, at ten o'clock we again set sail; and when I awoke very early the following morning, I found we were lying in the little harbour opposite the extensive Ruins of Bassein.

After taking the matutinal cup of tea or coffee, so indispensable at daybreak in India, we proceeded to explore the famous ruins, and returned much delighted from a profitable two hours' ramble. These have been so often described, that a few words will here suffice.

The ruins found at Bassein extend for miles, and were once important fortifications;—ramparts and bastions without the glacis, and within the fortified enclosure, vast and melancholy débris of fine Roman Catholic churches, convents and monasteries—lofty and imposing structures still remaining to testify to the bygone power of the Portuguese. There is a mournful look of utter desolation in the place which strikes the eye of the beholder, and forcibly impresses on the mind the nothingness of the greatest efforts of finite man. I remember experiencing this sentiment almost to oppression, when I visited the far more striking and extensive ruins of Mândoo (in Malwâ,)—the mountain-town whose circumference measures six-and-thirty miles, and whose area within the defences contains upwards of thirteen thousand English acres. This celebrated city, occupying the entire tabular summit of a mountain of the Vindhyan Range,* is separated by a vast chasm (resembling closely an artificial ditch of gigantic proportions) from the adjacent country, the whole of which is singularly wild and picturesque. Its magnificent edifices,—the fortifications, the water-palace, the Jumma Musjid, the white marble

* The Vindhya Mountains extend from the province of Behâr, (the former limits of which were between the 22nd and 24th degrees of North latitude,) with little or no interruption, to Cape Comorin, in latitude 8° 4' North, and longitude 77° 45' East, the southern extremity of Hindostan—bounding the vast *Gangetic* plain on the south. This extensive ridge of hills passes behind Mirzapore and Allahabad; and between Banda in Bundelcund, and Singpore in Malwâ, takes a sweep to the south; then bends north to Gwalior, behind Agra and Delhi in the northern boundary of the chain. In this quarter, the hills attain no great altitude anywhere. In the south this ridge extends east and west along the Valley of the Nerbudda. It is only in a few detached spots that it rises above two thousand feet in elevation. The highest peak of the Mândoo range (the "Shaizghur") is nearly three thousand feet high.

mausoleum of Hussein Shah, and many other grand and wondrous ruins—all tell of power *past*, of magnificence gone for ever. Alas! for what empty baubles man toils through the short career of life, and wastes his little span of existence!

The Portuguese obtained possession of Bassein by treaty with the Sultan of Cambay,* in 1531, and retained it until captured by the Mahrattas more than two centuries subsequently, in 1750. It was at Bassein that the celebrated treaty was signed, annihilating the Mahratta Power as a federal empire.

To people leaving Bassein, a most vexatious delay occurs in levying the *Mussool*, or tax, imposed by government on all boats touching at this harbour; and though we were very anxious to get away early, half the day was lost in absurd formalities before the business was got through. Altogether it is a tiresome arrangement, and entails a most unnecessary waste of time. We lost the morning tide in consequence, and when

* An ancient city in the province of Gujerat, situated at the upper part of the Gulf of Cambay, on the north-west coast of India. (This city was mentioned by Marco Polo, about A.D. 1295.) Latitude 22° 21' North, and longitude 72° 48' East.

we reached Tannah, it was late in the afternoon; and further water-travelling was impossible, as the narrow strait had become so shallow through the ebbing of the tide, that no boat could make any progress. We consequently landed at Tannah, and taking a phaeton, drove the remaining twenty-two miles to Bombay, as vellards now connect all the detached islets, and span the once severing arms of the sea.

Bassein is about thirty miles from Bombay, north of the Fort. Tannah is a town on the island of Salsette, and was once a famous fortress, which commanded the passage, about two hundred yards broad, between the island and the main land. It is situated north by east from Bombay, in latitude 19° 11′ North, and longitude 73° 6′ East. British troops are now cantoned here, and fine macadamized roads lead to Bombay and Poonah, south and north. Tannah is only famous for two things at present,—intense heat and insalubrity.

I fear I have but haltingly performed my self-set task of description in the diary of this day, but kind reader, as you read, "if to these pages any errors fall, think of the *heat*, and you'll forgive them all!"

To-morrow, (D.V.,) I leave Bombay, and as

the Monsoon is at its height, I may look forward to a stormy, and perchance dangerous passage to my "Vaterland." Qu 'importe? whether one sleeps in the bosom of the "dark blue sea," or in some lone churchyard? I am not sure that if I had to take my choice, I should not prefer the briny waters, "so deeply, darkly, beautifully blue." And what saith that ancient historian, Herodotus, making the sage Artabanus moralize thus to the great conqueror, his royal nephew— "We suffer during life things more pitiable than this, for in this so brief life, there is not one, either of these or of other, born so happy that it *will not occur to him, not once only but oftentimes, to wish rather to die than to live.*"* So the world has ever been the same after all! and happiness has ever been a—dream. As for me, I have betimes ceased to look for,

"Words which are things—hopes which will not deceive,"

because, Reader dear, they are all myths, untangible, unattainable—the more passionately they are sought, the more they elude the grasp.

"Who with the weight of years would wish to bend,
When youth itself survives young love and joy?
Alas! when mingling souls forget to blend,
Death hath but little left him to destroy!"

* Herodotus, "Book VII., Polymnia."

And this is exactly the substance of my mental arguments, when with wilful perversity I have put my life in peril even greater far than the stormy ocean is likely to bring. To judge by the past, my life is a charmed one, for the grim monster has fled at most unexpected times, and on most favourable occasions!

But to return to common-place once more, let me, *àpropos de bottes*, pay a farewell tribute to my gallant stud, the cherished companions of my wanderings. They are all gone to the hands of strangers, and I—" am desolate!" My favourite, the beautiful "Phœnix," with whom I have had so many hard-contested battles, was the last to be parted with, and I would fain have given him to any one who would have valued him as I did. But I could not manage this, and poor "Phœnix" has become the property of an alien! He had a will of his own, and rather preferred an eccentric style of progression—his fore-legs elevated to a proud approach to the perpendicular—whenever he felt disinclined to proceed; and though I finally mastered his haughty blood, he may break out in the old way again, if less experienced or more timid equestrians mount him. He was advertised as "a lady's horse," and if some fair one ride the gentle Arab, thinking she has secured a treasure, (which to me he really was,) I trust I may not have a broken neck to answer for. However lugubrious the idea, it rather amuses me to picture Phœnix's first return to his old habits, and the astonishment and horror of the rider on the "lady's horse." Poor Phœnix!

And now I must close this diary for the present, and prepare for my departure, which is to take place early to-morrow morning. I have not many hours to spare, for the shades of evening have long since closed around,—

> "It is the hour when lovers' vows
> Seem sweet in every whispered word!"

And all lovers, I am sure, will know what o'clock it is at this moment!

THE CONCLUSION.

"Farewell! a word that must be, and hath been—
A sound which makes me linger;—yet—farewell!"

POINT DE GALLE. (ISLAND OF CEYLON.)

12th July, 1852. *Monday.*—On Tuesday, the 6th inst., I left Bombay for Suez, in the steamer "Erin," sailing *via* this island of Ceylon to avoid the full force of the Monsoon, which must have been encountered on the direct voyage. I will enter into no description of this island, though its jungles teem with poetry, and savage beasts,—lovely wild scenery, and wilder elephants, *ad libitum*. This is an unusual and tempestuous season to commence the voyage Home, but increasing ill-health renders it imperative for me to leave this enervating, fever-generating clime. Besides, a deep fit of depression—partly mental, partly physical—renders me wondrously indifferent to the storm or the tempest;—

> "Let winds be shrill, let waves roll high,—
> I fear not wave, nor wind!"

I have wandered in the lone Cinnamon-groves of this jungly and beautiful island, and the time and the place have both been suggestive of serious thoughts on the past, present and future. My "Eccentric Marches" in the "Clime of the East, the Land of the Sun," have come, at last, to a finite termination; and it is not without "a pang of regret" that I sigh my adieus to a country endeared to me by recollections of past happiness, "soft as the memory of buried love." And turning with a shudder from the contemplation of the long, long months of sorrow, and hopeless, heart-wrung anguish, which preceded, I look back with kindling pleasure to my wanderings in the Himalayan Mountains, and with delight I picture to myself the icy regions of the Far North, and the boundless and incomprehensible deserts of wild Tartary. The perils past, and the unknown and remote regions explored, are deeply endeared to me from the very solace they gave to a stricken heart,—stricken indeed, in early youth, in "life's young day," when all ought to be bright and roseate, and full of hope and joy. It is because they did bring relief to my bruised and bleeding spirit, that I have a feeling of absolute fellowship with the scenes of my wanderings; and to me,

> "High mountains *are a feeling,* but the hum
> Of human cities torture: I can see
> Nothing to loathe in nature, save to be
> A link reluctant in a fleshly chain,
> Class'd among creatures, when the soul can flee,
> And with the sky, the peak, the heaving plain
> Of ocean, or the stars, mingle, and not in vain.
> And *thus* I am absorb'd, and *this* is life:
> —I look upon all *peopled* deserts past,
> As on a place of agony and strife."

Alas! how true!—and yet, from my loved and cherished haunts, I shall soon be far, far away. Soon will oceans and seas divide me from all I love and value most. I feel a prophetic warning of the resistless yearning which, *tôt ou tard,* will yet take entire possession of my faculties, impelling me to resume the fascinating society of far-distant mountains and savage deserts;—and then I know I shall regret not having created for myself a *home* in the wilderness. But, in the Anglo-Indian phrase, I must go "home" now to England. *Home?* what mockery! My "household gods lie shivered around," and if home be "where the heart is, wherever that be," all of mine that survived the shipwreck and desolation of my ruined and scattered "household gods," I have left in the "pathless deserts," and among the stupendous glaciers, far, far away!

It is a lovely night, and the bright stars are shining in the blue canopy above me. Would that I could read my fate "in those bright leaves of the poetry of heaven." Ah! I might perchance turn with sickening disappointment from the perusal, and the sweet dreams of delusion held out, even now, by that dear deceiver, Anticipation, might sink to everlasting nothingness—so I will not look on the starlight firmament of heaven, for fear some tell-tale twinkler *should* whisper the secrets of a dark futurity!

How faithfully does memory recall the many scenes I have visited, the many lands I have explored; though my years are yet green for such wanderings, and perchance 'tis a strange taste for youth to find delight in such solitary excursions—girt, too, with peril and toil on every hand. I know I must bid a long farewell to the said Travels, so I linger over these pages—the last of my self-appointed task. They seem to me the sole remaining link to the past. In a few short hours I shall have once more sailed away from the shores of India, and I cannot contemplate my departure without much regret. I left Bombay in a fearful gale,—wind and rain, thunder and lightning, in a wild and confusing mélange; and I have reason to anticipate a similar tempest tomorrow morning, when we sail away from India for the last time,—for the cloudless sky is dark and lowering, and where all was so still and peaceful a few minutes ago, there is nought but hurry and confusion now.

How typical of life and its uncertainties—its abrupt, unanticipated reverses—its unexpected changes—is the sudden storm, now howling through the rich and beautiful groves of this lovely island, the very gales of which are perfumed with the fragrance of myriads of delicious spices and orange blossoms. An hour ago, and—

"All heaven and earth were still—though not in sleep;
But breathless as we grow when feeling most;
And silent, as we stand in thoughts too deep."

But now, how changed is the scene;—the dark blue sky so clear and so glittering not many minutes ago, is black and lurid with the gathering clouds;—the thunder peals more distant, now more near, and the vivid lightning illumines the darkness without, while it dances with horrid playfulness through these large Oriental halls. The hurricane is blowing and the rain pouring wildly down, with a violence which the dwellers of temperate latitudes cannot even faintly imagine.

> —— "Most glorious night!
> Thou wert not sent for slumber! let me be
> A sharer in thy fierce and far delight,
> A portion of the tempest and of thee!"

But I must not trespass longer on the reader's patience, which is probably fairly exhausted. In closing these volumes, let me take leave of them in the most orthodox manner:—

> " My task is *done*—my theme
> Has died into an echo; it is fit
> The spell should break of this protracted dream.
> The torch shall be extinguish'd which hath lit
> My midnight lamp—and what is writ, is writ.
> Would it were worthier!"

THE END.

APPENDIX

TO THE

THIRD VOLUME.

APPENDIX A.

ROUTE FROM SIMLA TO KASHMIR, *via* BUSEHR, THE CHOOMOREEREE LAKE, ROOPSHOO IN LADAK, LEH (THE CAPITAL OF LADAK), ISKARDO, SOOROO, THE NANA-KANA PEAKS, AND WULDWUN VALLEY.

No. of Marches.	Names of Marches.	Remarks.	Miles.	Furlongs.
1.	Mahâsoo	Excellent road	8	0
2.	Fâgoo, (Dâk Bungalow)	Ditto	6	0
		(No servants at the Bungalows but a Chokeydâr.)		
3.	Theog ditto	Excellent road	6	4
4.	Mutiâna ditto	Ditto	6	4
5.	Nâgkundah ditto	Ditto	13	0
6.	Kotgurh ditto	Steep descent	10	0
7.	Nirtnuggur	Tolerable road	12	0
8.	Rampore (a city on the Sutluj; very hot.) Country of Busêhr	(No Bungalow.) Good road.	12	0
9.	Goura, (Country of Busêhr)	Steep road, ascent	8	0
10.	Surâhn ,,	Indifferent road	9	4
11.	Turanda ,,	Good road, but steep ascents and descents	13	0
12.	Nachâr ,,	Indifferent road	8	0
13.	Cheergâon ,,	Very bad road. Cross the Sutluj by a good bridge	11	0
14.	Meeroo ,,	Very bad road	5	0
15.	Rogee ,,	Ditto, and bad halting-place	8	4
16.	Cheenee ,,	Ditto. A sort of Bungalow available	8	0
17.	Punghee ,,	Indifferent road	8	0
18.	Leepee ,,	Steep and bad road	13	0

ii

19. Kánum, ,,	Bad steep road. Over the Kirmánung Ghat	7	4
20. Sōōngnum ,,	Broad and good road, though steep. Over Rōōning Pass, 14,508 feet in elevation above level of the sea	11	4
21. Hango ,,	Broad and good road, though steep. Over Hungrung Pass, 14,837 feet in elevation	9	4
22. Leo or Lee ,,	Steep and indifferent road	7	4
23. Chang or Chango ,,	Steep and very bad road	10	0
24. Changrëyzing ,,	Very steep and rugged road. A frightful torrent is crossed by a frail bridge in this march	6	0
25. Shoogoor (Country of China)	Shocking road, steep and rocky. A dangerous torrent crossed by a huge rock	8	0
26. Jëtoomdoh ,,	Road tolerable. Some parts narrow, and the soil crumbling	5	0
27. Lari, or Lurree (District of S'piti)	Road very bad,—only six inches in width; rocky and crumbling	10	0
28. Poh ,,	Road precipitous and rugged;—dangerous for horses	8	0
29. Dunkir ,,	Road precipitous and impassable for mounted horses	8	0
30. Kájeh ,,	Good road	12	4
31. Keebur ,,	Near the foot of Párung Pass. Road steep but pretty good	8	0
32. Tátung, (District of Rōōpshoo)	Foot of Párung Pass, which is crossed in this march. The road is steep and bad, and deep snow on the Pass. The elevation of the Párung Pass is about 20,000 feet. (Oojár.)	20	0

ROUTE FROM SIMLA TO KASHMIR—*continued.*

No. of Marches.	Names of Marches.	Remarks.	Miles.
33.	Phâlung-Palrâh (District Roōpshoo)	Oojâr encampment. Road shocking,—very rugged	10
34.	Choōmeeschūrtzoy ,,	Oojâr encampment. Very rugged	8
35.	Chângdoom ,,	Oojâr encampment. Very good road. Encampment on the banks of the Choōmorooree Lake	5
36.	Koorzuk ,,	Oojâr encampment about a mile from the lake. Excellent road	8
37.	Pōōgah (District Roōpshoo)	Steep ascents and descents. Oojâr encamping ground near the mines of Borax and Sulphur	12
38.	Neoūr ,,	Oojâr encampment. Road stony but tolerably level	14
39.	Toogjoh Chumboo ,,	Road perfectly level following the banks of the salt water lake. Oojâr encampment	6
40.	Deverung ,,	Excellent level road; Oojâr encampment, at the foot of Tungling Pass	11
41.	Ghia (Country of Ladâk)	First village in Ladâk. Over Tungling Pass	18
42.	Meeroo ,,	Road pretty good. Village. (Country of Ladâk)	8
43.	Oōpshee ,,	Ditto. ,,	8
44.	Mursilung ,,	Excellent road	7
45.	Teeksah ,,	Excellent road	8
46.	Lēh, the Capital city of Ladâk	Excellent road	9
47.	Snimo, or Neemo (Country of Ladâk)	Excellent level road	15
48.	Suspoola ,,	Bad road	6
49.	Noorlah ,,	Very bad road, narrow and dangerous	8
50.	Skeerebookchun ,,	On the whole the road is excellent; the latter part narrow	14
51.	Hânnoo ,,	Bad and precipitous path	12

iv

52. Poëyun	(District of Chorbut)	Over Hannoo Pass, about 15,000 feet in elevation; good path, but in parts steep; deep snow on and near the top	20
53. Khōppaloo	(Country of Bultistan)	Bad road	14
54. Blagârh	,,	Indifferent road, just below Khōppaloo; cross the Indus on a raft of skins	8
55. Keeris	,,	Road steep and rugged. The village is situated on the banks of the Singley-Choo or Indus	12
56. Nâr	,,	Road follows the course of the river, and is in parts very precipitous	9
57. Iskârdo	,,	This is the capital city of Bultistân or Bâlti. Road very indifferent. A mile below Iskârdo, the river Indus is crossed in a flat-bottomed boat	11
58. Thhorgōō	,,	Road pretty good	7
59. Gohl	,,	Ditto	7
60. Perkōōta	,,	Road execrable	8
61. Tōlti	,,	Road rugged, steep, and stony. The river Mântoka, which is 3½ feet at the ford, is crossed in this march	8
62. Karmânh	(District of Kartâkchun)	Part of road very rugged, following the river Sōōroo or Kârtse, a branch of the Indus. Below Tōlti, this river is crossed by a dreadful zampa, or bridge of twigs	10
63. Târkuttie	,,	Shocking road. The river is re-crossed just below the Fort of Kartâkchun by a bridge of twigs	9
64. Olding-Thung	,,	Part of the road tolerable, and part rugged	9
65. Gungunni	,,	Road steep and rugged; many dangerous places	8
66. Kirgitchoo	,,	Narrow and stony path, but tolerably level	6

ROUTE FROM SIMLA TO KASHMIR—*continued.*

No. of Marches.	Names of Marches.	Remarks.	Miles.
67. Kirghil	(Country of Ladâk)	Road very good, except two bad places, and a dangerous bridge over the Draüs river, crossed just below Kirgitchoo	5
68. Sōnkoo	,,	Road narrow but good, along the bank of the Kârtso river	18
69. Tisseroo or Sooroo	(District of Sooroo)	Road on the whole steep, narrow, and difficult	
70. Yelingkhōr	(District of Sooroo)	Oojâr encampment, at the foot of the Brâmoorj Punjâl. Stony road	
71. Kahinthul,	(District of Wurdwun)	Over Brâmoorj Punjâl. A difficult glacier-road, and a great deal of snow and ice on the ascent and descent of the Pass. Very steep and fatiguing path	12
72. Kohinâg, ditto	,,	Tolerable path across the Oojâr tract	6
73. Choomurpul, ditto	,,	Most rugged and difficult road	12
74. Soognuz (First Village in the Valley of Wurdwun)		A most rugged and breakneck path	4
75. Bussmun Fort	(Valley of Wurdwun)	Good road, at the head of the valley of Wurdwun	6
76. Unshun	,,	Good path, along the valley of Wurdwun	7
77. Hērh-Matteōōnh	(District of Kashmir)	Over Wurdwun Pass, 12,000 feet. A great deal of snow	15
78. Déoth	(Valley of Kashmir)	Road on the whole very tolerable	12
79. Makâm	,,	Good path through the valley	9
80. Islamabad	,,	Good path through the valley	
81. Sirinuggur, or city of Kashmir	,,	By water, 8 or 10 hours' sail in a light boat, down the Jhelum.	

vi

APPENDIX B.

Estimate of Time Employed on the Road from Bhimber to Kashmir, by Day and by Night.

These "Hours" are from Inference.

From Bhimber, to

Distance in Miles or Cosses.	Names of Stages.	By Day.	By Night, with Guides.
6 coss or 9 miles.	Shahabad Seraï. Going over the Bhimber Pass. Steep ascent and descent,—bad road. Supplies and village-ponies procurable at Shahabad.	3¼ hours. Riding a good pony, and taking advantage of every tolerable piece of road.	5½ hours. *Going at a walk.* Take a good pony; guides and mâsâls at night always.
6 coss or 9 miles.	Nouashēhra. Village ponies procurable at Nouashēhra, and supplies, &c.	2 hours. Riding as above directed.	4 hours. Going at a walk, &c. The rest as above.
6 coss or 9 miles.	Chingoos (or Chungus) Seraï. Nothing procurable here, neither men nor animals.	2¼ hours. Riding as above directed.	5 hours. Going at a walk, &c. The rest as above.
6 coss or 9 miles.	Rajoūrie City. Be sure to keep to the *right* bank of the Tōhi, and go to the city. Every requisite procurable here.	2¼ hours. Riding as above directed.	5 hours. Going at a walk, &c. The rest as above.

Estimate of Time Employed on the Road from Bhimber to Kashmir—*continued.*

From Bhimber, to

Distance in Miles.	Names of Stages.	By Day.	By Night.
8 miles.	Thunnah or Tannah. Good road.	2 hours, or less. Riding a good pony, as fast as possible where practicable.	4 hours. At a walk. Take guides and masâls (torches) always at night.
9 or 10 miles.	Burrumgulla. Ascend Rattun Peer. Good road.	3 hours. Riding, &c., as above.	5 hours. At a walk, &c. &c. The rest as above.
9 or 10 miles.	Ulliahabad Seraï. Over Peer Punjâl. Bad road.	5 hours. Take guides.	Dangerous road for night marching.
18 miles.	Shupayen. Good road.	3 or 4 hours. Canter the greater part.	7 hours. At a walk.
23 or 25 miles.	Sirinuggur, or Kashmir City. Very good road.	4 hours, or less. With a change of ponies. Level road.	With guides and masâls (torches). Probably 8 or 9 hours *en route.*

APPENDIX C.

ROUTE FROM JUMMOO TO KASHMIR.

No. of Marches.	Names of Marches.		
1.	Oogurbâhin or Hurmundur	15 Coss.	{ The cosses are from 1½ to 2 miles each.
2.	Kirumchee	10 ,,	
3.	Mēērh	10 ,,	
4.	Landurh	12 ,,	
5.	Nâssbun	10 ,,	
6.	Bâtlundur	11 ,,	
7.	Bunhâl (over pass)	12 ,,	
8.	Shahabad	10 ,,	
9.	Islamabad	8 ,,	
10.	Kashmir	from 8 to 12 hours by water, down the Jhelum.	

N. B. This route was given me by Sir Henry Lawrence. I know nothing of it, except that it is worse than the Bhimber one.

APPENDIX D.

ROUTE FROM JUMMOO TO KASHMIR.

1.	Seddie	14 Miles.
2.	Dhunsal	9 ,,
3.	Bulwalta	12 ,,
4.	Odumpore	15 ,,
5.	Bullee	8 ,,
6.	Chinneeânee	9 ,,
7.	Sonee	14 ,,
8.	Nâssbun	10 ,,
9.	Pooglah	13
10.	Bunhâl (over Peer Punjâl Pass)	11 ,,
11.	Shahabad	13 ,,
12.	Islamabad	12 ,,
13.	Kashmir, by water	from 8 to to 12 hours in a boat, down the Jhehum.

Total distance from Jummoo to Islamabad, 140 miles.

N. B. The above is according to native report, and in consequence may possibly be incorrect.

APPENDIX E.

ROUTE FROM KASHMIR CITY TO LEH, CAPITAL OF LADAK.

N.B.—On the whole, a good road for riding.

No. of Marches.	Names of Marches.	Miles.	No. of Marches.	Names of Marches.	Miles.
1.	Kungun	15	8.	Lōtsum	10
2.	Rēēwul	14	9.	Wukkah	7
3.	Sonamoorg (*Oojár*)	10	10.	Kurgoo	9
4.	Metchahoy (*Oojár*) over Draus Pass, 10,500 feet	12	11.	Lamēēroo	8
			12.	Khalach	9
			13.	Himmee	8
5.	Draus (town)	12	14.	Neemmoo	14
6.	Tashgâm	9	15.	Lēh (capital of Ladâk)	15
7.	Kirghil	13			

APPENDIX F.

ROUTE FROM KASHMIR CITY TO LEH *via* ISKARDO.

1.	Bundipore, on Ooler Lake (by water)	20 coss	11.	Blagârh	8 miles
2.	Pulwâree	12 miles	12.	Soormee	18 ,,
3.	Gorez	23 ,,	13.	Poēyun	14 ,,
4.	Pusswâree	10 ,,	14.	Urboodangha	10 ,,
5.	Boorzul	10 ,,	15.	Hânnoo	10 ,,
6.	Chikkum Kooroo	20 ,,	16.	Uchneethung	10 ,
7.	Allimalkamur	20 ,,	17.	Doomkhur	12 ,,
8.	Chochochoo	20 ,,	18.	Noorlah*	12 ,,
9.	Iskârdo (City)	9 ,,	19.	Suspoorla	8 ,,
10.	Keeris	23 ,,	20.	Neemmoo	6 ,,
			21.	Lēh	15 ,,

* A great part of this road, as far as Doomkhur, is through the Oojâr.

APPENDIX G.

DIRECT ROUTE FROM LEH TO SIMLA, *viâ* THE CHOOMOREEREE LAKE AND THE DISTRICT OF KANAWR.

		Miles.
1.	Teeksa	9
2.	Mursilung	8
3.	Oōpshee	7
4.	Ghēēa	16
5.	Deverung (over Tunglung Pass, 17,000 or 18,000 feet) Oojár	18
6.	Neoūr, by the Pēēmakingjing Lake. District Rōōpshoo. Oojár	17
7.	Poogah. District Roopshoo. Oojár	14
8.	Chōōmorēēree Lake. District Roopshoo. Oojár	10
9.	Koorzuk (Oojár)	2
10.	Chōōmorēēree Lake. Oojár	8
11.	Noorbogō	11
12.	Phâlung Palrâh	11
13.	Tâtung (foot of Parung Pass)	9
14.	Parochin. (Over Parung Pass, 20,000 feet in elevation)	14
15.	Keebur	8
16.	Kâjeh	8
17.	Dunkir	12
18.	Poh	8
19.	Lâri	8

		Miles.
20.	Sungrum (Hot Springs)	17
21.	Sheâlkur (10,000 feet)	10
22.	Nâko (12,000 feet)	12¼
23.	Leo	4
24.	Hango (over Hungrung Pass, 14,837 feet)	8
25.	Soongnum (over Roonung Pass, 14,508 feet)	10
26.	Labrung	12
27.	Rârung	17½
28.	Cheenee	22
29.	Meeroo	16
30.	Cheergâon	5
31.	Nachâr	11
32.	Turanda	8
33.	Surahn	13
34.	Gourah	9
35.	Cross Sutledge, to Rampore	8
36.	Nirt	12
37.	Kotgurh (or Komhârsin)	12
38.	Nâgkunda	10
39.	Muttiâna	13
40.	Theog	6
41.	Fâgoo	8
42.	Simla	14

APPENDIX H.

From Kurtarpoor to Jummoo.

Tanda	16 Coss.	
Dussooah	11 ,,	
Mookerian	11 ,,	
Deenanuggur	14 ,,	Cross Beâs.
Nainakot	11 ,,	Cross Râvee.
Aulutgurh or Aulgurh	7 ,,	
Ramgurh	15 ,,	
Kherie or Kherie Pullie	6 ,,	
Jummoo	10 ,,	Cross Tohi River.
Total miles	101	

N.B. This road is level to within one mile of Jummoo.

APPENDIX I.

From Kurtarpoor to Jummoo.

(Another route.)

1. Tanda	16 Coss.	
2. Dussooah	11 ,,	
3. Mookerian	11 ,,	
4. Deenanuggur	14 ,,	Cross Beâs.
5. Bubeâl	12 ,,	Cross Râvee.
6. Chunghee	10 ,,	
7. Hurmundur	12 ,,	
8. Kherie or Kherie Pullie	7 ,,	
9. Jummoo	10 ,,	Cross Tohi River.
Total miles	103	

N. B. This road goes through the lower and outer range of the mountains of the Himalaya, between Bubeâl and Jummoo, and is not so level as the one given in Appendix H.

The cosses are from 1¼ to 1½ mile.

APPENDIX J.

ROUTE FROM AGRA TO BOMBAY BY INDORE AND MALLIGAUM, the most direct road, with Dâk Bungalows at convenient distances.

No. of Stages.	Names of Stages.	Miles.	Fur.	No. of Stages.	Names of Stages.	Miles.	Fur.
1.	Munnia	B. 26		19.	Sindwah	13	4
2.	Sehore	B. 21		20.	Karoond	27	4
3.	Byrahia	B. 29		21.	Betawnd	17	
4.	Gohur	B. 29	4	22.	Dhoolia (Civil Station)	18	
5.	Tongra	B. 29	2				
6.	Budurwas	B. 30		23.	Arvee	12	
7.	Goonah	B. 29		24.	Malligaum	21	
8.	Bursud	B. 31	4	25.	Chandore	25	4
9.	Bioura	B. 29	2	26.	Surora or Surwala	14	
10.	Puchore	B. 18	2				
11.	Sarungpore	B. 21		27.	Nassick	22	
12.	Rojwâs	B. 25	4	28.	Warewarah	13	
13.	Dewas	B. 29		29.	Inkutpoora	17	
14.	Indore	B. 23	4	30.	Kurdeh	20	
15.	Jaum	B. 18		31.	Shahpore	11	
16.	Mundlaisir	B. 16		32.	Bhewndy	18	4
17.	Billuckwara	18		33.	Bombay (by water)	33	3
18.	Nagulwaree	28	4				

N.B. Beyond Jaum, I have not marked the Dâk Bungalows, as I am not sure of their localities, not having travelled on this route beyond Jaum, but I know there are staging Bungalows along the road.

" B." stands for Bungalow.

APPENDIX K.

ROUTE FROM LAHORE TO MOOLTAN, by the left Bank of the River Ravee.

Stages.	Distance miles.	Remarks.
Shoong	14	First part of the road good, remainder indifferent; encamping ground on the bank of the river. Country not much cultivated, and a good deal of jungle.
Mundhana	12	Road indifferent, open jungle, and little or no cultivation.
Bullookee	14	Ditto ,, ,,
Ulpeh	13	Ditto ,, ,,
Lesharie	10	Ditto ,, ,,
Fattehpore	16	Ditto ,, ,,
Ahmedshah	11	Ditto ,, ,,
Mahomedpore	13	Road very bad.
Harruppa	11	Road better. Small town and large Ruins, Tomb, &c.
Chackawalned	12	Indifferent road and jungle.
Dooboorgie	13	Ditto ,,
Paj Kooha	8	Ditto ,,
Toolumbah	7¼	Ditto ,,
Abdool Hakim	10	Ditto ,,
Serai Suddur	8	Country more open and cultivated. Road bad
Cirdarpore	12	Small town. Country slightly cultivated; road better.
Ameerghur	10	Ditto. Open jungle; road good.
Gogra	10	Open jungle. Road pretty good.
Mooltan	10	Road good.

APPENDIX L.

Elevation of some of the Principal Places in the British Himalaya, taken from "Gerrard's Heights."

Soobathoo	4,205	feet.
Hurripore	3,147	,,
Simla	7,886	,,
Fâgoo	8,017	,,
Theog	8,018	,,
Kotgurh	6,634	,,
Whârtoo or Huttoo	10,656 or 10,673	,,
Rampore	3,398	,,
Nirtnuggur	3,087	,,
Nâgkunda Pass	9,000	,,
Borenda Pass (much snow in June.)	15,000	,,